To Stroke A Cheetah

The Extraordinary Story
of a Very Ordinary Person

AN AUTOBIOGRAPHY BY
CAPTAIN D.B. HOPKINS

First published in 2002 on behalf of the author by
Scotforth Books
Carnegie House,
Chatsworth Road
Lancaster LA1 4SL
England
Tel: +44(0)1524 840111
Fax: +44(0)1524 840222
email: carnegie@provider.co.uk
Publishing and book sales: www.carnegiepub.co.uk
Book production: www.wooof.net

British Library Cataloguing-in-Publication data
A catalogue record is for this book is available from the British Library

ISBN 1-904244-07-6

Typeset in Bell 11 on 13 by
Carnegie Publishing
Printed and pound in the UK by
The Cromwell Press, Wiltshire

Contents

Foreword

TO BE ASKED TO WRITE A FEW WORDS by way of a Foreword to this autobiography is a real privilege. Despite the fact that our careers have taken each of us along very different paths, the author and I do share a common interest. We are both passionately fond of speaking and writing our native language. The use of English presents wonderful opportunities to those with a lively sense of humour and Derek Hopkins has filled each chapter of his book with colourful anecdotes and sensitive observations of those he has encountered during his three score years and ten.

From his schooldays, through his long career as a pilot, to his days as chauffeur to the famous, Derek practises the advice of the Headmaster who told him that he should seek to learn something new every day. Many of these 'learning experiences' will make you laugh – and some will make your hair stand on end!

I take issue with the use of only one word in the whole book. On the title page, the author describes himself as a very **ordinary** person. In the pages that follow we learn of his skills as a car mechanic, an aviator, a builder, a gardener, a diplomat and a humourist – not to mention his role as a husband and a father. In my opinion, his is an extraordinary story – not of an ordinary person, but of a rather special person. I am proud to be included among his many friends, and I commend to you his story – I know you will enjoy it.

John Davey

Formerly Chief Executive, Trinity College London

*An Autobiography
by Captain
D.B. Hopkins*

Introduction and Dedication

WHEN I STARTED TO WRITE THIS ACCOUNT of my life I never intended it to be other than a story my children and grandchildren might want to read, to see what I got up to over the years from 1930 to today. However several of my friends and acquaintances have read parts of it and encouraged me to try to get it published, saying it would appeal to a wider audience.

The fact that you are reading this means that I have been successful in finding a publisher and I hope you will enjoy the story of my life, which I think you will find slightly different to most people's. I have been lucky to have had such an exciting time, to have had such support from Mella, my wife of 46 years, and to have such a successful family.

I dedicate this story firstly to Mella, without whom I could not have done all the things I have. I am well aware that at times she has felt that she was left on the sidelines looking after our three sons, while I travelled the world earning a very respectable living. However we are both from that generation that believes that children are best brought up by having a mother at home while father provided the wherewithal. I am still firmly of the opinion that this is the best method of producing well behaved and balanced offspring, and when I compare the behaviour of today's generation of litter louts and vandals that the so-called equality of the sexes has produced, I think one could say that my case is proved.

Secondly I dedicate this book to our three sons, Trevor, Christopher and Austen, of whom I feel justifiably proud as they have all worked hard at their chosen careers.

Thirdly I dedicate my book to our four grandsons, who I feel sure will carry on upholding our family's motto 'The best is always good enough, but only just!'

*An Autobiography
by Captain
D.B. Hopkins*

I would like to thank all those friends who have read parts of this manuscript and encouraged me to have it published.

My grateful thanks are also extended to John Davey for taking the trouble to read my manuscript and write such a nice foreword.

The reader will notice that I have put certain things in as Annexes. I have done this as they may, or may not, appeal to everyone. Not reading them should not detract from your enjoyment of my story in any way.

CHAPTER ONE

The Writing on the Wall

'Y OU CAN NEVER SOMETIMES TELL what's least expected most'. So said Grandpa Marshall on many occasions (this was his rather quaint way of suggesting that one should always expect the unexpected), and now, after some 70 years of life, I know he was right. Definitely! I wasn't expecting to be born – well who is? But there it was – I had arrived in Bexley, Kent as a 'Kentish Man' for the rest of my life. For the uninitiated, a Kentish Man/Maid is born west of the River Medway while Men/Maids of Kent are born to the east of said river. It's curious how something one would have been totally unaware of at the moment of birth becomes indelibly fixed in one's subconscious for the rest of time, but this must be so for although I spent only the first 20 years of my life in the 'Garden of England', I still think of myself as belonging to Kent and am a supporter of the Kent cricket team rather than that of my adopted county, Sussex.

I made my first mark for posterity when I was three and still living in Bexley. Not a big mark, you understand, merely a tiny footmark in some concrete my Father had just laid for a path. I've often wondered if it is still there, at 'Adelaide', Parkhurst Road and if it is, whether any of the owners of the house since 1934 have contemplated the origin of such a small footprint.

Looking back, the next event that I can remember, albeit not very clearly, is being taken up in an aeroplane of Sir Alan Cobham's Flying Circus, from Rochester aerodrome I think, in about 1934. What I can remember quite clearly is looking down on the fields and mudflats around what I now know to be the Medway estuary. I learnt in later years from Mother that the seats in this aeroplane were of wickerwork and not fastened to the floor, so that they tended to slide about a bit during turns.

1931 – The Author aged 6 Months 'A drop of good stuff'

1934 – The Author Cleans His Car – A sign of Things to Come?

Probably my parents did not expect this experience to influence my choice of career but 'YCNSTWLEM!'

Although I have recently discovered where I first went to school, I have no recollection of my primary education, which started in Gravesend in about 1936, save that it was at a convent school. We had moved to a house called 'Sandhurst' in Central Avenue, Gravesend, where the above picture was taken, so that Father was near to Greenhithe and HMS *Worcester*, at which establishment he taught mathematics and navigation to young men who were destined for a career at sea. One would expect such a responsible profession to be fairly well paid, but it was not – to the extent that mother had to sell her diamond and sapphire engagement ring to be able to afford food to feed me! And they call £160 per week poverty nowadays!!

Some time in 1936/37 we moved to the house on the following page, in Dennis Road. The only notable thing about it, and the sole reason I've included the picture, is the fact that at the time we moved there, Father could not afford to buy it at a cost of just £275 – some £50 more per annum than his salary!

I have recently found and visited St Joseph's School in Echo Square, Gravesend. I do not remember going there at all even though I have now seen the place. I do, however, remember that the nun who taught singing told me that I had a voice like a frog! It put me off singing entirely and I have never sung in public since, nor do I intend to. I'm sure the good lady didn't mean me to abandon any thought of a singing career, but that is the effect it has had and any member of my family will vouch for the fact that I do not even sing in the bath for fear of upsetting them or the neighbours.

The Extraordinary Story of a Very Ordinary Person

The only other memory I have of my life in Gravesend is having my tonsils and adenoids removed. I can remember quite clearly a gauze mask being put over my mouth and nose, followed by chloroform being dripped onto it. The next memory is of the most dreadful sore throat, but how long it lasted I have no recollection at all!

The next significant event was the onset of World War II, and even today I can hear Neville Chamberlain's pathetic-sounding voice proclaiming to the nation that 'We are at war with Germany'. I must admit that I had no idea at the time of the significance of 'being at war', but I was to learn very quickly. The most immediate consequence was that HMS *Worcester* was moved to Footscray Place, near Sidcup. More accurately, the school was moved, leaving the ship still moored at Greenhithe next to the *Cutty Sark*. (The *Worcester* was broken up after the war, but I still have in my office a small piece of the ship made into a barrel, with a label that tells me that she was launched in Portsmouth in 1860. The *Cutty Sark*, of course, now resides at Greenwich).

Because it was thought by most people, including mother and father, that bombs were going to rain down upon us at any moment, so that staying in Kent would be dangerous, Mother took Steven (my brother) and me to stay with her parents. Grandpa and Grandma Marshall's house, 'Windycroft', was on the A1 (now the A638) just to the north of Retford. Directly opposite the gate, a footpath led across a field, first of all to the main railway line from Kings Cross to Edinburgh, then on to a plank bridge over a brook, where I could catch minnows and sticklebacks, and across another field up to the Worksop and Chesterfield canal. This was then in commercial use and I always found it exciting to watch the horse-drawn narrow boats laden with coal amongst other commodities slowly making their way, especially at the lock, which was but a short walk along the towpath. The bargees would always be happy to chat if I ran along the towpath alongside the boats. There, at weekends, there were always fishermen to watch, provided one was quiet and didn't cast a shadow over the water. There were some quite large fish in the canal and when it froze over in the winter of 1939, I could walk on it and see the fish under the ice. So together with train

An Autobiography by Captain D.B. Hopkins

spotting at the railway crossing, watching such grand locomotives as 'Flying Scotsman', 'Mallard' (which only a year previously had captured the world record by achieving 126mph), 'Green Arrow' and a host of others, time always seemed to pass quickly.

Grandma and Grandpa had a collection of brass water cans, varying in size from a half gallon to two gallons. These, normally used for the transfer of hot water from the wash boiler to the bath, came in very useful during the winter of 1939/40. The water supply to 'Windycroft' froze, so we had to collect a meagre supply from the next house along. This was an old farmhouse with a well that thankfully didn't freeze and I remember quite vividly trudging through the snow with the cans full of water.

Grandpa Marshall kept a shop in Cannon Square, Retford, where he sold grocery. It was typical of the period and always smelt invitingly of fresh ground coffee, intermingled with the aroma of the sides of bacon that were sliced on the hand-operated bacon slicer. Butter came in small

barrels and was dispensed with the aid of two butter pats that were ridged and left a nice pattern on each portion served. Cash taken at the counters was sent to the cashiers by means of containers 'fired' along an overhead wire by some elastic. The change was returned the same way – all very thrilling to a small boy!

Grandpa was helped by my Uncle Nelson, pictured on the left during WW I when he was a pilot in the Royal Flying Corps. He was shot down twice and, bearing in mind that parachutes were not then in use, it was something of a miracle that he survived both times. I learnt recently that he was called Nelson because Grandma Marshall, whose maiden name was Wessell, was distantly related to Admiral Lord Nelson. YCNSTWLEM!

As Hitler had neither invaded England nor bombed us by the end of July 1940, Father moved us back south to a house in Sidcup, into which he had moved while we were in Retford and which was only a stone's throw from Footscray Place. It was impeccably bad timing as the 'Battle of Britain' started almost immediately and we were able to watch the dog-fights taking place literally above our heads. I still have vivid memories of the contrails (for the meteorologically inclined – dense persistent) as the Hurricanes and Spitfires did battle with the German bombers and fighters in the lovely weather we had in September 1940. I remember, too, thinking what fun it must be to fly in a Spitfire!

In October I began the secondary part of my school education at the Chislehurst & Sidcup County Grammar School for Boys at Crittalls Corner. The building was a well-known landmark, one end of which resembled a tram. One can still just catch a glimpse of it as one whizzes over the flyover on the A20 enroute to and from London.

The headmaster was Mr C.R.McGregor Williams, whose basic dictum for education was, 'any day of your life you do not learn something new is a day wasted'. I have always tried to live up to this and I would like to see it used as the basis for education throughout the country. Mr McGregor Williams was known to all the boys as 'Jumbo', due to his diminutive stature. Diminutive he might have been but, like the law, he had an extremely long arm! Woe betide any boy who failed to wear his uniform properly or neglected to raise his cap when passing 'Jumbo' in the street.

In those days discipline was strict but fair and although caning was considered the norm for offenders in most schools, I don't recall any occasion when it was actually administered by 'Jumbo'. The very fact that he was known to keep a cane in his study cupboard and that he threatened to use it was sufficient to keep more or less every boy on the straight and narrow. However, I wouldn't want you to get the impression that we were all little 'goodies'. By no means! I recall being sent to 'Jumbo's' study on one occasion after I had poked the boy sitting in front of me in the rump with the nib of my pen, causing him to cry out and disrupt a detailed explanation of the proof of Pythagoras' theorem by Mr Grindrod, the maths teacher at the time, who was not amused! I forget now what caused this momentary degeneration from my normal behaviour, but off I was sent for a vertical interview with 'Jumbo'. Although I was about 14 at the time I was taller than he but this did not protect me from a series of jabs in the chest, as it was made plain to me what would happen should I incur his displeasure again. I hardly need to mention that I never had another summons to his study until I left school, and that was just for him to say goodbye, as he did to all the boys.

I wouldn't have been surprised if I had been sent for after The Great Coke Fight. I cannot remember exactly when this event took place, except that it was during the war. The school's central heating was fired by large coke-burning boilers. The coke was stored outside the boiler-room in huge heaps containing many tons of the stuff. What started the fight and who threw the first piece I shall never know, but within a very short time the majority of the boys spending their lunchtime in the playing fields were throwing pieces of coke at one another. The sky was, for a while, completely overcast due to the sheer

*An Autobiography
by Captain
D.B. Hopkins*

amount of coke that was airborne! Eventually the law, in the shape of one or more masters, arrived and put a stop to the proceedings. All the boys present were ordered to pick up all the coke that was spread over several acres of playing fields and return it to the bunkers. I am sure it was only the numbers involved that saved any individual from being punished, although the whole school was harangued by 'Jumbo' at assembly next morning and told the error of their ways in no uncertain terms.

I imagine that all schools had masters who were known as 'characters'. My school was certainly well blessed with these, and one of whom I have vivid memories was the PT master, a certain Mr Basri, who hailed from Iraq. He was an excellent teacher and his method of ensuring we all went through the showers like greased lightening after a PT lesson was novel to say the least. He had an old cricket bat with the blade sawn off to about six inches. He would stand at the exit to the showers and any boy he considered had been tardy would 'connect' with his bat on one cheek of the seat of understanding. Highly effective since the faster one dashed out of the showers, the less chance he had to connect with one's anatomy.

School dinners could also be quite exciting. We sat at tables of eight, three boys down each side and one at each end. The latter two were the servers and had to go up to the kitchen hatch and collect the plates of meat (spam fritters, sausages or whatever) and then go and collect the two dishes containing potatoes and the vegetable of the day. They would then serve these to each boy on his table. I was serving cabbage one day and in true schoolboy style I was plopping each spoonful of cabbage down with some force. The plate of the fifth boy I served broke! Investigation revealed a kitchen sink plug mixed with the cabbage – beautifully cooked of course!

My education proceeded fairly smoothly for the next two or three years, during which time we were gradually getting used to having our windows blown out and ceilings brought down by the efforts of the *Luftwaffe*. In order to be in a relatively safe place during air raids, we were in the habit, upon hearing the warning sirens, of retreating to a cupboard under the stairs wearing our 'siren-suits', which Mother had copied from that worn by Winston Churchill. As time went on we became rather blasé and stayed in our nice warm beds until the drone of the bombers or the 'thud' of exploding bombs got too close for comfort.

One memorable night we left it rather <u>too</u> late and I can still hear the noise of a bomb exploding in the road outside and see our front door coming straight at me as I came down the stairs. By deftly retreating a few feet I avoided being hit and was then able to run over the door and get into our 'safe' place. Steven had an even luckier escape that night.

When we went into his bedroom on the ground floor in the morning after the 'all-clear' had sounded, we found a foot-long shard of glass had gone, like an arrow, straight through the hollow in his pillow where his head had been only moments before the bomb exploded. After these close shaves we went back to our routine of going to our 'shelter' as soon as the siren sounded.

Food was, of course, rationed but like all young boys with hollow legs, Steven and I were perpetually hungry. Mother and Father rose to the occasion by growing an assortment of vegetables and animals in our small garden. We had chickens, ducks, rabbits and goats. The latter gave us a supply of tuberculosis-free milk, which we drank and from which we also made cheese. To supplement the butter ration we used to collect the cream from the top of the bottles of milk, put it in a sterilised 'Heinz' salad cream bottle and shake until a small blob of butter appeared, which helped to eke out the meagre ration.

Somewhere in the vicinity of Sidcup there was a Smith's Crisps factory and by some devious means we used to get a regular supply of potato crisp sweepings from the factory floor to augment the feed we gave to the chickens and ducks. These sweepings came in old hessian sacks and tasted fine to me, although I'm sure they had been declared unfit for human consumption. Working on the old adage that *you have to eat a peck of dirt before you die*, I feel sure I had my fair share, which has stood me in good stead since I have never been one to have allergies, asthma and the like. (Modern parents should perhaps take note and although I am not advocating feeding floor sweepings to one's little darlings, perhaps a little less of the current overly sterile world would do wonders).

Steven and I did a lot of collecting during these years. We would go out first thing in the morning after an air raid and pick up as much shrapnel as we could find, a considerable amount, from our garden, where it fell after bouncing off the roof. This was mainly from the anti-aircraft guns, which were positioned all around for the defence of London. We also collected grass and dandelions for rabbit feed from the grounds of Footscray Place. Here there were 'tank traps', deep ditches with a vertical side nearest to London, designed to prevent or delay enemy tanks on their way to the Capital. Fortunately they were never needed, but after a while they filled with rainwater and became a wonderful place for all the local lads, including Steven and myself, to collect newts, both common and great crested. The latter were to be found in great profusion, although where they came from remains a mystery.

Unfortunately I do not know the history of Footscray Place, but from the grounds one could tell that people of substance had lived there in some style. There were 'ice houses', where ice from the ponds was collected in the winter months and stored for use during summer and

*An Autobiography
by Captain
D.B. Hopkins*

there was a particularly fascinating swimming pool with summerhouse in the grounds. The latter had two storeys but no obvious staircase to get to the upper floor. After much searching, we eventually found that on either side of the fireplace at the end of the ground floor room was a concealed door. Behind these were the two sets of rather narrow stairs leading to the room above. Why the place was constructed in such a manner is a mystery and one can only surmise that its purpose was to facilitate secret trysts between lovers.

In 1944 the 'doodlebugs' started to fly over us. There seemed to be some six different tracks for these, one of which came straight over the top of our house. These weapons were highly unpredictable in their behaviour. Sometimes the engine would cut out and the bomb would immediately dive into the ground and explode; sometimes they would carry on gliding after the engine stopped and disappear from sight before we could hear the explosion in the distance; sometimes they would dive into the ground with the engine still at full power. When we heard one coming, we would rush outside to see which track it was on. If it was not on 'our' track, or once it had passed us, we would continue with what we had been doing. Also about this time the V2 rockets started landing and since they travelled faster than the speed of sound, the noise of their arrival was only heard after they exploded. One night a V2 landed on the lodge of Footscray Place, some 200 yards from our house, killing the parents of a boy we knew. We cared for him and he stayed with us for a few days until he could be sent to relatives.

As Mother was pregnant with my sister Nola, Father decided that enough was enough and on 19th July 1944 we were once again sent up north to Retford to stay with Grandpa and Grandma Marshall – just in the nick of time it seems, as Nola was born on the 29th! Once again I went to school in Retford, again at the King Edward Grammar School. I walked there and back each day from 'Windycroft', a total of six miles. This was not, as one might suppose, a great hardship as I was able to go along the towpath of the Chesterfield and Worksop Canal and then by footpath across fields to home. Another reason was that we were at that time sharing the school building with another school (from Worksop I think), so that we only went to school three days a week. We went on Monday, Wednesday and Friday, while the other school attended on Tuesday, Thursday and Saturday. The footpath I used crossed, as I mentioned earlier, the LNER mainline from Kings Cross to Edinburgh and I spent many a happy hour watching more of the famous engines such as 'Silver Link' and 'Papyrus', especially on the non-school days. I also had the novel experience of being taught carpentry by the same master who taught my father when he was at KE Grammar School during the 1914/18 war.

Speaking of being taught things, occasionally I would come across two tramps, 'Ebb and Flo' as they travelled around the area. Ebb and Flo were reputed to be respectively the son of a wealthy family and their maid who had taken to the road, and listening to them haranguing the general public certainly increased my vocabulary of swear words to a considerable degree! The two of them were decidedly odd. Ebb towed all his worldly goods behind him in an old-fashioned basket invalid chair, whereas Flo pushed hers before her in a large pram that had seen better days.

We returned home to Sidcup on 19th April 1945 just in time for VE Day and a welcome change back to some sort of normality in our lives, although my schooling had suffered to some degree. Early in my years at secondary school I had been in the 'A' stream, but for whatever reason, I was not keeping up sufficiently and I was put down to the 'B' stream in my third and fourth years. This caused my father to give me a lecture on the subject of 'pulling my finger out' and by the end of the fourth year I had done just that and received the form prize! Thenceforth I was put back in the 'A' stream, where I remained until I left school.

In August I went with many of my friends to a school harvest camp in South Petherton in Somerset. Here we had a grand time, although the work was hard, especially when a few of us were given the task of *pulling* ten acres of flax by hand. This involved pulling up the ripe stalks of the flax and tying them into bundles. If you have never done this, you will be unaware how sharp flax can be! The trick to avoid tearing ones hands to shreds, we soon learnt, was to grip each handful of the stalks extremely tightly so that they couldn't slide through one's fingers. I forget how many days we took to do this, but I do remember that the weather was very hot and sunny, so we welcomed the offer from the farmer to refresh us with some cider. It was homemade on the farm and we were somewhat surprised, not to say disgruntled, when we were only given a couple of inches of the golden liquid in the bottom of a tumbler – that was until we drank it!! It was real 'scrumpy' and as we were all only about 14 or 15, the effect on us was dramatic, to say the least. However we soon got the taste for it and many of our gang were to be seen carrying a bottle of the stuff down to the fields for the remainder of our time in that delightful county.

Our camp was only a few miles from Montacute House (now National Trust, but then still privately owned) and there was a beacon on a hill nearby. We learned from the locals that Montacute had a ghost, which occasionally walked abroad and announced its presence by lighting a fire in the beacon. Now to schoolboys of our age this was not only an opportunity for fun but a challenge as well. Consequently, one night we cycled to the beacon and with a suitable supply of dry sticks, paper and matches etc. lit up. The talk in the village and pubs next day

*An Autobiography
by Captain
D.B. Hopkins*

had to be heard to be believed, because prior to this everyone only knew someone who knew someone who had seen the beacon alight but now <u>everyone</u> had actually seen it!

Another of my interests at this time was collecting engine numbers. It started during my second evacuation to Retford. There was a series of books by Ian Allen, one for each of the railway companies, i.e. LNER; LMS; GWR and Southern Railway. Having twice lived cheek-by-jowl with the LNER, I had seen most of the named engines and living in Sidcup as I did, I had easy access to many of the Southern locomotives. A pal and I would occasionally go up to Clapham Junction, then the largest railway junction in the world, and spend many happy hours spotting. My favourites were the 4-4-0 Schools Class engines, named after the most famous public schools. One of them still survives on the 'Bluebell Line' not far from where I now live. On another occasion my pal and I went up to Liverpool Street Station to spot engines not seen on the main LNER east coast line. At the time coaches were brought into the station from the sidings by a tank engine. We were hovering around one after the train had departed when the driver invited us on to the footplate. We accepted this unexpected pleasure with alacrity and, to our considerable delight, we were allowed to 'drive' to the other end of the platform. This was my first experience of 'driving' anything bigger than a bicycle.

In spite of the discomforts of pulling flax, it would seem that I was not put off harvest camps and in the summer of 1947 I was to be found at Kidlington near Oxford. Curiously I cannot remember the work we did, but I do remember that it was here I was introduced to the game of 'pudducks'. This game is greatly suited to those gatherings where numbers are large, as any amount of participants are allowed, indeed positively encouraged. It is a mixture of cricket and rounders and the rules are fairly lax. 'Hit and run' is enforced and there is a bowler at each end of the pitch 22 yards. The ball is bowled by whichever bowler has it. There are only two stumps and the two batters have a rounders bat apiece. A tennis ball is used, which prevents injury, as one way of being 'out' is to be hit by the ball being returned by any fielder. Everybody fields, and all the players get a turn at batting, thus all are involved all the time. As can be seen, it is an ideal game for large gatherings of people, and it teaches you to keep your wits about you.

Speaking of games, I never liked soccer; it is in my view totally boring. Instead I played lacrosse, a much faster and more interesting game. I also played tennis and swam a lot, once I had taught myself to swim. I did this by cycling to Eltham, the nearest swimming pool, every Saturday morning for an entire winter and although I couldn't swim a width at the start, by the time spring arrived I could, and did, swim a mile each time I visited the baths.

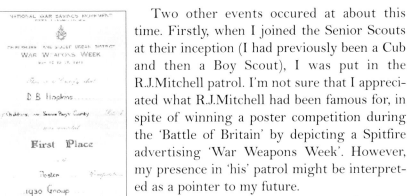

Two other events occured at about this time. Firstly, when I joined the Senior Scouts at their inception (I had previously been a Cub and then a Boy Scout), I was put in the R.J.Mitchell patrol. I'm not sure that I appreciated what R.J.Mitchell had been famous for, in spite of winning a poster competition during the 'Battle of Britain' by depicting a Spitfire advertising 'War Weapons Week'. However, my presence in 'his' patrol might be interpreted as a pointer to my future.

Secondly I was a very enthusiastic builder of model aeroplanes, including the one pictured. The Sea Fury was the fastest single engine plane built in this era and my model, with its 2cc engine, was also fast. It was a control-line job and I calculated its top speed to be something over 60mph! I also built several gliders, one of which was so good that when I launched it on its maiden flight, it soared away over some nearby houses and I never saw it again despite chasing after it on my bicycle.

During my time in the sixth form I was involved in several pranks. In retrospect some of these now seem to have been quite dangerous, although no harm was done to anyone and the following is one of the more harmless. The 'senior' chemistry lab had four benches, each equipped with four workstations with sink, water tap and gas tap with Bunsen burner attached by rubber hose. It was the practice for the laboratory assistant to turn off the water supply at the main tap in his office during the lunch hour, presumably to prevent unauthorised use of the lab by us students, who were known to be keen to try various illicit experiments, such as the construction of fireworks. Anyway, on the day in question, after the water had been turned off and the assistant had gone for lunch, a few of us nipped into the lab and disconnected all sixteen Bunsen burners from the gas taps and re-connected them to the water taps, turned all these full on and retired to a suitable vantage point to witness what happened next. The result was far beyond our expectations, because on his return the lab assistant unlocked his office, went in and turned on the water at the main tap. We were rewarded by the sight of sixteen fountains of water jetting up to the ceiling of the lab. Now I, and no doubt the reader, would have immediately turned off the water at the main, but this chap, no doubt in a panic, went and

*An Autobiography
by Captain
D.B. Hopkins*

closed each of the sixteen taps individually, getting soaked in the process. We all made ourselves as scarce as frog's feathers and kept a low profile for the rest of the day. It was just as well that 'Jumbo' never got to hear about my part in this as I might not have got such a glowing reference when I came to end of my school days.

Another event that made my sixth form days memorable was the visit to the 'Scientific Society', of which I was secretary, of the well-known broadcaster, Wynford Vaughan Thomas. He had recently been with King George VI and Queen Elizabeth during their visits to the U.S.A., South Africa and India. During his address he told anecdotes to illustrate the differing philosophies of life in those three countries. In India a railway company was building a new line which involved making a tunnel through a mountain. An American civil engineer was in charge of the project with an Indian as his number two. The normal methods were being used, i.e. the tunnel was being excavated from both ends so that they would eventually meet in the middle. Blasting and digging continued for some months, but due to a mis-calculation, when they met the two ends were mis-aligned by some two feet! The American was most upset, saying, 'Back in the States there would be a Congressional inquiry if this happened, etc., etc.' His Indian colleague was not in the least worried, saying, 'In India we don't mind if we miss altogether, because then we would have <u>two</u> tunnels!!' When I visited the Subcontinent in later years, I realised just how accurate a summary this was.

In the summer holiday of 1947 I finished building my new bicycle, for which I had saved up pocket money and any other money that I gleaned from birthdays etc. At the time it was my pride and joy and in many ways could be said to be the start of my interest in mechanical engineering, which in later years I have heard described as 'tinkering with cars'! I cycled from Sidcup to Retford, a distance of about 160 miles, to visit Grandpa and Grandma Marshall at 'Windycroft'. This took me about 12 hours and my route was through London and up the A1, or 'Great North Road' as it was then known, and when it was just a road of one lane each way. Apart from being quite surprised by my arrival by bicycle, I think Grandpa was quite impressed by my feat, as he had been a keen cyclist in his younger days and I still have the medal he received for regular attendance at his club's outings. The cycle he rode was a penny-farthing and I am sure his feats of riding exceeded mine by a long chalk.

It is interesting to reflect that today it would be difficult to repeat my ride, as the A1 is now a prohibited road for cycles. I suppose the only way to do it would be to plan a route along country lanes, etc. I say that Grandpa was surprised by my unannounced arrival because they didn't have a telephone. In fact they still didn't have electricity and I will always remember Grandma filling the oil lamps every day and Grandpa walking down to the local garage once a week to take the lead/acid battery for re-charging and returning with the one he left the previous week. This way they were able to have a wireless for listening to special programmes. Too much listening and the battery went flat before the end of the week!

In May and June 1948 I sat my Higher School Certificate examinations in Chemistry, Applied Maths, Pure Maths and Physics. Unfortunately I managed to contract mumps at about this time, so I had to do several papers in isolation in the school secretary's office.

In September, having passed the exams and gained Inter B.Sc, I started work as a laboratory assistant with the Prince Regent Tar Company in Silvertown. At the same time I started a degree course, part time, at Sir John Cass College in Jewry Street in London. The hours and conditions under which I worked, which were quite normal for the time, would have modern students organising protest marches on the streets. After the usual hours, 9 to 5, at Silvertown, I would travel to Jewry Street for three hours of lectures or laboratory work from 6 to 9pm. This happened every weekday except Thursday, and on Wednesday afternoons I had lectures from 2 to 5. On Saturdays I worked from 9 to noon. I recall that my pay was £4 10 shillings per week before tax! After two years of keeping my nose to the grindstone, I managed to persuade the Kent Education Committee to award me a grant so that I could attend University full time, starting in October 1950.

Although my time at Silvertown was hard work, it was not without its lighter moments. On one occasion we were larking about in the lab and I was wielding a 'Pyrene' fire extinguisher of the type with which one pumps carbon tetrachloride on to a fire, with the intent of spraying a fellow lab assistant. At that moment the Chief Chemist 'Jock' walked through the door just in time to catch the blast. Fortunately for me he had a reasonable sense of humour and I got away with a light wigging!

The main 'character' of the lab was an elderly cockney lady called Maud, who did all the cleaning and washing of the equipment. At Christmas she always brought a bottle of gin to work with her and insisted that we all have a drink with her to celebrate the 'festive season'. We drank out of beakers and the whole occasion has been

*An Autobiography
by Captain
D.B. Hopkins*

forever etched in my memory, as we had to drink the gin undiluted!! Yuk!!

During 'Rag Week' a number of amusing incidents took place, one of which was the cementing of a WC to a pavement in Trafalgar Square. This was done under the cover of a PO Telephone's repair tent and it was some three weeks before it was discovered, by which time the cement was well and truly set.

In 1948/49 I passed my driving test and for a couple of years I went around on a 250cc BSA motorbike.

In January 1951 we moved to Sutton Lodge, Sutton-at-Hone, near Dartford and soon after this I decided that I'd had enough of motor cycling for the time being – I'd fallen off a couple of times, once on an icy lane and once on the wooden blocks in London, which were absolute death traps when wet! As a matter of historical record, the Prince Regent Tar Company, for whom I was then working, made these wood blocks. Fortunately they were in the process of being removed. Although ideal for the horse-drawn vehicles for which they were meant, as they deadened the noise of the iron-rimmed cartwheels, they were less than ideal for vehicles with rubber tyres.

Thus I exchanged my BSA for my first car, a 1932 Wolseley Hornet Daytona Special. I rebuilt the engine, having it re-bored on site, and re-sprayed it bright green using a spray gun and an air supply from a vacuum cleaner. The result, whilst not of prize-winning quality, was surprisingly good and Mother named it 'The Green Dragon' – picture above. It was a very advanced design for 1932, having a six-cylinder-in-line engine with an overhead camshaft at a time when most cars of similar size had side valve engines. I don't know who fitted it, but the exhaust was a straight through Servais system with a copper tailpipe, which looked magnificent after it was polished, although this shine didn't last long once the engine was started! It had a rather small petrol tank and I used to carry an emergency supply in a WW II-vintage 'jerry' can, which I still have and still use to store petrol!

Sutton Lodge had a most interesting garden, which must have been a grand sight in its heyday. It had two giant redwoods and a large orchard of fruit trees. It also had wells, an icehouse and the remains of a 'Pineapple House'. In addition the north wall of the garden was hollow, with a chimney at one end and a fireplace at the other. In the days when both coal and labour were cheap, this fire was kept going during cold weather in the winter, allowing vegetables to be grown out of season.

During our time there we carried on keeping chickens, much as we had done in Sidcup, although on a somewhat larger scale. At one time we were sure that someone was stealing the odd bird or two, so I rigged up an alarm system to let us know if the gate to the chicken run was opened. My 'alarm' consisted of a jam jar containing photographic flash powder and a piece of fuse wire connected to two terminals, in turn connected to a car battery via a contact on the gate. The jar was put in an empty 5-gallon drum to hide it and prevent injury from flying glass. I calculated that the device would make sufficient noise for it to be heard in the house, which was some distance away. To be sure it worked, I thought it best to conduct a trial. To say that the trial was a success would be a considerable understatement. When I set it off there was a tremendous 'BANG' and the bottom of the drum became completely hemispherical. At this point I had second thoughts about the enterprise and abandoned it. Curiously, though, we never lost any more chickens, so perhaps the thief got the message somehow!

About this time Mother decided to keep pigs and after Father and I had made suitable accommodation for them three Wessex Saddleback sows arrived. Soon it was time for them to be mated and I was despatched to a friendly pig farmer in nearby Horton Kirby to borrow his boar, which fortunately for me was completely docile, as I had to 'walk' it along the lanes to enable it to perform its duty, after which I had to 'walk' it home again.

After my parents moved from Sutton Lodge to Eastbourne in 1953, the house and grounds were sold to a developer who demolished the house and there is now a housing estate on the site. The first I knew of this was when I flew over the area in a helicopter sometime in the 1970s. We circled the area twice before I could convince myself that the house really had gone!

Whilst we lived in Sutton-at-Hone I became a member, and before long, the President, of the local Young Conservatives. This was not so much an expression of my political beliefs as an opportunity to meet lots of quite delightful girls! One year we went to the national conference at the Grand Hotel in Brighton and had a jolly good time finishing

*An Autobiography
by Captain
D.B. Hopkins*

with a party in someone's room. One of the hotel staff remarked the following morning, 'We can always tell when the Young Conservatives have been here because all the tooth mugs from the rooms are found in one room!'

In October 1950, when I started full time at university, I felt that a career in chemistry was not for me and I told Father so, suggesting that I should join the Royal Air Force instead. Father, however, insisted that I stick with my degree course and so I spent the next two years full time at Sir John Cass College. I passed the mathematics part of the course with flying colours, but my heart wasn't really in chemistry, so it came as no surprise to find I'd failed the theory, although my marks in the practical were sufficient for a first class degree. This seemed to be a considerable setback at the time, but had I been the proud owner of a 'crystal ball', I would have seen it was for the best. YCNSTWLEM!

In August 1952, having finished at university, Steven and I decided to tour Scotland in the 'Green Dragon'. We set off with high hopes of being able to eke out our meagre funds by camping, or rather sleeping out under the stars, since we didn't possess a tent. Once we got to Scotland, this idea proved to be impossible as the weather was less than co-operative. We travelled to Scotland via the east coast as far as John O'Groats, taking in such sights as Lincoln Cathedral, Durham Cathedral, the Forth Bridge and the Tay Bridge.

Having reached John O'Groats, we headed west along the north coast then southeast along the A838, which you can see from the picture below is nothing much more than a dirt track. Nowadays it looks more like an 'A' road as it has been covered in tarmac. You may wonder why I've bothered to include this picture as the scenery hardly

merits its inclusion. The shot was taken just at the northern end of Loch Merkland and it is a pretty wild spot. We had stopped to top up the radiator of the 'Green Dragon', something we had to do with monotonous frequency due to a slight leak. We hadn't seen anybody on or off the road for hours, but while we were filling the radiator two men in deerstalking attire with telescopes hove into sight coming towards us. Naturally we stood up from our task and wished them 'good morning', but to our utter astonishment and disbelief they strode past us noses in the air, without saying a word. So much for Scottish hospitality or to take a charitable view, maybe they didn't understand English!

From here we proceeded to Lairg and on to Inverness, the well-named 'Granite City', then along the south-eastern side of Loch Ness. This particular day we were having nice warm sunshine and we felt that a swim in the loch would be just the thing! Having donned our trunks we went into the water, which was quite shallow for some 30 yards from the shore at this point. This was when we discovered why people do not swim in Loch Ness – by the time we reached water deep enough to reach our calves our feet were more or less suffering from frostbite so we left the water in a hurry!

It had been our intention to return home down the west coast, but due to the rough road surfaces one of the springs on the front of the car broke. This, coupled with the fact that we had by now nearly run out of funds having had to stay in B & B's most nights as the weather did not allow us to sleep under the stars, made us decide to return to Kent by the most direct route possible. This we did, arriving at some time in the middle of the night, much to the surprise of our parents. Not quite the sort of tour I might want to do today, but at 17 and 21 respectively, Steven and I felt it had been a worthwhile experience.

Another of my interests while living at Sutton Lodge was amateur dramatics. I took part in a production of *Mr Pym Passes By* in 1951 and in 1952 I played the part of the detective in *The Late Christopher Bean.* Sir Alec Guinness I was most definitely not, but the experience taught me a lot about play acting which was to stand me in good stead some five or six years later, although I didn't know it at the time. YCNSTWLEM!

I've never been what you might call a talented sportsman, but while at Sutton-at-Hone I did play a bit of cricket for the Farningham Village team. I think the main reason I got into the team was to make up the numbers. However it did give me the opportunity to play in a charity match against a team who had managed to secure the services of Godfrey Evans as wicket keeper. If you have never had the privilege of batting with one of Kent and England's most famous keepers behind your stumps, you will be unaware that in village games he was wont to crack jokes, which, although funny, definitely put you off your stroke. I

*An Autobiography
by Captain
D.B. Hopkins*

went in at number eleven and managed to score eleven, no thanks to Godfrey. Great fun though!

As you read the following chapters you may come to agree that although it would be going a bit far to say that one's destiny is written in the stars, it is entirely on the cards that looking back at one's early life can give an insight into what happens in later years. Recalling my early life, I can now see, with the 20/20 hindsight that comes with age, that a lot of my interests in my formative years could have acted as pointers to my career(s)!

CHAPTER TWO

Plan 'B' – I Join the Royal Air Force

As I MENTIONED PREVIOUSLY, I had had the idea of joining the RAF in 1950, only to be told by Father to finish my studies at university first. Now that I had done that and decided that a career in the chemical industry was not for me, I took myself down to the nearest RAF recruiting office, which rather oddly was in Chatham, the home of the Royal Navy. I went off to Chatham as soon as I had repaired my car's front spring with the help of the local blacksmith. At this time National Service was in being and so I would have had to 'do' my two years in one of the armed services in any event. However, I had decided that I wanted to make a career in the RAF so I was welcomed with open arms, so to speak.

I wanted to fly, preferably as a pilot, but would have accepted training as either navigator or flight engineer if I had been deemed unsuitable for pilot training. Having undergone a medical examination and various aptitude tests, I was accepted for aircrew training. A few days later I received 'the Queen's shilling', which was actually a four-shilling postal order! Acceptance of this means one is in the service of the monarch, the custom going back to the days when the 'King's shilling' was pressed into the hand of reluctant citizens by the 'press gangs'. This was the basis for the expression, 'one volunteer is worth ten pressed men.'

I reported to RAF Cardington on 20th October 1952 to be attested and collect my uniform.

The attesting ceremony consisted of each of the new recruits, about 20 of us if my memory serves me correctly, holding a bible in our right hands and repeating the oath of allegiance to Her Majesty Queen Elizabeth II. It was at this point I was became aware of the gravity of my commitment not that I had any intention of changing my mind – although up to being attested I could have withdrawn from the process and remained a 'civilian'.

An Autobiography by Captain D.B. Hopkins

The uniform I received was that of an Aircraftman 2nd Class or AC2 for short, which consisted of heavy serge trousers and battledress top, a 'best blue' top, overcoat of the same material, blue shirts of the hair variety, black shoes, boots [army pattern], PT kit with plimsolls, various items of underwear, socks, beret, knife, fork and spoon, a housewife and a button stick. Finally we were issued with a canvas kit-bag in which to keep everything on our travels.

If the reader has never been in the services, they may be forgiven for not knowing the purpose of either a housewife or a button stick. Unlike housewives found around homes then and now, the standard RAF issue housewife in 1952 comprised needles, thread, spare buttons and other such accoutrements as were deemed useful by the 'top brass', all wrapped up neatly in a sort of purse made of calico. The button stick was a six-inch long piece of brown plastic, with scalloped edges and a slot along some four of its six inches. I, like my fellow recruits, had absolutely no idea what one was supposed to do with such an odd looking piece of kit. We soon found out!

All the buttons and badges on our uniform were brass. Some weeks later we had become 'officer cadets', as signified by white flashes on our collars and caps, although we were still technically AC2's. Brass buttons and cap badges were specifically designed, we thought, to 'make work for the working man to do', as they had to be polished every day to a very high degree of lustre. The purpose of the button stick was to enable even the most ham-fisted recruit to get the desired lustre without getting 'brasso' on the material of the coat or cap.

Two other jobs had a high priority. First we had to get our berets reduced in size from the dinner-plate diameter they had when received. The method for doing this was to soak them in water to shrink them. The second task was to get a mirror-like finish on the toecaps of our boots, which were received from stores with the dullest finish one can possibly imagine – rather like the skin of a black orange! The method employed to achieve the mandatory lustre was to rub the toecap with an old toothbrush handle liberally smeared with black boot polish and spittle. Eventually, after many hours and much elbow grease, this produced the desired effect. Thereafter it was only necessary to 'bull' the cap with a yellow duster, polish and spittle to keep it in fine fettle ready for inspection by the most critical NCO. We also learned how to get a crease in our serge trousers and, more importantly, how to keep it there. The former was achieved by ironing them under a sheet of brown paper and the latter by the simple expedient putting them under the mattress and sleeping on them. I imagine recruits nowadays are issued with permanently creased trousers so they don't have the 'fun' we 'enjoyed'. We were at Cardington for four days, during which we started to learn to run everywhere unless we were marching. But this was all fairly gentle and gave a decidedly false impression of what was to come!

On 24th October we were all shipped off by bus and train to the Aircrew Transit Unit [ACTU for short] at Cranwell in Lincolnshire. Lest the reader should get the wrong impression, let me hasten to add that ACTU had absolutely nothing to do with the elite RAF College. ACTU was merely a holding unit for recruits destined for aircrew training. From here they were posted to the various Initial Training Schools, which were situated at Digby [Lincolnshire], Jurby on the IOM and Kirton in Lindsey [Lincolnshire]. As I mentioned earlier, National Service was still in being, and as those chosen for aircrew training during their national service had only two years in which to complete it, they were given priority. We arrived at Sleaford Station to be greeted by some of the loudest voices I had ever heard in my life. These came from a number of Corporal DI's whose aim in life, besides teaching us drill, discipline and esprit-de-corps, seemed to be to make life as unpleasant as possible. DI stands for Drill Instructor or, more aptly as we soon discovered, Dim and Ignorant!

My pay at this time was £1 one week and £1 10 shillings the alternate week. In order to receive these princely sums, we gathered every Thursday morning at 0900 for pay parade outside a particular hut. One of the DI's, it was the same one every week and you must imagine the voice, which sounded as though someone was trying to strangle him, would shout the following instructions: 'Right you 'orrible lot. When I call out your alphabetical numeral you will line up inside. A's,' and all those men whose surnames began with the letter A would troop inside and form the first row. 'B's,' 'C's,' followed until he had gone right through the alphabet. One week he had got to the 'M's' when one man ran up and apologised for being late as he had been on sick parade. 'Orl right,' he says, 'What's your name?' 'Phillips, Corporal,' came the reply. 'Right' shouts the DI, 'Get in there with the F's!'

For the next six weeks or so I spent the majority of my time polishing my kit, doing drill, PT, sports and 'education', and all my money in the NAAFI supplementing the meals provided. When I joined the RAF I was a somewhat skinny 10-and-a-bit stone. By the time I had been in the service three months, I was about 13 stone (and none of it fat!) and I have been much the same weight ever since. 'Education' was something of a laugh and seemed to be aimed at anybody who hadn't been to school. Bearing in mind the selection procedures we had all passed, it was nothing short of insulting, but it helped to keep us occupied!

Our accommodation was old wooden huts dating back to the 1914–18 War, with pot-bellied stoves for heating and service issue brown lino on the floors. Provided the stoves were stoked really well so that the chimney glowed red, the people within a radius of about six feet could keep

*An Autobiography
by Captain
D.B. Hopkins*

tolerably warm, but as soon as one stopped stoking, i.e. at 'lights out', the heating effect dropped rapidly to that of a candle!

The lino was required by the DI's to be kept polished to a very high lustre. Bearing in mind that it was winter and the ground was muddy, the only way to keep a reasonable shine was to walk, or rather, shuffle about on squares of old blanket. Anybody coming in and failing to do this was exceedingly unpopular with the other 13 members of the hut and was swiftly shown the error of his ways. One chap let the side down on several occasions, so eventually we decided to teach him a lesson. He had a habit of being the last into bed before 'lights out', so one night while he was away completing his ablutions, we moved his entire 'bed-space', consisting of bed, locker and wardrobe, out of the room into the storeroom. By the time he eventually returned to the room all the other 'bedspaces' had been shifted to take up the room left by the removal and the lights switched off. He counted his way to where his bed had been and tried to climb into bed, only to find it already occupied. From this he was expelled very firmly. He then tried the next one with a similar result! Finally he finished up in the storeroom, trying to sleep in his own bed propped up against the wall at a steep angle. Unfortunately he was so stupid that he didn't learn his lesson!

Friday night was 'bull night', ready for the Officer's Inspection on Saturday morning. If the standard was insufficiently high, then nobody got a weekend pass, a severe sanction since it meant we were confined to camp for the entire weekend. Consequently no effort was spared to make 'our' hut the best of all. Imagine, then, our total surprise and considerable annoyance when at about midnight on a Friday around the 5th November, when we were all soundly asleep after working hard the previous evening 'bulling', to be awoken by an enormous bang and to find, when we put on the lights, that the entire inside of the hut was covered in flour. Somebody from a neighbouring hut had crept in and placed a two-pound bag of flour on one of the stoves in the middle of the hut, lit the 'tuppenny banger' that had been inserted within and retired the way he had come. Let me inform you that two pounds of best self-raising distributed by this method goes an extremely long way! All 14 of us spent the rest of the night clearing up the mess and we just got it ready for inspection in time. You might think that the affair ended there. Not a bit of it! We bided our time until a couple of weeks later and after our rivals had retired for the night, we crept into their hut and discharged a soda-acid fire extinguisher all around their domain which had been painstakingly readied for inspection the following morning. It was with some satisfaction that we watched them spend the entire weekend cleaning and 'bulling' their hut and forfeiting their weekend passes!

Eventually my turn came to pass on to the next phase of training. It was known as 'grading' and consisted of a short course of basic flying instruction on a Tiger Moth. For this I was posted to RAF Digby, near Sleaford on 9th December 1952. In the course of this you were tested after five hours' flying, eight hours' flying and a final test after eleven and a half, after which one was given a grading mark on a scale of 1 to 9. 1 to 4 meant you were unsuitable for further pilot training, 6 to 9 meant you continued and if you got a 5 you were borderline and had a further test. We were never told what our marks were, but as I was allowed to fly solo, and only those with marks of 8 or 9 were given this privilege, I suppose, in retrospect, I should have been somewhat complacent about my future career. However I was not in the least complacent since I was decidedly under-confident in those days and lived each day one at a time. I would not have been surprised to be told that I did not have 'what it takes'. This is not false modesty and even if I had been given a glimpse of my later flying career in a handy crystal ball, I probably wouldn't have believed it.

The value of this grading was demonstrated when one cadet was being shown spinning. He had been shown how to get into and out of a spin, and was then told to do it himself. Apparently he froze completely with both hands gripping the coaming of the cockpit and no amount of cajoling by the instructor could persuade him to try the manoeuvre himself. This is the sort of behaviour that cannot be revealed by the most searching selection procedure, so grading saved the RAF a lot of money and time. Incidentally, this was the same cadet whose bedspace we had moved, so none of us were surprised when he got the 'chop'!

My first solo took place on 17th January 1953. I got airborne and immediately felt completely lost. No doubt this is a feeling common to quite a lot of new pilots on their first solos, but in my case it was compounded by the fact that the surrounding countryside was covered in snow and everywhere looked the same. At this point I'm sure my sense of self-preservation took over, as I soon rediscovered the airfield, no runways, just grass, and all too soon I was back on terra firma. I felt sure I had been airborne for at least an hour, whereas in reality it was only ten minutes. I cannot remember whether I had a feeling of exhilaration at going solo or sheer relief at having got back to earth successfully. Most likely it was a bit of both! Over the years I've always passed off the 'Biggles' picture (right) as taken on the day of my first solo. In fact it was taken a few days later after the snow had thawed and before I was

posted to RAF Jurby on the Isle of Man to become, hopefully, an officer before continuing training as a pilot.

So it was on 27th January that we were off to Liverpool by train and on to the IOM ferry for the somewhat rough crossing to Douglas. Jurby was a whole new experience. In the first place we were accommodated in barrack blocks, which were a great improvement over the wooden huts of Cranwell, and secondly we donned the white flashes on our collars and berets that denoted our status as officer cadets. A third, and not inconsiderable, benefit was an increase in pay, which was most welcome. Having seen recent TV pictures of officer training I realise that not much has changed over the past 47 years, as the picture (above) reveals. Here we can be seen attempting to build a bridge across a river under the direction of one of our number and using a hotchpotch collection of various pieces of lumber, rope and angle iron. It was great fun and invariably all participants take it in turns to fall in the water, which was thankfully not deep!

On another exercise we were supposed to be attacking an enemy force of some sort and although I cannot remember the details, I do remember that we were issued with a few thunderflashes apiece, which we hurled about with seemingly careless abandon, much to the surprise, and no doubt concern, of the inhabitants of a level-crossing keeper's house around which some of the action took place!

As at Cranwell, there was inter-block rivalry and this led to several skirmishes. One such was the occasion when our neighbours raided our block in our absence, collected all our PT shoes and suspended them in a kitbag from the roof of their block. This caused us some inconvenience until we retrieved them, but probably not as much as we caused them when we retaliated by collecting every piece of their cutlery and hiding it! You can be forgiven for thinking that the 'authorities' might have frowned on such escapades, but while they did not positively encourage them, they did not actually *discourage* them on the grounds that this sort of thing inspired a certain 'esprit-de-corps', which was to be commended.

Of course all this time we were being taught the intricacies of drill by a battery of DI's and our general fitness was catered for by participation in various sports. In my case, not being a football fan, cross-country running kept me as fit as I probably have ever been, before or since. On the subject of marching, I have enjoyed the experience of marching as part of a well trained body of men, but particularly so when accompanied by a military band. There is nothing to beat it! And there is no other nation that does it as well as we do!

One other aspect of our training was taken care of while we were in the IOM and that was to experience GAS. We had to go into a small, specially sealed building for a mercifully short time while different gases were released. These included tear gas and a minute dose of nerve gas. As we came out of the building coughing our hearts out, we were instructed to run round the building to get some fresh air into our lungs. I can truthfully say that those few minutes were the most uncomfortable in my life! By the latter part of April we completed the course with a passing out parade and were sent on leave as Acting Pilot Officers before onward posting to Basic Flying Training Schools.

I wouldn't want to give the impression that my time in the IOM was all work and no play. In fact we had most weekends to ourselves and on one occasion a group of us hired a car, specifically so that we could drive right around the famous IOM TT course and see for ourselves how difficult it must be to drive a motorcycle at high speed along the narrow winding roads.

Incidentally, one of the group, Bas Harris, was a very talented player on the organ. He was roped in by the station Padre to play at church parades on Sundays and he kept us all amused listening to a piece of 'pop' music of the day skilfully interwoven into the hymn tune he was playing.

Also in the group was Cliff Hill, whose main claim to fame, besides being a very good friend with whom I've regrettably lost touch over the years, was that he could not march to save his life! He was not like some unfortunate folk who march with the left arm swung forward at the same time as the left leg and vice versa. No, Cliff's failing was that he was always just half a step out of synchronisation with everybody else, rather like Corporal Jones of 'Dads Army'!

At this time in 1953 we were quite a military family, as can be seen right, and I wonder how many families could boast having members of all three services. Father still had his Home Guard uniform, Steven was a cadet at Pangbourne College, from where he later joined the Fleet Air Arm for a four-year stint as a pilot, and I am wearing my <u>very</u> new 'best blue' uniform from Gieves. Quite why father still had his old home guard uniform eight years after the HG was disbanded remains a mystery, although he

might well have used it while still teaching at HMS *Worcester* as part of his duties with the combined cadet force. Regrettably neither Steven nor I can shed any light on the subject!

I left Jurby as a commissioned officer and although I did not receive the actual document until several years later, this seems an appropriate place to include it in my story.

When first commissioned my cap badge had the crown of the late King George VI, but once The Queen had been crowned, the badge was changed to hers so my 'housewife' came into its own with the sewing the changeover entailed. Fortunately by the time I got my wings, the change had been made so I had only one sewing session to endure!

Elizabeth II, *by the Grace of God* OF THE UNITED KINGDOM OF GREAT BRITAIN AND NORTHERN IRELAND AND OF HER OTHER REALMS AND TERRITORIES QUEEN, HEAD OF THE COMMONWEALTH, DEFENDER OF THE FAITH.

To Our Trusty and well beloved   Derek Bryan Hopkins   Greeting :

WE, *reposing especial Trust and Confidence in your Loyalty, Courage, and good Conduct, do by these Presents Constitute and Appoint you to be an Officer in Our Royal Air Force from the* Twenty Ninth *day of* April 1953 . *You are therefore carefully and diligently to discharge your Duty as such in the Rank of Acting Pilot Officer or in such other Rank as We may from time to time hereafter be pleased to promote or appoint you to and you are in such manner and on such occasions as may be prescribed by Us to exercise and well discipline in their duties such Officers, Airmen and Airwomen as may be placed under your orders from time to time and use your best endeavours to keep them in good Order and Discipline. And We do hereby Command them to Obey you as their superior Officer and you to Observe and follow such Orders and Directions as from time to time you shall receive from Us, or any superior Officer, according to the Rules and Discipline of War, in pursuance of the Trust hereby reposed in you.*

GIVEN at Our Court, at Saint James's
the Twenty First *day of* July   1953 in the Second   Year of Our Reign

By Her Majesty's *Command*

CHAPTER THREE

Flying Training – I Get My Wings

APRIL 1953 saw me and 14 fellow trainee pilots arrive at No.1 Basic Flying Training School (BFTS), RAF Booker for the start of my flying training proper. Booker is now Wycombe Air Park and you can see it on the left as you whiz up the M40 on your way to Oxford.

Once again 'home' was a wooden hut, but with a difference. Now that my rank was enhanced to the dizzy heights of Acting Pilot Officer (APO) on probation, I had a batman, or at least part of the one that was allocated to each hut, which meant that the four of us who shared the hut no longer had to clean and polish as if our lives depended on it. We had it done for us. And how!

The batman I shared was a true professional, who believed that serving an officer was not a job but a vocation and certainly not demeaning in any way. He was one of a dying or even dead breed who believed it was his privilege to look after us. I doubt if I've ever been so well looked after, before or since my four months at Booker. Every day my suits and uniform would be pressed, whether I had worn them or not. Likewise all my shoes would be polished until they gleamed. Bert, for that was his name, believed that 'his' officers would be the best turned out of any in the entire unit.

After I had been there about a week, Bert asked me to put all the clothes that needed laundering on the floor ready to be sent to the laundry. This I did, shirts, socks, vests, underpants, pyjamas, etc. all in a big heap. When I wandered back into my room a few minutes later I found Bert putting the shirts in one pile and the rest in another. I told him I wanted the shirts to be laundered as well as the rest, but he informed me, in a kindly but very firm way, that he always took the shirts home to launder and iron himself as the laundry didn't make a proper job of them! A man who took more pride in his work would be hard to find.

Another difference was that the hut was furnished rather more

An Autobiography by Captain D.B. Hopkins

lavishly than I had been accustomed to hitherto, with an armchair and a desk at which I could sit when studying. The latter was quite essential, because from now on I was required to learn a great deal, not only about the aircraft I was going to fly, but also about such subjects as Air Law, Meteorology, Airmanship, Navigation, Morse code, Customs of the Service (i.e. how to behave as an officer) and many other things.

As at Digby, all the instructors were civilians employed by a company called Airwork. I imagine the reason for this was the rapid build up of the RAF at that time due to the Korean Conflict and that the Air Ministry needed many more instructors at short notice. So they recruited retired RAF instructors on short-term contracts. My instructor was a Mr Heelas, who took me through the mysteries of straight & level flight, turns, stalls and spins and circuits and landings. It lasted for just over 5 hours, at which time he sent me solo. This was consolidated over the next few weeks and then after about 15 hours flying, came instrument flying, both simulated and real, and aerobatics. During the latter I learned to <u>do</u> a loop, not, as those ignorant of proper terminology insist on saying, 'loop the loop'. We were also taught how to do a 'short landing', but the one in above photograph is slightly too short and definitely beyond a joke.

By the beginning of July I was ready for my 25-hour test, but before this I did a dual cross country navigation exercise, landing at the old London Airport at Croydon. I went there again just after I had my final test towards the end of July, mainly because the instructor I went with on both occasions had business to conduct.

Earlier in July on my solo landing-away navigation flight I flew to Hamble and whilst there I witnessed an unusual incident involving an Avro Anson communications aircraft. This had flown in to collect some VIP or other but on landing the undercarriage collapsed as I was watching from the control tower. I can hear to this day the amusement of the controller as he rang the Anson's base to ask for another aircraft to be sent ASAP! Fortunately there was no chance of a similar collapse happening with the Chipmunk as the undercarriage was fixed.

Another memorable event whilst I was at Booker was the RAF Flypast for the Coronation of The Queen on 2nd June. The rehearsals for this meant lots of formation flying for the instructors and days when we students had little or no flying. My second trip to Croydon was on 20th July 1953, making me possibly one of the last people to land there before the airport was closed and turned into an industrial and housing estate.

The course finished on 22nd July and after a couple of weeks leave, I was posted to the RAF Police Depot at Netheravon in Wiltshire for 'holding' until my next course started, and here I spent my time doing any odd job that was given to me.

During my very short stay there I met and fell in love with a WRAF officer who was a god-daughter of Marshal of the Royal Air Force Sir Phillip Slessor. The romance came to nothing as you will see, but I've sometimes wondered if it had blossomed whether I might have achieved a higher rank. YCNSTWLEM!

Once again I was put into the hands of another 'real' batman, who immediately set upon my clothes as if they had never been pressed/polished in their existence! After only a week of this delightful existence I made my way to RAF Pershore in Worcestershire and joined Number 10 Advanced Flying Training School for training on the Airspeed Oxford and hopefully to get my 'Wings'.

Incidentally Airspeed was the company set up by Neville Chute and his book, *Slide Rule*, is supposedly based on his experiences at that time. The Oxford was a twin-engined aircraft powered by two Cheetah X engines (no, this is not the reason for the title of this book, though getting them started on a cold winters day might have tempted one to stroke them), originally built as a bomber, and there is one on view at

*An Autobiography
by Captain
D.B. Hopkins*

the Imperial War Museum, Duxford. I saw this in the summer of 2000 and that is the first time I've seen one since the course finished in 1954. We were the last course in the RAF to gain our wings on the Oxford and at the morning briefings toward the end of the course, we were told to ignore fires on the airfield as it was 'just Oxfords being burnt!' But I'm jumping ahead somewhat.

After some time in Ground School, learning about the Oxford and most importantly being introduced to the problems and theory associated with asymmetric flight, we were introduced to our instructors. Mine was Sergeant Alec Hammond and the first thing he told me, an officer, was that on the ground he was required to call me 'Sir', but whilst in the air I would call him 'Sir', and I would have to mean it! In fact he was an excellent instructor and we got on like a house on fire. Sadly a few years later he was killed in a motoring accident in the USA whilst on a course training as a Thor Missile operator.

Most instructors I have ever met have their own particular idiosyncrasies, rather like schoolmasters, and Alec was no exception. If I did something wrong, he would say, 'What are you Hopkins?' And I would have to reply, 'I'm a clot, Sir'. One morning we took off with me at the controls when he shouted, 'Fire in the port engine'. I went through the routine of closing the throttle, pulling up the fuel cock, waiting a few seconds and then switching off the ignition, and finally pretending to operate the fire extinguisher. 'I have control', he said, 'that was ok but not quick enough. I'll fly the aircraft and you announce a fire in one engine and I'll show you how it <u>should</u> be done'.

After a few moments I called out, 'Fire in the starboard engine'. Alec's hands fairly flew around the cockpit and the starboard engine stopped, followed after a short pause by the port one, Alec having shut off the fuel on one engine and the ignition on the other. In the silence that followed, during which you could hear the proverbial pin drop, Alec's hands flew even faster round the cockpit while he restarted both engines. 'What am I?' he asked sheepishly after they were both going and we had regained level flight, 'You are a clot, Sir', I replied. This was a highly amusing incident that I used to tell <u>my</u> students about in later years to illustrate the point that it is better to get the drill correct by doing it at a reasonable speed instead of getting it wrong at high speed. I suspect that the accident at Kegworth was caused by a similar keenness for speed rather than accuracy!

Because the Oxford was not cleared for either aerobatics or spinning, we kept our hands in at these two important parts of flying training in the Chipmunk. There had never been a problem until the day my fellow student, Bob Brown and his instructor, failed to pull out of a spin and the aircraft finished up in some woods near Pershore town. All pilots will tell you that any landing you can walk away from is a good one, but this one…! Both Bob and his instructor were injured but fortunately not seriously and Bob completed the course successfully with the rest of us. (Tragically Bob Brown and his navigator Plt Off Alcock were killed in a Canberra whilst doing his conversion course at Bassingbourn and cynics might be tempted to remark that Bob was living on borrowed time after his first crash). Chipmunks were modified soon after this incident, with two 'strakes' on the aft part of the fuselage and I think I am right in saying that no further problems were ever encountered with spin recoveries.

Another exercise we did quite regularly was to practice forced landings. The idea was to close both throttles and pretend that both engines had failed, then pick a suitable field and get yourself into a position from where you could land in said field. We didn't actually land, but just did a low overshoot at about 200 feet AGL (Above Ground Level).

One of the traps for the unwary in the Oxford, which, with the best will in the world, couldn't be said to have been ergonomically designed, was the position of the VHF radio control box. Sitting in the left-hand seat, as one did when flying solo, the box was just behind one's left elbow. It had four push buttons with which to select one of four VHF channels and below these a switch. In the upright position one could receive messages and by pressing the button on the control yoke one could transmit. However the switch in its other position, pushed over to the left, was in the continuous transmit mode, so that everything one said was broadcast to the world. It was <u>very</u> easy to knock this switch into 'continuous transmit' with one's elbow and not realise it.

One day I was flying solo doing 'general handling' in the area over the Severn Estuary, as was a fellow student, John Gradwell, when the following was heard by all and sundry, 'F*** it – engine failure – check fuel – check switches – pick a field. I think I'll have a go at that one over <u>there</u>. Hmm, no, I think I'll try that one over there'. This was followed by the sort of noises small boys make when they are pretending to be aeroplanes, succeeded by, 'Mayday, Mayday, Mayday, this is Gradwell in the shit again!' Needless to say that he was indeed deep in the fertiliser business when he landed back at Pershore. Sadly, soon after this incident, which had us all in fits of laughter, John was 'scrubbed' from the course for failing to reach the required standard and I never saw him again.

There was some excitement in early February when the second prototype of the Bristol Britannia had a fire and was crash-landed in the Bristol Estuary, sufficiently close to Pershore to allow Alec Hammond and I to fly over the crash site and see the event. Little did I know then that one day I would be flying a very similar aircraft. (See chapter 11).

In November we had an Escape and Evasion exercise. The scenario is that you have been shot down in enemy territory and you must try to

*An Autobiography
by Captain
D.B. Hopkins*

avoid being caught and use your initiative to get back to a friendly country. To simulate this we were taken in a blacked out lorry to the middle of nowhere some miles from Pershore. We were each allowed to carry 4d (4 old pence) to make a phone call for help in case of a dire emergency. Otherwise we had no money or food at all. The 'enemy' forces looking for us consisted of the regular police plus specials and some units of the Territorial Army, all of whom were to touch us and say the code word 'Starling Jaunt' for us to be captured.

I was in a group of five and we soon recognised our location when we could see Bredon Hill in the distance. It was about 5pm and dark, being November, so off we set in the general direction of base. The weather was cold and foggy so by dawn we were feeling pretty miserable and hungry. It is all very well living off the land when there is something to eat, but all we found were left over potatoes in one field and some beetroot in another. Neither was much good as we had no means to cook them. In accordance with good practice, we holed up in a wooded area with the intention of staying there until darkness allowed us to move again with a fair chance of not being caught. After a few hours of trying to sleep and getting steadily colder and more miserable we all decided that enough was enough and moved off cautiously, avoiding habitation, towards our goal.

We were crossing one of the few fields that still had crops in it – mangle wurzles I think – when we saw what we thought was an irate farmer coming our way. Since we had been told not to antagonise the local communities in any way we stopped to explain what we were doing. Bad mistake! The old man, who looked about 90, laid his hand on my shoulder and in a thin reedy voice said, 'Starling Jaunt'. Thus I was caught. I was so amazed that this old man could be a Special Constable that it never entered my head to leg it across the field! The next thing I knew I was being taken to a Worcester city police cell, where I was locked up stark naked and interrogated leaning on a wall on my fingertips. Most uncomfortable, I can assure you. After repeating my name, rank and number for what seemed an infinite number of times, my interrogators got bored and I was returned to Pershore, a hot bath and a welcome bed!

The course proceeded steadily for the next couple of months and then on 18th December we had the Officers Mess Christmas Ball, arguably *the* social event of the year and certainly for the seven months duration of the course. I had arranged with my WRAF friend at Netheravon that she should accompany me, but she had reasons to change her mind at the last moment, which meant I would have no partner.

One of my fellow students had arranged to take a nurse from The Worcester Royal Infirmary to the ball but he had no car. Since I still had the 'Green Dragon,' he asked me to take him to the Nurses Home to collect his date, Betty. When we got there we met Betty in the guest's sitting room, which was reasonably full of nurses, and I thought there might be a chance of finding someone to accompany me for the evening. However it seemed that all those present had other plans or were about to go on duty. At that point Betty suddenly rushed off saying she had just thought of someone who might be persuaded to go. This 'someone', it seemed, had just come off duty and

was in the bath and intending to go to bed after a very long day. However, after considerable persuasion, and after I had agreed that a short evening dress was acceptable as her long dress was kept at home, the 'someone' reluctantly, I found out later – agreed to come with me. After some delay while she dried herself, and got dressed Staff Nurse Pamela Harley appeared. A vision in her short, black cocktail dress, our eyes met literally 'across a crowded room' and we were both instantly in love. Sounds incredibly 'corny' but it led to a romance that has gone on ever since and as I write this in the year 2000 we are very soon to celebrate our Sapphire (45 years) Wedding! YCNSTWLEM!

Soon after we met, my mother started calling Pamela 'Mella' to distinguish her from my cousin Pam. She is known as Mella to this day and I expect you can see why I fell in love so totally.

From the above it sounds as though we were engaged and married quite quickly. This was not so for various reasons, not least of which was the fact that I was under 25, the age after which one did not need to get permission to marry from one's commanding officer. Also – and this was quite a consideration – until you were 25 you did not qualify for 'married allowance', which meant a difference of about 20% of salary. We did, however, go out together quite a lot during the rest of my time at Pershore and spent much of our time off driving up to and walking on The Malvern Hills.

I should explain that just prior to our meeting Mella had had an operation on both her big toes and was having to be careful how she walked to avoid hurting herself. I'm surprised that I managed not to tread on her toes during the dancing we did at 'The Ball', but it appears that I was successful in that endeavour. In 1953 The Goon Show was at the height of its popularity on steam radio, to the extent that if one didn't get into the anteroom in the mess in good time one couldn't get

*An Autobiography
by Captain
D.B. Hopkins*

near enough to the radio to hear it. It was thus that during our forays to The Malverns I spent much time shoving Mella uphill, and preventing her sliding downhill, both to the accompaniment of various voices from The Goons

About this time we had started formation flying and in the picture on the left my right shoulder is visible while I am trying to keep station in line astern some ten feet from the Oxford in front. Alec Hammond is on the right. It looks quite difficult, but is really fairly easy provided you keep close enough to the aircraft on which you are 'formating'!

In January I passed my Instrument Rating test, thus gaining a 'White Card'. (As one gained experience one graduated to a 'Green Card' and eventually to a 'Master Green Card). This meant that I was now able to progress on to night flying, for which it is essential that you can fly competently solely by reference to the instruments.

In order to practise instrument flying, the Oxford was fitted with a system known as *two-stage amber*. With this system amber screens were fitted in the side and front windows of the cockpit. It was possible to see through these, thus enabling the instructor to keep a good lookout while the student was flying on instruments. The student used to wear a pair of dark blue tinted goggles, which allow him to see the instruments but stopped him looking through the windows. To stop the goggles steaming up, which they invariably did, a narrow tube from them was poked through a small hole in the side of the cockpit. A set of the screens and goggles were kept in each aircraft. The amber screens were old like the aircraft and quite brittle when cold, so it was quite common for them to break when being taken out of the window clips.

One of my fellow students, John Mullins, was the proud owner of a Morris 8 with a soft top and side screens, one of which was missing. On one occasion he had just completed an hour of instrument flying and was taxiing back to the dispersal when his instructor said, 'I have control Mullins, you can take out your screens now.' In doing so John broke both, as they were very cold. 'Now look what you've done, you've broken them,' says his instructor, 'You have control, I'll take mine out now.' Whereupon he promptly broke both on his side. With a somewhat red face, 'Tell you what, Mullins,' he says, handing John eight pieces of broken amber screen, 'You can have these for your car.' I never did find out what John did with his prize, and regrettably I never will as John was later killed flying a Hawker Hunter off the Dorset coast, while flying as a target for the Navy.

Around this part of the course I was doing some low flying with Alec Hammond and on the way back from the low flying area where I had been practising the art at 250 feet AGL (above ground level), Alec said, 'I have control, I'll show you some real low flying!' We were crossing a large area of market gardens to the east of Pershore and were over a very large field of Brussels sprouts. Alec took the aircraft down to within a few feet of the tops of the sprouts so that the two propellers were almost cutting a swathe through them when suddenly a man stood up from picking the crop, only some 25 yards in front of us. He almost immediately dropped flat on the ground, but not before I was able to see the expression of abject horror on his face, an image that will remain with me to my dying day!

Later that month I was able to put my newly gained proficiency in instrument flying to good use during the final navigation exercise of the course. This involved flying solo to another airfield, landing and returning to base. The airfield chosen for this was Feltwell, just to the west of Thetford forest in Norfolk. Five of us were doing this exercise taking off one after another.

I was the first to go and last was Pete Smallbone. At the briefing 'Met' told us that the layer of stratocumulus had a base of about 1500 feet with tops at 4500 feet. As the Oxford was not fitted with any anti-icing systems on the wing, we were briefed to climb to 500 feet above the cloud layer. As was so often the case, 'Met' were wrong in their estimate of the top of the cloud. It was, in fact, 10,000 feet and so I levelled out at 10,500 feet and set a heading for Feltwell. It was January 29th and the Oxford's cockpit heating system was so inadequate that by the time I reached my destination I was extremely cold! I landed, followed in fairly rapid succession by numbers 2, 3 and 4.

We were all in the crewroom warming ourselves with a most welcome cup of coffee when Pete Smallbone arrived. He taxied in, parked, shut down the engines and opened the door at the rear of the fuselage, whereupon a white hand flew out, hit the frozen ground and splintered into a hundred pieces. What on earth, we wondered, was that? When Pete got to the crewroom and had thawed out sufficiently, he told us that he had been taken short during his trip. In these situations during dual flying one could get the other pilot to take the controls while one went to the back of the aircraft, opened the door and relieved oneself, but solo was a different matter. Pete could not think what to do until he got so desperate that he took off one of his white cape leather flying gloves and filled it. Of course he couldn't put it down straight away, but since the temperature at 10,500 feet was many degrees below freezing, the glove with its contents soon froze solid. Definitely a case of YCNSTWLEM!

To open the door of the 'Oxbox', as it was affectionately known, one merely pushed down on a leather-covered chain rather like that in the early Minis. However, should one need to bale out, it was necessary to jettison the door and to do this one pushed down on the lever provided for that purpose. One day a student was taken short while flying dual and after asking the instructor to fly the aircraft for a few moments, waddled aft to the door. I should say at this point that we wore parachutes which were attached to the pilot at all times while flying and walking with one strapped to ones bum was quite difficult. When the student got to the door, he mistakenly used the jettison lever. The door immediately flew off into the slipstream pulling him out with it. With considerable presence of mind, he pulled the rip-chord and parachuted safely to ground – still holding the door! After hitching a lift from a passing motorist, he arrived back at the guardroom with his parachute in a big bundle under one arm and the door under the other. The latter was replaced where it belonged and the aircraft was flying again in a very short time! Definitely an instance of 'look before you leap'!

Early in February I had my final handling test, in which one had to demonstrate that one had learned sufficient about flying to be worthy of being awarded ones 'wings'. Naturally I was very nervous, still being, unnecessarily as it transpired, somewhat under-confident, but I passed with flying colours. Quite a milestone in my life! My final flight was on the 16th February, when I took part in the *spot landing* competition. The top five students on the course were given the opportunity to take part in this, the idea being to land the aircraft 'dead stick' as close as possible to the middle line of three on the runway. Three lines were put on the end of the runway in white paint so that they were clearly visible from a considerable distance.

The five of us chosen for this competition took it in turn to join the

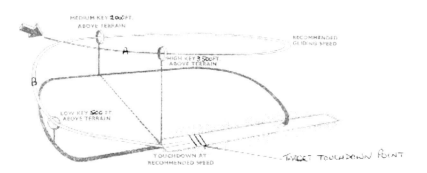

circuit at point 'A' and close the throttles and attempt to put the aircraft on the runway with the main wheels as close as possible to the centre line of the three. We were each allowed to open the throttles only once during this circuit, at point 'B', to check that the engines would open up to full power in the event of an overshoot being necessary. Generally speaking one aimed to be at the 'key' points at the height shown in the diagram. I mis-judged the last one of these and was rather lower than I should have been. I therefore resorted to what was known in the business as a 'split arse' turn on approach to correct my mistake. Notwithstanding the fact I was the only one of the five of us to touch down with my main wheels <u>exactly</u> on the middle line, I didn't win. I was disqualified for making the Runway Controller flee for his life from the '*Runway Caravan*' opposite the three lines. I hadn't thought my final turn to be half as hairy as it looked to observers, but apparently they thought it highly likely I was going to crash and all the fire crews jumped into their rescue vehicles. C'est la vie!!

Some of the cadets I had been with at Digby and Jurby had gone on to their wings training on Harvard aircraft and from one of them I heard the following cautionary tale. A particularly keen student had arrived at the flight lines one morning and seen his name down for a solo sortie in a Harvard. He didn't wait to be briefed by his instructor, but went straight to the aircraft, started up and got airborne. Not only did he not get briefed but he also forgot to check the fuel contents in his hurry to show his keenness. Consequently, not long after he was airborne, the engine stopped for lack of fuel. With considerable skill he found a suitable field and landed without damage to either himself or his aircraft. He found a farmhouse nearby and phoned base and told them what had happened. He was told to go back to the aircraft and wait.

In due time a fuel bowser arrived and put some petrol in the tanks. An instructor also arrived to fly the aircraft out of the field and back to base. To his consternation he found the plane parked very neatly, tail towards the hedge, in a field about the size of a postage stamp. Assuming that it had been turned round by the refuelling crew, he thought to himself, 'If this idiotic student can get it into this field I can get it out!' Without more ado he climbed in, started up and with the throttles wide open set off towards the line of trees at the other end of the field, into which he unceremoniously crashed!

Fortunately he was not hurt, but the aircraft was wrecked, and after extracting himself from the remains he said to the somewhat abashed student who had been watching proceedings from the safety of the ground, 'How the blazes did you manage to land in this tiny field?' To which the student replied, 'Oh, I didn't land in this field Sir. I landed in that big one next door and bounced over the hedge!' Moral of the story: Never assume – check!

*An Autobiography
by Captain
D.B. Hopkins*

The next excitement was the passing out parade and 'Wings' presentation by Air Marshal L.F. Pendred, the Air Officer Commanding Flying Training Command, seen in the photograph pinning mine on to a very proud chest. This was followed by sherry in the Officers Mess. Mother had come to the ceremony and met Mella for the first time.

After it was all over, Mother and I left in the 'Green Dragon', dropping Mella in Pershore on the way. She told me later that as she saw me and Mother disappearing down the road she wondered if she would ever see me again! I spent the next three weeks on leave in Arundel Road, Eastbourne the house to which Mother and Father had moved. I was waiting for my next posting and there was a possibility it would be on to Sunderland flying boats, which Alec Hammond had recommended. It was not to be, as those wonderful aircraft were about to be phased out of service and no more crews were being trained. YCNSTWLEM!

CHAPTER FOUR

Jet Propelled

Having now got my Wings and not being sent on to fly piston-engined aircraft, I was posted to RAF Worksop for conversion to flying jet-propelled aircraft. I arrived there on 24th March 1954 and commenced my arrival procedure. This is something one has to endure whenever one is posted to a new unit. It consists of taking a form around various sections and getting it signed by the person in authority to say that your presence on the unit has been recorded. One does the whole thing in reverse when the time comes for one to leave the unit. Very tedious!

The big difference at Worksop was that the first item on the agenda was to take possession of a standard issue RAF bicycle from the Bicycle Store. Strange, you may think, as I did until I found that everything at number 211 Advanced Flying School (AFS) was stretched out over a very large area and a bicycle was definitely essential to get from, say, the officer's mess to the airfield. You may be forgiven for asking, 'why not use your car?' Simple answer: not everyone was lucky enough to own a car and nobody but senior officers were allowed the privilege of driving round the station as room for parking at the various units was limited. More importantly, to get to some of the squadrons required travelling around the taxi track. Cars mixing with aircraft would have been very dangerous, whereas on a bike one could easily dodge taxiing Meteors by taking to the grass!

The course started with the customary ground school, before which the new course was welcomed to the mess with a dining-in night. The Chief Flying Instructor was a Wing Commander Coward, who had lost a leg during the war and now sported a tin one. His 'Dining-In Night' party trick was to pick on a likely young pilot officer from the new course, 'Come here young man!' 'Yes, Sir?' 'Kick my leg!' 'Pardon, Sir?' 'Kick my leg, that's an order!' Whereupon the Plt Off would kick the leg nearest him, which, the Wingco made sure, was the tin one. This made a resounding clanging noise and was greeted by hoots of laughter from

An Autobiography by Captain D.B. Hopkins

all present. Wg Cdr Coward did this for every new course that arrived, and caused much amusement all round.

However one course arrived and someone must have tipped them off, as when the order, 'Kick my leg' was given, the Plt Off concerned kicked his real one, leaving the Wingco dancing around on the tin one and howling with pain. I never saw him repeat his party trick after that!

During Ground School we learned about the differences between piston and jet engines, particularly from the handling point of view. The major difference is that while a piston engine gives you power very quickly when you open the throttle, a jet engine, having to overcome much more inertia of rotating parts, is considerably less responsive. The result is that with a jet one has to anticipate the need for power changes. It may not sound much, but the jets then in use had centrifugal compressors, which had a large rotating mass and it was quite difficult to get used to the idea and avoid being caught out with too little, or too much, power. Today's engines do not suffer from this drawback quite so much, largely because they use axial flow compressors with a much smaller rotating mass, but it is still a consideration one has to bear in mind.

Because we were now going to fly at high altitude, where it is necessary to breathe oxygen, we had to have a High Altitude Decompression Test. For this we were put in a decompression chamber with a Medical Officer and taken up to a simulated altitude of 37,000 feet, all the while breathing oxygen through the sort of mask we would wear in the aircraft. The aircraft in question was the Gloster Meteor Mk 7 for dual training and the Mk 8, shown above, for solo flying. The latter was, with the De Havilland Vampire, the mainstay of Fighter Command at that time, the former having seen service just at the end of the Second World War.

The first part of the decompression test was a climb to 25,000 feet, during which we were told to remove our masks so that we could experience the effects of anoxia (nowadays usually called hypoxia). These effects are quite insidious and it is important to know and recognise them in order to avoid becoming unconscious due to lack of oxygen. We were told to write our name on the piece of paper provided, and keep writing it. When we had become almost unconscious the MO restored our oxygen supply, and we were then able to see for ourselves, from the way our writing had deteriorated into unreadable scribble as we were slowly overcome by the lack of oxygen, just how insidious the effects are. Quite a few pilots have lost their lives over the years by not being sufficiently aware of the dangers of anoxia.

After this we were taken up to 37,000 feet, at which height an 'explosive decompression' was simulated as the chamber was rapidly depressurised. The first thing you notice is that you cannot see the man sitting opposite you, only 3 feet away, due to the fog that immediately forms. The second most noticeable effect is that everyone in the chamber breaks wind. It is important to do this, since not doing so would mean you might explode or, at the very least, suffer great pains in the alimentary tract. The quality of the resulting atmosphere I leave the reader to imagine!

In 1954 the RAF was still using the old phonetic alphabet which started – A for Able; B for Baker; C for Charlie...; K for King...; Q for Queen and so on. My instructor, Squadron Leader Tommy Ormiston's call sign was KB (King Baker) as he was the Officer Commanding No. 2 Squadron and since I was his student, mine was QB. Thus for the next six months I hurtled around the skies of Nottinghamshire calling myself 'Queen Baker'! Fortunately in those days 'queen' didn't have the connotation it does today!

During the first few flights I was taught how to handle the aircraft and it's engines and how to use the airbrakes, which were new to me since none of the aircraft I had flown up to then had this facility. I was also taught how to fly with one engine shut down or 'flamed out', to use the correct terminology, and, very importantly, not to use the airbrakes when flying with asymmetric power. The reason for the latter was to avoid the so-called 'Phantom Dive', which was caused by having too low a speed with a large amount of rudder input towards the live engine. Doing this caused the aircraft to flip on its back and dive into the ground. Many Meteor pilots were killed in this way, giving rise to the aircraft's nickname of 'Meatbox'. Although all this might give the impression that it was difficult to fly, it wasn't. In fact the Mk 8 was one of the nicest aircraft I ever flew in my career, and in fact it was so easy to do a smooth landing that it was known as 'a gentleman's aeroplane'!

After some six hours of this routine, plus lots of circuits and landings I was sent solo in the Mk 8. This was a strange experience in one particular respect since the Mk 8 was not fitted with an intercom. Well, to whom would you talk in a single seat aeroplane? So unless you were using the VHF to speak to Air Traffic Control or another aircraft it was more or less silent in the cockpit even with one's microphone switched

An Autobiography
by Captain
D.B. Hopkins

on, so much so that until you got used to the idea, it tended to add to the feeling of loneliness when out of sight of the ground.

Soon after this I was taught how to do bad weather circuits, keeping below a low cloud base of, say, 250 feet above ground level. This required a different technique from a normal circuit done at 1000 feet AGL, but was great fun since it gave you a legitimate excuse for some moderately low flying! We also did high-level circuits at 2000 feet AGL for use on those hazy days when forward visibility is restricted, especially into sun. Then another dual exercise was a High Speed Run, when I was shown how to control the aircraft at high Mach numbers. I forget the actual Mach number, but it must have been about 0.8, that is eight tenths of the speed of sound, at which speed the aircraft feels the effects of compressibility of air. It manifests itself as buffeting and pitching, terminating, if not controlled, in a dive from which it can be very difficult to recover, until you reach thicker air lower down. Instrument flying and aerobatics were also high on the agenda, as was map reading at low level and navigation at high level.

I passed my instrument rating test (IRT) in the middle of June and so was able to progress to night flying. On the night I was doing my first solo another aircraft landed on the runway. Nothing unusual in this you may think, but in this particular case the pilot omitted to lower his undercarriage, and whilst he was not hurt, it blocked the runway. At the time I was doing circuits and landings and I was instructed by ATC to orbit the airfield until the runway was cleared. This I did, flying for endurance, as I didn't have much fuel left. After a while I could see the situation was getting quite serious and so I suggested that I should shut one engine down to save fuel. This caused a near panic in the control tower, as single-engined landings were not considered the thing for a pilot on his first solo at night! I eventually landed safely, but I gathered from the ground crew that there was little more than the <u>smell</u> of fuel left in the tanks by the time I shut down the engines! If you think this a mite hairy for a pilot of my limited experience, think what it was like for some pilots in the Battle of Britain, who had very much less experience, some as little as 10 hours, and were thrown straight into the deep end of fighting the enemy, whereas I had some 250 hours under my belt!

Then came formation flying and the next picture shows just that. As I mentioned in chapter three, the art of formation flying is to keep close to the leader. That is the middle aircraft in this photo, and provided you do this, the rest is easy, even if the leader does steep turns or aerobatics – you just ignore the background view and keep 'station' on the leader. Part and parcel of formation flying exercises was 'tail chasing'. This was to teach you to keep another aircraft in sight so that you could, in theory, get close enough to shoot it down.

On one occasion the formation leader called, 'Tail chase GO!' and

broke hard right towards some cumulus cloud with the obvious intention of losing me in the cloud. I was trying to keep up with him and getting faster and faster as we were diving quite steeply. When you increase speed in a Meteor you need to keep winding the elevator trim forward to keep the stick forces to a level at which you can control the aircraft. I got myself into a position where I had to use both hands on the stick to keep the nose down far enough to enable me to see the other aircraft. It was a sort of catch 22 situation as I couldn't take one hand off the stick to wind the trim forward without the nose coming up and my losing sight of the leader. Suddenly, he did a sharp left climbing turn, and I immediately followed. As soon as I relaxed the forward pressure on the stick I went into an extremely high 'g' turn during which I completely blacked out! The next thing I remember was slowly regaining consciousness, finding myself in a cockpit and wondering for a split second where the hell I was and what the hell I was doing. Gradually I regained control of both the aircraft and my brain and finally managed to find the leader and regain formation on him for the return to base. Moral of that incident – always keep the aircraft in trim!

On another occasion I was coming back to base from some exercise or another and found myself over some broken cloud and not quite sure where I was. I thought that if I descended through the cloud I would soon be able to identify my position. I very soon saw some very lumpy hills all around me and realising that I was among the Pennines, I put on full power and went in the direction of UP like a homesick eagle. And the moral of that incident is – never let down through cloud unless you are certain where you are!

We did a lot of our circuit and landing training at Gamston Airfield, just south of Retford, so with a small detour I could fly over 'Windycroft' so that Grandma and Grandpa Marshall could see me. I have often felt they must have seen great changes in their lifetimes as

*An Autobiography
by Captain
D.B. Hopkins*

they were born well before the advent of the motorcar and now were seeing their grandson in a jet aircraft.

When I had a weekend free I used to go down to see Mella in Worcester and when this coincided with her day off, we spent time together touring around Worcestershire and our beloved Malvern Hills. Some time during the summer Mella moved down to Eastbourne to stay with my parents and work at the Princess Alice Memorial Hospital. This arrangement allowed me to go home during long weekends and see both my parents and Mella.

I finished the course on 31st August with an 'Above the Average' assessment overall and an 'Exceptional' rating for formation flying. Pilots were then assessed, and may still be, as far as I know, as Exceptional, Above the Average, Average or Below Average. To my considerable surprise, I received an Above the Average assessment on my wings course on Oxfords, so it seems I needn't have worried about my chances of success as a pilot, but then hindsight is a wonderful thing!

Having given me such a high assessment on the Meteor, Tommy Ormiston strongly recommended that I should be posted on to day fighter/ground attack aircraft, but the Air Ministry in their wisdom gave me a posting on to night fighters. (It is the same in any of the Services – if you are a qualified electrician you will finish up as a cook!) I had just about resigned myself to a tour flying the Meteor NF14 when that posting was cancelled and changed to a tour on bombers. Consequently, after spot of leave and cooling my heels at Worksop until the end of September, I was sent to the Bomber Command Bombing School at RAF Lindholm (near Doncaster and now one of HM's Prisons) to learn how to drop bombs.

During my leave I decided that I had to part with the 'Green Dragon' as it was getting to the stage in its life when it needed more repairs than were economically viable. I exchanged it for another motorbike, a Royal Enfield 350cc. Soon after I got it, Mella and I decided to have a day out on the Medway at Tonbridge. So we packed a picnic and off we went. We hired a boat and I rowed up the river until we found a suitable spot for our picnic. I tied the boat to a handy tree root, got ashore and took the picnic from Mella. I then attempted to help her out, but she was too near the stern and as she was trying to get onto the riverbank the boat gradually swung out leaving Mella suspended over the water into which she inevitably fell to the accompaniment of much splashing and hilarity. Fortunately it was a lovely sunny day so I rigged up one of the oars to make a clothes line upon which we hung Mella's soaking wet apparel. She had to strip off to her foundation garment and have her picnic wearing my mackintosh to preserve her modesty. The look on the faces of passers by in other boats, as they saw all this laundry hung out to dry, was nothing short of incredulous and made me wish I had a camera with me! In fact her rather thick skirt was still damp by the time we got back to Eastbourne, even with the draught on the back of the bike. The only ill effect from this incident is that ever since Mella has only liked water in a bath!

It is interesting to note that when the first jets entered service with the RAF, it was rumoured that only pilots below the age of 32 would be allowed to fly them as it was thought that the strain of flying at high speed would be too much for anyone older! What a load of balderdash that idea turned out to be, because a good friend of mine was still flying them as an instructor at the ripe old age of 60!

Often, returning to Worksop in the Meteor 8, we used to come in at maximum speed, break left to join the circuit and extend the airbrakes to lose speed ready for landing. This produced a sort of howling, whistling noise and was known as 'spreading the blue note'. Because my new motorbike sometimes made a similar noise, I christened it 'Bluenote', painted the fuel tank to match and it was always referred to by that name until I sold it.

I arrived at Lindholm on 29th September for a two-week course of bombing instruction on Varsity aircraft. All the take-offs and landings were done by very experienced staff pilots, many of whom had been flying during World War II, so all I was required to do was fly straight and level over the bombing ranges (Otmoor near Oxford and Wainfleet in the Wash). Also on the course were navigators who were being trained to become navigator/bomb aimers. They gave the instructions, 'left, left' or 'right' or 'steady' and the instructors stressed the need to us to fly the aircraft at a steady height and speed, keeping the 'ball in the middle'. The slip indicator, as it was properly called, consisted of a ball in a curved tube of liquid which showed whether the aircraft was sliding sideways or 'slipping'. If the aircraft is slipping when the bomb is released, the bomb will not go where the aircraft is pointing, but off to one side and has even less chance than normal of hitting the target. This is as popular with bomb aimers as dropping catches is with bowlers in a cricket match!

I did five trips in the Varsity, which included visual bombing at 4000 feet, simulated GH bombing and 'high' level bombing at 7000 feet. The staff pilots were all ex-wartime veterans and on the return from my first exercise, the pilot, a Pole, got the staff bomb aimer to give him a 'bombing run' to keep him on the runway centreline until we were only some 100 yards from touchdown. I thought this particularly amusing until I found out later that it was necessary for his crew to do this, as he was getting quite myopic in his old age! YCNSTWLEM!

I then had about ten days leave before I reported to number 231 Operational Conversion Unit (OCU) to learn to fly the English Electric Canberra light bomber.

*An Autobiography
by Captain
D.B. Hopkins*

But before I move on to the next chapter, the incident with the 'no wheels' landing reminds me of the Atcherly twins. These two, who were well known throughout the RAF, were what one would call 'characters'. One of them had rather poor eyesight and the other some problem with his waterworks. In order for them to pass their medicals when joining the RAF, one twin did both eyesight tests and the other provided both urine samples. Unfortunately one twin was killed when he disappeared over the Mediterranean in a Meteor, but the other rose through the ranks and at one point in his career was the AOC (Air Officer Commanding) of one of the Groups in Training Command. It was during this time that a student at a flying training school landed with his undercarriage still up. Upon hearing about the incident, AVM Atcherly decided that he had better interview the student and give him a 'bollocking'. He decided that rather than have the student report to his office he would go to the unit concerned and see the young man there. He organised a single seat Vampire Mk5 and off he flew. As he got near to his destination he got somewhat lost and not wanting to embarrass himself was refusing to answer ATC's increasingly worried calls. Finally the ATC controller asked him where he was, to which he replied, 'I'm shulking!' (He spoke that way.) Eventually he found the airfield and landed, yes you've guessed it, wheels still up! Having skidded to a halt on the runway he was sitting in the Vampire with the hood still closed when a corporal from a fire vehicle started to wield a fire axe thinking the hood was stuck, when the AVM wound it open with words, 'What's the matter, lad?' To which the corporal replied, 'Hurry up and get out of there Sir, the AOC will be here in a minute!'

Later the AVM met the student who was the cause of all this fuss and bother, and told him that he should be more careful in the future, but as he too could make the same mistake he told him, 'I'll meet you half way, I'll buy you a beer in the bar!' Quite a character! I also heard that once while he was inspecting some students before presenting them with their wings, he passed a particularly tall and thin student with fair hair who was sporting a wispy moustache and remarked to him, 'Shave it off, lad, its sapping your strength!'

In chapter three I mentioned the runway caravan. I need to mention it again in connection with the next incident. The caravan was just what its name suggests positioned at the side of the duty runway and manned by a member of Air Traffic Control. Among his duties, the controller would have to watch for aircraft approaching to land and check whether their undercarriage was down or not. In the latter case he would fire a red Verey light warning the pilot to go around. Another duty was to clear aircraft for take-off when radio silence was being observed so as not to alert an enemy of a raid. In this incident a Meteor flown by a student at night called 'downwind', was 'cleared to finals', then called 'finals one, two, three greens' and was 'cleared to land'. After this there was no sign of the aircraft until about half an hour after it had been cleared to land. At that point the pilot appeared at the door to the runway caravan, *having completed the approach on foot!* He said that he had undershot the runway and landed in a wood, but that the aircraft was more or less undamaged. Next morning a search party took several hours to find the wreckage of the Meteor, the largest remaining portion of which was the nose back to the rear of the ejection seat. The pilot was adamant that he had scarcely scratched the thing, which shows just how disorientated he was and even more lucky to have walked away from it without injury. YCNSTWLEM!

During my course at Worksop the well-known cartoonist Pat Rooney visited the mess and, like most of my contempories, I had my 'likeness' done. The spanner in my hand is to illustrate my love of amateur engineering, the aircraft are Meteors and the car is a not very good likeness of the Green Dragon. The original cartoon hangs in pride of place on my office wall to this day, a constant reminder of sunny summer days at RAF Worksop.

'DEREK'.

*An Autobiography
by Captain
D.B. Hopkins*

CHAPTER FIVE

Bassingbourn –
First Time Round

I ARRIVED AT NO. 231 Operational Conversion Unit (OCU), RAF Bassingbourn in Cambridgeshire on 20th October 1954, to train as an operational bomber pilot on the English Electric Canberra. This was the first jet bomber to be operated by the RAF and in 1954 was quite new, having first flown on 13th May 1949 and entered service with No 101 Squadron in 1951, replacing the ageing piston-engined Lincolns. It is interesting to note that as I write this in 2000 the Canberra is still in operational service with the RAF in the form of the PR 9 (Photo Recce) version shown below.

English Electric also built the RAF's first truly supersonic fighter, the Lightning, which was capable of speeds around 1,500mph. Quite a record for a company whose name has long been forgotten by most people! Not by me though, as the Canberra was a truly great aircraft, with which I had a long association, as you will see.

Because many squadrons were being equipped with Canberras in 1954, there was a need for large numbers of aircrew. To meet this requirement, 231 OCU was bursting at the seams with students. This being so, accommodation in the Officers Mess was totally insufficient to house every new student. Thus I found myself sharing a caravan with another new student. The weather was unseasonably cold, the heating in the caravan poor and the insulation even poorer. The heating consisted of a coal burning fire which was just about adequate if stoked to the point where the chimney glowed red, but as soon as we went to bed and the fire went out, we practically froze, making sleep

impossible. We stuck this out for about a week, after which we persuaded the mess to find us warmer accommodation.

As I was destined for a bomber rather than a PR squadron, it was necessary to find two navigators with whom I would train, then join a squadron and fly together for the next two and a half years. All the new students, pilots and navigators, met up on the first day in ground school and after getting to know one another, joined up as crews. I crewed up with David Brown, known for some inexplicable reason, as 'Jim', who was to be the Nav Plotter, while Sam Slatter was the Nav Observer/Bomb Aimer.

When travelling from 'A' to 'B', Jim navigated the aircraft and Sam provided 'fixes' every few minutes using the 'Gee' set. Gee was an airborne radar device that saw use in the Second World War and the system comprised a number of Gee chains covering most of the UK. Each chain consisted of a master transmitter and two or three slave transmitters. The master transmitter transmitted radio pulses, which were received by both the aircraft and the slave ground stations. The slaves automatically retransmitted each pulse at a fixed time interval after reception, so that the aircraft received pulses from the slaves as well as the master transmitter. By timing the intervals between receiving the various pulses, the navigator could find his position. Generally speaking a fix could be taken to be accurate within two miles. Crude compared with present day GPS, but all we had at the time! The equipment in the aircraft consisted of a cathode ray tube and controls, by which the observer used to get the time differences. He then used a special chart to work out the fix. This took around a minute for each fix and Sam would pass the information to Jim to plot on his chart and calculate whether we needed to alter course to keep on track.

For accurate navigation a fix was required every three minutes and the conversation from the nav's compartment was either, 'Have you got that fix yet, Sam?' 'No, the signal keeps breaking up!' or 'Here's the fix Jim', 'Hang on a minute, I'm not ready for it yet.' On a navigation exercise lasting anything up to three hours, this conversation could get somewhat repetitive, not to say boring, but fortunately it was usually interspersed every so often with a loud bang from Sam's side of the nav compartment. The first time this happened I very nearly ejected in shock, but once I discovered it was Sam giving the Gee set what was known as a 'technical tap' by thumping it on both sides at once, I was able to relax. The Gee sets being full of radio valves were notoriously unreliable and the 'technical tap' was the recognised method of restoring normal service!

The course started with three trips in the dual control T4, lasting in total about three hours, after which Jim and I launched ourselves in the B2 version, like the ones shown on the following page, which actually

*An Autobiography
by Captain
D.B. Hopkins*

belonged to No.9 Squadron and which we were to fly later, although we didn't know it until the end of the course. Then came a dual check followed by flying as a complete crew doing cross-country navigation exercises, visual bombing and GH blind bombing. GH was an offshoot from Gee, again used during the war, and it enabled bombs to be dropped through cloud from very high altitude. It was used up to 45,000 feet and experienced crews could achieve an accuracy of around 200 yards, presumably close enough if one was using nuclear bombs, but not very effective with conventional explosives.

Visual bombing was carried out up to a maximum of 25,000 feet, that being the limit of the capabilities of the T2 bombing computer and sighting head. Once again these were leftovers from WW II and are now museum pieces.

The computer fed information such as height, drift and airspeed to the bombsight both of which were situated in the nose of the Canberra to the left of the bomb-aimer's couch, on which he lay in a prone position whilst guiding the pilot to the target with the familiar, 'left, left' or 'right' or 'steady' and, 'bombs gone' after release. You will have noticed that 'left' is repeated while 'right' isn't. This is so that the pilot, who is listening to this on the intercom, which can be pretty noisy at times, doesn't get confused and turn the wrong way. It sounds unnecessary, but I can assure you that it isn't. Because there is always a slight lag between the height and airspeed information getting from computer to sighting head, it is vital that the pilot flies very accurately and without 'slip'.

One of the targets we used for practice was 'The Ship' in the Wash and it was every crew's ambition to get a bomb down the funnel of this old coaster sitting on the mud on the north shore of the Wash. Given the shortcomings of the system, it was largely a matter of good fortune if the bomb landed reasonably close to the target, so you can imagine our delight when we achieved this seemingly impossible feat on one joyful occasion!

The bombs used for practice were quite small, weighing 25 pounds, and exploded on impact with the ground with a flash and a puff of smoke so that the observers on the range could plot them and give you the result by radio. The main problem with them was that at the sort of height used for GH bombing, where the temperature could be as low as −60°C, they had a tendency to ice on to the release mechanism and not fall off when 'released'. If they stayed put, it was no problem. You simply closed the bomb doors and returned to base. They might drop off once you got down to lower and warmer altitudes or if you went through some turbulence, and while this usually didn't cause a problem as they were not supposed to explode before they had gone some distance from the aircraft, it did mean that once you had landed, the armourers had to meet the aircraft with a sort of stretcher with which they could catch the errant missile as the bomb doors were slowly opened using the hand pump. But if they dropped off a second or so after they should have done, they would probably land outside the danger area. Getting an ODA was cause for an official inquiry and so to be avoided if at all possible. Fortunately we never had one, but that was due more to luck than good judgement.

One of the methods of finding the runway in poor weather was a Ground Controlled Approach or GCA. The GCA control caravan sat close to the far end of the duty runway and the controller had two radars, one showing him the aircraft's position relative to the correct flight path in azimuth, the other in height. Thus the controller could give the pilot headings to steer to keep on the extended centre-line of the runway and information about whether he was on, above or below the glide-path. As I completed a GCA one night, the last aircraft to land before the airfield closed, I was somewhat surprised to hear a fanfare of trumpets over the VHF. To my enquiry as to the reason the controller informed me, 'Trumpets to welcome you home.' YCNSTWLEM!

We continued with lots more of the same mixture of navigation and bombing exercises, both by day and night until we finished the course on 2nd February 1955. I went home to Eastbourne for some leave, Jim went to his home in London and Sam to Wales, during which we learned that we had been posted to No.9 Squadron at RAF Binbrook, near Grimsby. This was a great privilege as 'Shiny Nine' is a very old squadron, whose battle honours include the first 1000 bomber raid on Cologne, the sinking of the Tirpitz with 617 Squadron and the raid on Hitler's retreat at Berchtesgarten just before the end of the war. The list of commanding officers is peppered with famous names like 'Stuffy' Dowding and 'Huff Puff' Lloyd. The squadron was formed on 8th December 1914 and since my birthday is 8th December, one might consider this more 'Writing on the Wall'!

*An Autobiography
by Captain
D.B. Hopkins*

CHAPTER SIX

There's Always Bloody Something!

J IM, SAM AND MYSELF arrived at RAF Binbrook on 21st
February 1955, ready to join No.9 Squadron. The official motto of
the squadron is *Per Noctem Volamus* meaning *We Fly By Night*. The
unofficial motto is *There's Always Bloody Something* or TABS for short,
which was adopted by the squadron in 1941 when they were based at
Honington and flying Wellingtons. The validity of TABS became
apparent when the then CO, Wing Commander Arnold, flew his
damaged aircraft level long enough for his crew to bale out but was
then killed in the crash that followed.

Having settled into our accommodation in the Officers Mess, I found
that mine was once again in a hut, this time shared with a pilot from 50
Squadron. We reported to No.9 to meet the CO and the other crews.
The CO was Squadron Leader George Bastard and it is to his lasting
credit that he used the obvious pronunciation of his name. If anybody
used B'stard (and many people did) he would say, 'My name is spelt
Bastard and pronounced Bastard!' He made us feel most welcome and
explained the nature of our role in the RAF, namely to be part of the
deterrent against the USSR in the cold war. He also told us that at the
moment we were an unclassified crew (i.e. useless) and our first task
would be to achieve 'Combat' status, followed in due course by 'Combat
Star', 'Select' and finally 'Select Star'. The latter two would require a lot
of work and experience on our part!

At this juncture it is interesting to note that there were five
Canberra squadrons based at Binbrook. Besides 9, there were 12, 50,

101 and 617. Each squadron had 10 aircraft so that on an exercise involving all the squadrons there could be anything up to 50 aircraft taking off at half-minute intervals. Quite a sight!

Once I had had a check ride with the Squadron QFI (Qualified Flying Instructor), the three of us started our training to become a 'Combat' crew, which involved visual bombing either on 'The Ship' in the Wash, Otmoor near Oxford or at Chesil off the Dorset coast, where the target was a raft moored in the sea and painted Day-Glo red. In addition we did GH bombing at Theddlethororpe off the Lincolnshire coast, at Chesil and Luce Bay in Scotland. This was interspersed with long-range navigation exercises and General Handling. We normally took 8 bombs to drop on the selected target, either visually or by radar and usually one at a time, but occasionally a stick of two. All these bombs were recorded and our average scores were entered on the squadron 'Bombing Ladder'. Naturally there was considerable competition to be top of the ladder.

In 1955 there were few restrictions on where we could fly, there being only one 'Airway', Amber One, and it only went up to 10,000 feet. Occasionally when we were detailed for a 'general handling' sortie we would take the opportunity to 'visit' our homes by making a round trip over Wales, London and Eastbourne. When we got to Eastbourne, I used to fly up over the pier which took us directly over my parent's house and Mella and Mother would appear on the back lawn waving a large tea towel, which we could see quite easily. I hate to think what would happen today if a Tornado pilot did something similar!

Around this time a Canberra of one of the other squadrons suffered a starter explosion. The result is shown by the series of pictures, which

*An Autobiography
by Captain
D.B. Hopkins*

graphically illustrate how well and how completely an aircraft full of fuel burns despite the best efforts of the fire crews. The lesson to be learnt is not to hang about the vicinity should you be unlucky enough to have it happen to you, although this was the only starter explosion I ever heard of, until the B6 version appeared. This had a new starter with three cartridges in it. On one occasion one of these fired all three cartridges at once and thereafter only one cartridge at a time was loaded.

In July I went back to flying a Chipmunk for a change of scenery as it were, and to give a number of Air Training Corps cadets flying experience. Most of the cadets were in their teens and had no previous experience of flying, so it was interesting to see how they reacted to being airborne. We were not allowed to suggest to the cadets what the trip would comprise. Instead we had to ask them what they would like to do, the idea being not to put them off flying by doing violent manoeuvres like aerobatics and so on, unless specifically asked.

One afternoon a cadet asked if he could fly in cloud, so I obliged by climbing up to about 4000 feet, which took a considerable time in a Chipmunk. It being summer, the cloud was small fair-weather cumulus, but nevertheless quite turbulent inside and this young man was promptly sick into the paper bag so thoughtfully provided for the purpose. We then descended and joined the circuit at Binbrook for a few landings and take offs. When we finally taxied back in, he asked me somewhat sheepishly not to tell his fellow cadets that he had been sick, presumably because he didn't want to appear less resilient than his peers. I was able to reassure him of this and I have kept his secret ever since. I have often wondered if he took up flying as a career or settled for a less stomach-churning occupation on the ground!

By the beginning of August Jim, Sam and I had become sufficiently skilled in our respective roles to achieve 'Combat' status and by way of a reward we were allowed to go on what was called a 'Lone Ranger' exercise, which meant flying to some RAF base abroad. We went to RAF Wunsdorf and spent a pleasant weekend looking around Hanover. You might be tempted to think that a Lone Ranger was just a jolly, but you would be wrong. For the navigators it was training in navigation over unfamiliar territory, and for the pilot, good experience of landing at a new and different airfield.

Life carried on in the same vein for the next few months with the added excitement of Bomber Command exercises, which simulated war conditions and involved fairly long flights by day and/or night, culminating with an FRA on a target on a bombing range in Germany. An

FRA or First Run Attack was done with the aid of GH and meant you had only one chance of dropping your bomb, actually a 25lb practice weapon to simulate either a stick of conventional HE bombs or a nuclear weapon. One such exercise was called 'Beware' and took place on 2nd October, when we dropped a bomb on the range at Nordhorn from 40,000 feet. The day after we dropped four more bombs at Luce Bay using GH, then did a high speed run up to about .83 Mach and returned to base.

For the next three weeks my log book is strangely lacking in entries. This was due to a very special occasion. *Mella and I got married.* We had got engaged on 6th February, Mella's birthday, and as there had been no sign of Mella's parents organising our nuptials, originally planned for 18th May, we went ahead with our own arrangements with the help of my parents. In the days leading up to our wedding I had found a small house to rent in Louth, which was within easy commuting distance of Binbrook. By today's standards, this was not a terribly well appointed abode, being in a terrace and having an outside loo, which was jolly cold in winter, no hot water, and a bath which was got to by raising the hinged dining table above it! But it was ours and we were happy there for the next couple of years. We had nice neighbours and one couple in particular, Joan & Eric Stanley, became very good friends, whom we still visit from time to time.

In July we had bought a new Hillman Minx to replace the 'Blue Note'. I had also applied for, and received, permission to marry from the CO, this being necessary as I was still a few months short of my 25th birthday.

All preparations being complete from my end, I went on leave and on 7th October 1955 we became Flying Officer and Mrs Hopkins in the Town Hall, Eastbourne. We then went to the Cavendish Hotel on the

*An Autobiography
by Captain
D.B. Hopkins*

seafront for our reception, which was a luncheon and of which both Mella and I have absolutely no recollection as the whole day seems to have passed in a complete fog. Since the reception was a luncheon, we repaired to 'Woodleigh', my parents home, for the cake-cutting ceremony before setting off for our honeymoon in the Hillman.

We got away at about 3.30pm but didn't get very far before we had to stop to quench our considerable thirsts with several cups of tea in a suitable café in Shoreham. From here we made our way to Midhurst, where we spent our first night at the Angel Hotel. The following day we drove to Lyme Regis via Stonehenge, and it is interesting to note that one was allowed on to the stones, in the days before they became such a magnet for tourists and hippies alike.

Over the next couple of days we wended our way to Lands End, crossing Dartmoor and Bodmin Moor. We stopped in Penzance and rather than have lunch in a restaurant, we bought genuine Cornish pasties fresh from the oven and took them with us. They were still piping hot when we got to Lands End and so big that we had some bits left over to feed the gulls! On then to Lynton and Lynmouth, where we were able to see the devastation caused by the dreadful floods that had occurred only recently. Next day, on along the north coast of Somerset to Bridgewater, then up the Cheddar Gorge on our way to Priddy to stay with my Aunt Mary and Uncle Ron, who worked at Wookey Hole Caves as guides.

At this point I must mention the controversy we engendered by driving up the Cheddar Gorge. If you have driven up it yourself, you will know that it is quite a long drive and that the gradient changes frequently from steep to shallow and back to steep again. It was while we were travelling *up* one of the less steep parts that Mella observed that we were now going *down* the gorge. I tried then, and have been trying for 45+ years, to explain that she was experiencing an optical illusion and that we were still going *up* the gorge. We have repeats of this discussion at fairly regular intervals and it usually has us writhing about in fits of laughter after only a few moments. I'm convinced that it is small things like this that help to keep a marriage alive over such a long time.

After six days of touring and laughing we got back to Eastbourne. We packed all our belongings, which didn't take very long as we hadn't much, and off we set for Louth to install ourselves in our tiny house by the canal next to the gasworks. It was this aspect of our abode that was a contributory factor in our changing our car for a saloon rather than a soft-top, but I'll come back to this later. Recently we went back to Louth to see where we had started our married life only to find that both the gasworks and our house no longer existed. YCNSTWLEM!

At the beginning of November, 9 Squadron re-equipped with

Canberra B6's, which were a considerable advance on the B2's. In the first place they had more powerful engines and greater fuel capacity and secondly a much improved oxygen system. The uprated engines also had progressively variable guide vanes to replace the two-position ones on the B2. This was a great improvement in respect of engine handling, particularly on the approach to landing in icing conditions. Just six days after our conversion, Sam, Jim and I dropped 16 bombs at Wainfleet with an average error of only 86 yards advancing us to the top of the visual bombing ladder and qualifying us for 'Combat Star' status.

On the 19th November a Sycamore arrived to give some of us experience of being winched up into a *helicopter*. (I have never been able to say or write helicopter without a smile, since an instruction to amend AP129 (Manual of Flying) appeared, which instructed the owner to change *Heliopter* to read *Hicopleter*). The winching was good fun, although the chap whose turn came immediately after mine may have thought otherwise when the strop broke when he was a few feet off the ground! Fortunately he was unhurt, but the incident brought forward the change to strops made of nylon rather than canvas, the latter rotting after being repeatedly dunked in the sea.

Around this time the squadron was told that it was to be detached to the Far East as part of 'Operation Mileage' to replace 12 Squadron, who were already out at Butterworth in Malaya. This was an ongoing operation to end the 'emergency' of CT (communist terrorist) infiltration into the region. Each squadron spent about 4 months at Butterworth, on the west coast of Malaya opposite Penang Island; the first was 101 Squadron, who had been replaced by 12, and now it was our turn. Since this operation involved area bombing, we started to practice formation flying and then low level bombing in formation.

While all this training was proceeding smoothly, but without too much urgency since we were not due in Malaya until March, the Squadron was told that it was to make a goodwill tour of West Africa, before going to the Far East, leaving Binbrook on 25th January 1956. Despite the flurry of activity this engendered, on 19th December the three of us flew to RAF Habbaniya in Iraq via RAF Idris (now Tripoli) in Libya and back, as our reward for gaining Combat Star status. We had to return via Marham due to bad weather at Binbrook, and during the evening we spent there I won a kitchen clock playing bingo for the first, and last, time in my life.

I arrived home in Louth the next day, in time for Christmas, loaded with new potatoes, oranges, grapefruits and other goodies purchased in Idris, plus the clock, which we had hanging in the kitchens of various houses for many years. My parents and sister Nola had come up to spend the festive season with us, although quite how we all fitted into our tiny house I can't remember.

*An Autobiography
by Captain
D.B. Hopkins*

Once Christmas was over it was back to formation training combined with the demonstration flying that we would be doing in front of large audiences in Africa, including The Queen and Duke of Edinburgh. We also had to be kitted out with gabardine uniforms for ceremonial wear in the tropics, in addition to the usual khaki drill shorts and shirts for everyday wear. Unfortunately for Sam, it had been decreed that only pilots and plotters were to go on the tour. The picture on the following page shows us posing by one of our aircraft. I'm second from the left and the 'Boss' is sixth from the left. Surprisingly none us appear to be shivering despite the snow.

Whilst keeping cool was not a problem in wintry UK, it is fair to say that climbing into a Canberra that had been standing for any length of time in the tropical sun was something none of us looked forward to as the temperature in the cockpit could be well over 100°F. To help alleviate the problem, we were issued with Air Ventilated Suits (AVS). They were meant to be worn over a string vest and underpants and were plugged into a cold air source in the cockpit, which blew refrigerated air through pipes all over the suit. They were not particularly comfortable, but did help to keep one cool.

Air Vice Marshal Whitley (eighth from the left) had been appointed to lead the tour. He was a man blessed with an amazing ability to remember people's names. He visited us soon after the tour was announced and we were all assembled in our crew room so that the fourteen of us could be introduced to him. Immediately after this had been done he was able to go round the room and identify us all by name. A month later he came back to see how the training was proceeding and met us all again in the crew room. Once again he was able to identify each one of us. Not only that, but some six months later I met him in Malta and he immediately remembered my name. Quite amazing when one considers he had only clapped eyes on me for a few hours!

Incidentally the pilot standing just to the right and behind AVM Whitley is the late Gordon Corps, who in later years became well known in flying circles as one of the Air Registration Board test pilots who were responsible for testing the Concorde for its Certificate of Airworthiness. Gordon and his wife Janet were very good friends of Mella and me, and he and I were great rivals at bombing and later we both went to CFS (Central Flying School) to become instructors. Sadly Gordon died in the mid-1990s whilst investigating the crash of an Air India airbus about 10,000 feet up a mountain near Kathmandu. As I understand it, he fell victim to mountain sickness.

On the morning of 25th January seven Canberras left snowy Lincolnshire and headed off towards the steamy heat of Lagos, Nigeria stopping overnight in Idris. Six aircraft arrived at Ikeja Airport, Lagos on the 26th, the seventh reserve aircraft going to Kano, as parking

space was very limited at Lagos. We spent the following day preparing the aircraft for all the forthcoming demonstrations and inspections. On the 28th we did our first show, starting with a flypast over Lagos, then on to Enugu for a demonstration, followed by a flypast at Port Harcourt and return to Lagos. Next day we did a flypast over Lagos city followed by a full demonstration over the harbour area. At 0940 on the 1st February the crews and aircraft were inspected by the Queen and the Duke, after which we had to do a quick change into flying suits ready for a series of flypasts at Bida, Minna, Kaduna and Ibadan before returning to Lagos.

Whilst staying at Ikeja, we were living in bell tents, six to a tent. With a temperature outside in the region of 90°F you can imagine what it was like inside!! Trying to get into mess kit in the evening to attend the many functions was akin to donning ones clothes having stepped straight from the shower.

Another of my purchases before we went to Nigeria was a brown Trilby hat for wear with 'civvies'. It was deemed by Air Ministry that officers should always wear a hat, even when off duty. Whoever dreamt up this ridiculous rule had obviously never been in Nigeria.

The next day the six Canberras flew to Accra in what was then the Gold Coast. Here we did demonstrations over Accra city and Takoradi. When the Prime Minister, Dr Kwame Nkrumah, expressed a wish to fly in a Canberra, I was chosen to give him a 15-minute trip over the city and harbour. A local reporter took the photograph of us through the door of my aircraft after the flight. The feature in the local paper said that Dr Nkrumah was the fastest Premier in the world, having flown at over 500mph! Personally I felt that the PM looked decidedly pale after his experience, but I suppose that was only to be expected, especially as

An Autobiography by Captain D.B. Hopkins

he did not have the luxury of sitting in an ejection seat.

On the 5th February we all flew to Kano to resume our part in the Royal Tour, commencing with fly-pasts at Enugu and Macurdi on the 6th, and then three more on the 8th at Maiduguri, Potiskum and Azare. On the 10th, by request of the Queen, we did an extra demonstration at Apapa Wharf in Lagos immediately after the Queen's inspection of the facility. For me this was a particularly memorable occasion and not only because I was operating in front of the Royal Party.

Our demonstration consisted of a number of flypasts in a 'box four' as shown on page 99, both at high and low speed, with and without bomb doors open, while the remaining two individualists performed aerobatics in between our passes. We completed our display with a run in and break followed by individual high-speed runs past the Royal party. It was during this that I was following Gordon Corps' aircraft and he seemed to be getting further and further away from me. I kept increasing power in an attempt to keep up as I zipped along just above the mastheads of the ships in the harbour until I glanced down at my instrument panel and saw that my airspeed was an amazing 540 knots! I could scarcely believe my eyes, and bearing in mind the maximum permitted speed of 450 knots I immediately reduced power. I didn't dare open the airbrakes, as this would probably have produced the first swept wing Canberra! I wonder if anybody has ever been faster in a Canberra at low level? Somehow I doubt it as this airspeed equates to nearly .82 Mach, just short of the point at which compressibility becomes a serious consideration.

After demonstrations at Ibadan on two consecutive days and two more at Sokoto and Kano, Jim and I had four days off to see the sights of Kano while the other five aircraft went on to Lungi Airport, Freetown, in Sierra Leone. Two sights we were taken to see in Kano were the Mosque, the 'Mud City' and the groundnuts. Officially we were not allowed to enter the Mosque as we were not Muslims, but our guide explained that we should give the old man at the entrance to the left hand minaret a shilling and we would be able to climb to the top and look at the view of the 'Mud City'. The concept of building in mud seemed strange to me, used to rainy Britain, but in Kano, where it seldom rains, mud gets as hard as concrete, is practically as durable, readily available and costs practically nothing.

After the splendours of the 'Mud City', we went to see the place where the groundnuts were stored after harvest while awaiting transportation. Each of the pyramids shown in the picture was said to contain 1000 tons, so I leave it to your imagination to work how many there might have been in total. Enough to fill all the packets of peanuts in all the pubs in Europe, I would imagine! Our four days as

tourists came to an end on the 20th when we left Kano to fly to Bathurst (now Banjul) in the Gambia and join up with the other five aircraft flying in from their stay in Sierra Leone. We did a demonstration the next day followed by a static display the day after so that the local population could see our aircraft at close quarters. On the 23rd we flew to Gibraltar before flying back to the snows of Binbrook on the 24th.

We all had something of an adventure getting into 'Gib'. The weather was atrocious and all the navigation and landing aids at 'Gib' were unserviceable at the time. The latter became the subject of an inquiry by the AOC (Air Officer Commanding) of The Rock and I heard later that the Senior Air Traffic Controller was the recipient of a vertical interview by the AOC. After descending from 45,000 feet and breaking cloud over the sea between the mountains of North Africa and Spain, thanks to the unerring accuracy of Jim's navigation, it took me some time to find the rock, due in no small part to my being unfamiliar with the layout of the place as well as the lack of Nav. aids. I was under the impression, for some reason, that the runway was on the seaward side of the rock rather than between the rock and Spain. When I did eventually find the rock, it was straight ahead and looking extremely solid. I quickly made a right turn and passed close to another Canberra going in the opposite direction, also lost or, as navigators say, temporarily uncertain of its position! At this point I realised where the runway must be and on completing a circuit of the rock landed successfully, although with very little fuel remaining after a four-hour flight. This, as you will see in a later chapter, was not the only close call I was to have at Gibraltar.

I then had a week's leave, which was a welcome break for Mella as well as myself, as she had been having to fight her way through the snow to get to work as a theatre sister in the hospital in Louth all the time I had been sweltering in the sun of West Africa.

Back on the squadron on the 7th March, reunited with Sam, we

An Autobiography
by Captain
D.B. Hopkins

dropped six 'time-expired' 1000lb bombs on the range in the Wash in preparation for 'Operation Mileage' in Butterworth in Malaya. We left on 9th March, a week earlier than the rest of the squadron, with our bomb bay full of new fuel pumps to be fitted on 12 Squadron's aircraft. These pumps are of the swash plate and plunger variety and are fuel lubricated. Further lubrication is provided by silver flashing on the ends of each of the plungers.

The fuel tanks at Butterworth had become contaminated with seawater, killing some micro-organisms therein, which decomposed into a sulphur-containing compound. This in turn took the silver flashing off the plungers of all the pumps in all of 12 Squadron's Canberras, rendering them unable to fly. We flew via Idris, Habbaniya, Mauripur (near Karachi) and Negombo (Ceylon). We cruise-climbed on each leg to conserve fuel, as was the normal practice, and on reaching Negombo had reached a height of 55,000feet (for the mathematically minded = 10.42 miles) mainly to avoid flying in the top of an enormous cumulo-nimbus cloud. The lightning from this was spectacular in the extreme, it being dark at the time.

When we came to descend, Jim had developed a very severe toothache, which necessitated a slow descent to avoid damage to his choppers, not to mention crew morale. We arrived in Butterworth on 11th March to be greeted by a welcoming committee from 12 Squadron, who had been out there for four months and were dying to get back to Binbrook and their loved ones. Needless to say the fuel pumps were fitted without delay and off they flew towards a snowy home.

In the meantime Jim, Sam and myself settled into the mess and life in the tropics. Our rooms had 'air-conditioning' provided through half doors of the kind one sees in bars in Westerns. Mosquito nets were a 'must', and a useful accessory to have in one's room was a gecko. I had a nice creamy yellow one that lived behind my bedside light and popped out in the evenings to devour whatever insect lay within his reach. He was a very well fed gecko, which tells you all you need to know about the quantities of mosquitoes and other flying/biting insects in that neck of the woods.

During the day we wore khaki shorts and shirt, but after 7pm long sleeve shirt with trousers was mandatory. The food was excellent, the mess being run by a Warrant Officer of the Royal Australian Air Force. In particular, Sunday curry tiffin was looked forward to with relish. The curry came in three strengths; hot; hotter and Jesus Christ! But we weren't here for the food and on 27th we did our first flying, in forma-

tion, to Changi (Singapore) to refuel, as the contamination problem at Butterworth still existed. Some excellent sleuthing by a Rolls-Royce engineer, Mr A. Burns, eventually solved the problem, but it was early in May before we could refuel at Butterworth. Until then we had to terminate each trip at Changi, refuel and fly back to Butterworth ready for the next strike at the terrorists.

There were two methods of dropping our bombs. The first was on a map reference in the jungle. This sounds a bit hit or miss, especially as the jungle looks very much the same all over Malaya. The second, preferred, method was for an Auster of the Army Air Corps to drop a smoke marker on the target and we would fly in with three aircraft in formation, each carrying six 1000lb Medium Capacity (MC) bombs and drop the whole lot together. The basis of the system was for the pilots of the AAC Austers to keep an eye on their piece of the jungle, which they knew like the back of their hands, and as soon as they saw signs of crops being grown, a strike was laid on. The aim was not to kill the CT's, but to deny them access to food so that they were eventually forced to give themselves up. The minimum height for dropping 1000lb MC bombs was, if my memory serves me, about 3,700 feet. We therefore flew at 4,000 feet and you can rest assured that one is well and truly aware when they explode! It was rather like the effect of driving over a particularly vicious 'sleeping policeman' at 70mph in a car with inadequate springing!

The pilots of the AAC were a breed apart and as mad as hatters. One of our navigators was offered a trip in an Auster and like a fool he accepted. He was shown some incredibly low flying and at one point they were flying down a road, only a few feet off the ground, and were rapidly approaching a line of tall trees. It was obvious that the Auster would not pass the trees without tearing the wings off, but the pilot suddenly tipped the plane on its side and went through the line of trees, wings vertical, levelling the wings on the other side. His passenger was suitably impressed, and, as he told us later, determined never to fly with them again! These intrepid pilots reported on the success of our bombs almost as soon as we dropped them and we thought they must have 'hidden' behind a tree as the bombs exploded!

On days off several of us liked to get the ferry across to Penang Island and wander around. The most popular spot for having a bite to eat was the Singapore Cold Store, as it was the only place on the island with air conditioning. It was also the place where I learned to handle chopsticks and by the end of my stay I could pick up slices of cucumber with ease!

I particularly enjoyed rambutans, which one could buy from sellers on the ferry terminal for a few coppers. However, I did not even have the courage to try durian even though it was available. One could tell when it was in season by the awful smell, which was detectable half a mile away. Pity it smells so much, as I'm assured that it tastes delicious! A common sight in Penang was joss sticks drying in the sun. These ranged in size from about six inches to six feet long and had a very pleasant smell all their own, even though they were not lit.

*An Autobiography
by Captain
D.B. Hopkins*

Our main relaxation was swimming, but when we first arrived at Butterworth the pool was out of use so we swam off the beach behind the mess until we heard about a local boy getting bitten by a sea snake. After this we waited until the pool was back in use! Speaking of snakes, I'm told that Malaya has a comprehensive selection of indigenous snakes, many of which are poisonous. It was, therefore, something of a surprise only to see one snake the whole time I was there, and that was lying dead in the road.

The other wildlife that we occasionally saw around the mess consisted of small (about four feet long), Komodo dragons. These had a habit of wandering off the beach along the verandah in front of our rooms. One evening we were all in the bar and one of the navigators went to his room to fetch something. He came rushing back a few seconds later looking as white as a sheet. He had got to his room and under the half doors could see two beady eyes staring at him. He didn't wait to find out to what the eyes belonged and by the time we all went to investigate, the dragon was wandering slowly along the verandah back towards the beach. The other animals that caused a certain amount of inconvenience were bullocks, which were used to pull small carts. There was a road crossing at the seaward end of Butterworth's runway, and quite frequently we had to overshoot to allow a slow-moving bullock cart to clear out of the way before we could land.

In early June a cruiser of the US Navy visited Penang. The officers were invited to have Sunday tiffin in our mess and each of us was given an American officer to host. Mine was a young ensign and it was obvious he had never before eaten curry, so he was following my example by taking only the hot curry and leaving the hotter varieties well alone. When he came to help himself from the proffered dish of sambols, he did fine until he got the dish containing sweet mango chutney. You will probably be aware how slippery that stuff can be and when he took hold of the dish it shot out of his hand like a cake of wet soap, went vertically upwards and alighted upside down right onto the middle of his plate. Going red from the neck up he came out with, 'Gee, that was almost embarrassing.'

By the end of April the 'emergency' was all but over, the remaining few terrorists having been rounded up. It seems that there was a stock of 500lb and 1000lb bombs left over and presumably transporting them back to UK was not economically viable, so we proceeded to use them for practice using a range near Song Song island up to the North of Penang. The actual target was a rock in the sea and due to the general prowess of the crews it was hit repeatedly. This would have been fine but for the fact that the local Sultan had a palace quite close to the seashore on the mainland and he took umbrage at having his home shaken to the core at regular intervals. Thus our practice with live bombs came to an end!

At the end of May we took part in the Queen's Birthday Flypast over Penang and I did a final strike on 12th June with six more 1000lb bombs, destroying more trees in the jungle, but by this time the emergency was pretty much over as most of the terrorists had been caught or had given themselves up. I flew home in a Hastings by courtesy of Transport Command, arriving back in Louth on 25th June for three weeks' leave, during which time our eldest son became more than just a twinkle in our eyes!

All too soon I was back in harness, both literally and figuratively, and on 10th August I flew someone to Tangmere, the only time I ever landed there. The weather was rather poor and on take-off a seagull passed close on the right hand side. Air Traffic informed me that he thought we had had a bird strike. I replied that I thought we had missed the gull, but ATC convinced me otherwise with, 'You should see the bird!' When we got back to Binbrook we found traces of the unfortunate creature on part of the undercarriage leg. This was fortunate for us as such big birds can do considerable damage if they hit the wing or get ingested into an engine. While out in West Africa, one of our aircraft hit what the locals called a 'Turkey Buzzard' (a sort of vulture with a five foot wingspan) at high speed, which made a very large hole in the leading edge of the wing. Although this was patched up to enable the plane to carry on with the tour, extensive work was needed on return to base to remove the remains of the bird from inside the wing!

At about this time Jim, Sam and myself became a 'select' crew which meant that we could drop GH bombs from 45,000 feet and play a full part in the squadron's operations.

In early September we started rehearsals for the 'Battle of Britain' display we were to do on the15th. This passed off without a hitch, but soon afterwards we were put on standby to go to an unspecified destination because of the looming crisis over the Suez Canal. For the first two or three weeks of October I went to work each day with a suitcase, neither Mella nor I knowing if I would be returning home that day.

Finally on the 30th I flew with the rest of the Squadron to Hal Far, a Royal Naval Air Station on Malta. Mella, of course, did not know where I had gone and although she was by then four months pregnant, nobody from the RAF went to see her, quite unlike today's 'Nanny State' when everybody seems to need, and get, 'counselling' for even the smallest amount of so-called 'stress'. Fortunately neither of us has ever suffered from the lack of moral fibre that seems so common among the population of today! But then both of us had been trained to be self-reliant.

Upon arrival in Malta, our aircraft had to have wing-tip fuel tanks fitted, have identification stripes painted on the wings and be loaded with four bombs apiece. We were issued with an escape kit in case we

*An Autobiography
by Captain
D.B. Hopkins*

were forced to land in enemy territory. The kit consisted of a .38 revolver and 12 rounds of ammunition; a silk map of North Africa; a piece of 'wire' with a ring on each end, with which we were told it was possible to cut through steel bars, and 6 gold sovereigns. The last were intended to save vital parts of our anatomy being removed from our bodies in the case of capture. How useful all this kit would have been I don't know, but when the time came for me to hand back my .38 I tried to 'break' it only to find that this was quite impossible. I suppose I might have been able to throw the weapon at an enemy followed by the box of bullets!

On the 31st Jim, Sam and I flew the first of two raids on Egypt. The target was the airfield of Abu Sueir and involved a round trip of 5 hours fifteen minutes. We carried four 1000lb MC bombs and to have any chance of getting back to Malta with the available fuel, we cruise-climbed all the way, both outbound and inbound, finally reaching a height of 55,000 feet before we descended to land in Malta. Although I had previously reached such an altitude, this was the first time I had been so high for such a long period. Although the aircraft were pressurised and heated to some extent, neither system was designed for use under such extreme conditions, i.e. −60°C outside and a height of 55,000 feet. The effect of this led to all three of us suffering from 'the bends', which manifested itself as pains in joints such as elbows, ankles and knees. Thankfully it vanished as soon as we descended.

By the time we reached our target we had climbed to 44,000 feet, from which height we were to drop our bombs, aiming at a marker flare laid by a 'pathfinder' of 139 Squadron, whose Canberras were based at Akrotiri in Cyprus.

The Extraordinary Story of a Very Ordinary Person As I mentioned in chapter five, the visual bombsight and computer with which our aircraft were fitted could only operate up to 25,000 feet. Consequently we employed a method using the sighting head only. The bomb aimer, Sam, was provided with a table of settings to put on the sighting head, which had been disconnected from the computer, dependent on the height from which we were to drop the bombs. As there was no computer to allow for variations in height, heading and airspeed, this method called for some extremely careful and accurate flying, which is pretty tricky at very high altitudes. That the system worked, though, was amply demonstrated when our stick of four bombs hit the ground two each side of the marker flare. A 'direct hit' if ever I saw one! Having offloaded 4000lbs, the aircraft immediately ascended a few thousand feet as we headed back to Hal Far. Thankfully there was no opposition from the Egyptian Air Force, whose Meteors had no chance of reaching our dizzy altitude.

We left Hal Far at 30-second intervals and with navigation lights off and radio silence. Now 30 seconds might sound enough to give a safe separation between aircraft. But it is soon eroded over a period of 5 hours or so. As a result we felt the turbulence from the slipstream of other aircraft quite frequently on the return journey, and when we got back to the point where we switched on our navigation lights, I was not entirely surprised to find myself surrounded by other aircraft. Two nights later we repeated the whole exercise with a raid on Huckstep Barracks in Cairo with, I'm happy to say, equally fine bombing results. With the crew with whom I had the privilege to fly this was not diffi-cult, but it does demonstrate the value of lots of practice and very good training.

At this point the USA got into the act, which brought an end to our efforts. We spent the next six weeks keeping our hands in at flying in general and bombing in particular using the islet of Filfla as a target, the Squadron moving from Hal Far to Luqa at the end of November. We also managed to set up some inter-service liaison with the Royal Navy. There was a submarine stationed in Valetta, named HMS *Sentinel* and having met some of the crew, we arranged to give them rides in our Canberras in exchange for a day out on their boat.

Jim and I presented ourselves at the submarine base early on the appointed day and went aboard. There were just five officers in the crew, all Lieutenants, of whom one was the Captain. He arrived after us looking smart in his best uniform and after being piped aboard he disappeared below, reappearing a few minutes later dressed in his 'working kit' of slacks and a fairly grubby white sweater. Jim and I were somewhat puzzled by this change of apparel, but we soon understood the reason when we went to diving stations soon after we had put out from Valetta. The control room was extremely small and pretty dirty. I found that wherever I stood during the diving process, I was in someone's way. I had no sooner moved out of one spot to be elbowed aside by some rating so that he could operate a valve or other piece of

*An Autobiography
by Captain
D.B. Hopkins*

equipment. Squashing up against the bulkhead I soon got spots of grease on my best uniform and could see why the skipper wore what he did.

Having submerged for an exercise being hunted by an RAF Shackleton, we went down to periscope depth, 48 feet I think, and the skipper turned his uniform cap back-to-front and ordered 'periscope up', peered through it for about 45 seconds, ordered 'periscope down' then after about a minute, reordered 'periscope up' and so on. The periscope was going up and down like a yo-yo and I remarked to the Lieutenant who was showing me around the boat, 'there's no need to do the John Mills epic stuff just for us!' He then explained that this yo-yo business with the periscope was certainly not for our benefit, but essential to keep the thing lubricated else the seawater would act on the lubricant and it would seize in the 'up' position. I imagine that with modern lubricants this is no longer necessary, but it certainly was in 1956!

Next I was taken to see the engine room, where one of the two diesels was having some new pistons installed, notwithstanding the fact that the other one was in use propelling the boat with the 'snorkel' up. Then up to the sharp end to have a look at the torpedo room. I was quite unprepared for the size of torpedoes, which were stored one above the other, three high on each side of the boat. On top of the uppermost torpedo was a sailor lying on his back reading a book. I asked the Lieutenant what he was doing; 'Oh, that's his bunk' came the reply. How the other half live, I thought to myself! However, the officer's accommodation was only a little better, the wardroom consisting of a table, enough to seat five providing you were all very friendly, and three bunks. As there were always a minimum of two officers on watch, three bunks was sufficient for those not on duty. This was known as the 'hot bed system'.

I was allowed to have a shot at keeping the boat at periscope depth using the hydroplanes. I found this to be quite easy, as it required the same technique as an aircraft does to keep it level at a particular height. You just have to allow for the inertia of the boat/aircraft, which will take you through the level you are trying to achieve if you don't anticipate the need to start levelling out before the desired depth/height. All this was great fun, although I'm not sure I would want to do a 30-day patrol cooped up in such small spaces as was the norm for these chaps.

After spending the whole day submerged, being sought by the Shackleton and its sonobuoys, we returned to port and, once tied up, we adjourned to the wardroom for a few pink gins in the best tradition of the Senior Service. When I went aboard in the morning I had to negotiate a narrow gangplank. When the time came to go ashore, I found that we were tied up alongside another boat, so there were two gangplanks to cross. How I did this in my advanced state of inebriation without falling in the water I shall never know!

Mella, and presumably the rest of our wives, got to know our whereabouts by quite a clever device to evade the censor. One of my colleagues wrote to his wife and drew a cow on the top of the letter, which, although being censored, reached her unaltered with instructions to take it to Mella who, being a nurse, realised the significance of the cow – bovine fever and Malta fever being one and the same thing!

At the beginning of December Jim, Sam and I flew to Gibraltar and back for another 'lone-ranger', this time with no problem as I now knew the layout and the aids were working. While there we heard the story of a National Service airman who celebrated his imminent return to UK by painting the letters YO in front of the GIBAIR on a Dakota of the local airline. You can work out for yourself how this read!

On 12th December we returned to Binbrook in nice time for some Christmas leave, after which life continued somewhat less hectically than the one we had got used to in the past 12 months. On 11th January I flew to Lindholme to collect our new CO, Wing Commander Beresford Horsley, George Bastard's tour of duty having come to an end. The squadron were all very sorry to see George depart, but it was inevitable as a new policy of having a Wing Commander as CO had just come into force.

Some time during my tour with 9 Squadron, I can't remember precisely when, we caused something of sensation one night after we became a 'UFO'! It was during one winter depression that there was a very strong jet-stream over the UK, in the order of 150 knots I seem to remember, so by turning our Canberra into wind at 45,000 feet above London and reducing our speed to around 150 knots we effectively 'hovered' over the City. We stayed there with our landing light on for a good ten minutes, then turned 180° and opened up to full power thus increasing our groundspeed to something like 650 knots. After a moment at this speed I turned off the landing light. This resulted in headlines in one or two of the more sensational newspapers along the lines of 'UFO HOVERS OVER LONDON!'

Another night while flying at 45,000 feet I witnessed some weird lights far away to the east. As I recall, they were multicoloured and lasted for only a few seconds. I imagine there was as mundane an explanation of this phenomenon as of my antics over London. YCNSTWLEM!

Jim, Sam and I continued with the routine of visual and GH bombing interspersed with exercises until 21st March, when I did my last trip on the squadron before being posted to the Central Flying School (CFS) at Little Rissington to become an instructor. I had put my name forward for this earlier in the year when volunteers were being sought.

My course at CFS was due to start early in April, but our baby was due to arrive on 3rd April so I had asked to go on the following course starting in June. Consequently I spent a couple of months without flying and making myself useful doing odd jobs around the squadron. I left 9 Squadron officially on 10th May with an 'Above Average' rating in my log book and my name at the top of the bombing ladder, which I felt was a most satisfactory end to my tour.

Speaking of odd jobs, one of my ancillary duties was that of Squadron Flight Safety Officer. In order to become suitably qualified to do this, I was sent on a week's course with the Accident Investigation Branch (AIB) of the Civil Aviation Authority in London. In the course of this we were given a basic idea of how to carry out an accident investigation, including how to plot the trajectories of pieces of wreckage backwards to find out when and where an aircraft broke up in the air and how to look for parts of wreckage showing signs of metal fatigue. We were told that should we find a metal part displaying the typical crystalline structure of metal fatigue, we should be aware that this would have happened before the accident and may well have been the cause of the accident.

We were also told of the perils of taking eye witness accounts too literally, as they could be very unreliable, particularly if the witness had anything to do with aviation. It seems that pilots and other aviators tend subconsciously to build into their accounts their own theories as to the cause of any incident/accident. The instructor told us that the most reliably accurate eye witnesses were schoolboys around 15 years old and the next best were old ladies! When asked why old ladies, we were told that it was because they always provided a nice cup of tea on a cold day!

In the AIB headquarters where the course was held there was a 'black' museum containing pieces of aircraft wreckage that were significant causes of various accidents – for instance there was a non-return valve from a fuel line in a Blackburn Beverley that had caused it to crash in North Africa, killing all on board, because it had been fitted back to front. A perfect illustration of Murphy's Law.

The exhibits in the museum were kept in glass-topped cabinets and in the front of one of them was the handle and a short piece of the stem of an umbrella. I asked why it was there, whereupon the instructor whipped it out from the display and stuck it under my nose asking what I could see. There was obvious evidence of metal fatigue and I said so, asking what accident it had caused. The instructor told how he had been leaning on it during an investigation when it had snapped and caused him to fall flat on his back. YCNSTWLEM!

I mentioned earlier that living next to the gasworks was one reason for us to get rid of our 'ragtop' Hillman in exchange for a saloon – the ragtop suffered badly from the effect of the soot that was liberally distributed by the gasworks. The second reason was the imminent arrival of the baby, which both of us felt would not benefit from the excessive supply of fresh air, the only heater being one I had made myself! We went to a garage in Grimsby to purchase the new Hillman. This was the sort of garage which prided itself on your being able to eat off the showroom floor, but which knew very little about engineering. Right from day one it was obvious to me and anyone with the tiniest bit of mechanical knowledge that the crownwheel and pinion in the final drive needed setting up properly to stop the incessant whining noise it made.

When I took the car for the 1000-mile check I mentioned this noise and was told that it would wear off in due course. Now you probably know as well as I do that no mechanical noise ever goes away on its own, and I said so. The 'engineers' insisted that I should drive it for a further 1000 miles and if the noise did not disappear I was to bring the car back. The noise remained – surprise, surprise – so I took it back. They informed me that they would change the six half-shaft and pinion bearings! I told them that it was the pinion that needed setting up properly with the crownwheel, but they insisted it was the bearings at fault. It will come as no surprise that this made not the slightest difference. So I again complained and, this you will hardly credit, they said they must have installed six faulty bearings!! So six more were installed, fortunately at their expense, but naturally these made no difference.

At this point two things happened. First I lost my temper and second we moved house to Stow-on-the-Wold. Before we moved, I wrote to Lord Roots and explained the shortcomings of their suppliers in Grimsby and by the time we had settled into our house in Stow I had a reply apologising and suggesting I go to see a certain garage in Stow. This I did early one morning, and to my delight found a really untidy place run by one man and his dog. I immediately thought to myself that I would get satisfaction here. Sure enough, the proprietor who had had a copy of my letter, came out in the car and agreed that the crownwheel and pinion did indeed need setting up. I left the car with him and collected it later that day minus the terrible noise. This story amply illustrates the difference between technicians and engineers. The former, at Grimsby, knew only how to change things. The latter, in Stow, knew how to fix things at a basic level and get proper results very efficiently.

I've jumped ahead slightly because on 29th March Trevor Paul arrived much to our delight, as we had wanted a son. When Trevor was six weeks old, we moved to Stow-on-the-Wold, close to RAF Little Rissington, home of the CFS and where I would be stationed for the next four months.

*An Autobiography
by Captain
D.B. Hopkins*

Before I close this chapter, I must mention what became of Jim and Sam. Soon after I left 9 Squadron Jim went to the V-Force as a navigator on Victor bombers. Sadly he was killed when his aircraft crashed on take-off at RAF Akrotiri in Cyprus. I am uncertain of Sam's fate, but when I last heard of him he was managing the Victoria Wine shop in Brecon. YCNSTWLEM!

CHAPTER SEVEN

If You Want To
Learn – Teach

I 've often heard it said that the only way to learn about anything in depth is to teach it. This is particularly true about flying,
as I was to find out in the course of the next few years. It is also
said, with good reason, that a pilot is at his most vulnerable when he
has accumulated around 1000 hours experience. This is when he begins
to think that he has become a SHP (shit hot pilot), and quite often has
resulted in accidents happening due to over-confidence. So it was a very
good thing for me to go to CFS at this point, as I was close to accumu-
lating the magic 1000 hours.

Number 188 Instructors Course started on 3rd June 1957 shortly
after Mella, Trevor and I had moved to 7, Enoch Terrace, Oddington
Road, Stow-on-the-Wold, Gloucestershire, a mere twenty minutes
drive from RAF Little Rissington, the highest military airfield in UK.
The garden, although small, was very untidy when we arrived, so with
the course work, gardening and a small son I was kept pretty busy for
the next four months. The cottage, one of a terrace built of Cotswold
stone, was very cosy if rather small. One nice thing about it was that it
backed on to a field of raspberry canes allowing us to open the kitchen
window and help ourselves!

I didn't know what to expect on the course, but I soon found out that
a lot of play-acting was needed, so my earlier somewhat limited thespi-
an experience stood me in good stead,
proof if proof is needed, that no experience in life is ever wasted as
YCNSTWLEM!

The course was in two halves. In the
first half I flew the Percival Provost T1
for exactly 50 hours. Those who were to
become basic QFI's (Qualified Flying
Instructor) spent the second half of the

course doing a further 40 hours on this aircraft, while the others, including myself, who were to become advanced QFI's, converted to the De Havilland Vampire T11. Our time was divided fairly equally between flying and ground studies. After going solo in the Provost, we started learning to 'patter' our way through the different exercises, like 'straight and level', 'turns', 'stalling', 'spinning' and so on. One would do each exercise with a CFS instructor and then go up with a fellow student and each try to 'teach' the other. I found it all very strange and not to say difficult at first, but I gradually got used to the idea that it was all a big 'act'. We were also shown how to use a blackboard to the best effect. If you have ever tried doing this, you will, I'm sure, agree that knowing the right way is essential if your students are to gain the maximum benefit from your expertise.

The end of the first part of the course gave us an opportunity to have various members of the family present at Trevor's christening early in August, and this was the first and last time both Mella's and my parents got together.

I then went on to fly the Vampire T11. The format was much the same, with ground school sessions interspersed with flying, although with the latter there were many more different exercises to master, such as high speed flight, steep turns and night flying. It seems quite incred-
ible to me now that during the steep turns we used to patter whilst pulling $6\frac{2}{3}$ 'g'. With no 'g' suits it was a matter of practice at clenching your stomach muscles so that you could remain conscious during this

exercise, although I suspect that the student on the receiving end spent most of the exercise blacked out.

We also did a lot of aerobatics and the Vampire (above) was an excellent aircraft for this, both at low and high altitude, and I remember well during my night final handling test I had accelerated to about .8 Mach for the high speed run at 40,000 feet when the examiner said, 'do a loop'. So there I was, 42,000 feet upside down over the centre of Birmingham with nothing on the clock except the makers' name, when the examiner observed, 'I wonder how much nooky is going on down there?' I can only assume that he felt entirely at ease with my flying skills to be able to make such a seemingly trite remark whilst in such an attitude. Anyway I passed the course, winning, to my surprise and considerable delight, the Gross Trophy pictured below.

This trophy gained its name as it was presented to CFS by the graduates of No. 144 course and was awarded to the student who achieved the highest marks in ground school and I was presented with the trophy at our 'dining-out' by the Commandant of CFS, Air Commodore Hyde, who was known to all and sundry as 'Chaps' Hyde. He earned this strange nickname by his habit of addressing people as 'Chaps' even when only one person was present. He was also well known as having a love of pyrotechnics, so much so that at our dining-out the naval lieutenant who had just won the wooden spoon terminated his very brief speech by lighting a 'tuppenny banger' and throwing it in front of 'Chaps' where it exploded amid a great deal of hilarity.

Having done both my final handling tests, I was entered for the Brabyn Trophy for the best aerobatic display. Alas I didn't win this one, but it was fun trying!

The course finished on 24th September and I was posted to No 8 Flying Training School (FTS) at

*An Autobiography
by Captain
D.B. Hopkins*

RAF Swinderby, alongside the A46 between Newark and Lincoln. Once again Mella and Trevor, now six months old, and I were on the move, this time to Collingham, a village north of Newark where we settled into a rented semi-detached house next to a Mr & Mrs Willis. They were an elderly couple, but were incredibly kind to us, and 'Auntie' Willis as she soon became known, often baby-sat for us when we had a function to go to. Old Mr Willis was typical of his generation, a man of few words with a droll sense of humour. He was cutting his front hedge one day when one of his cronies came past, slowly pedalling an ancient bicycle. The only words that passed between them were, 'Are you level?' from the man on the bike!

QFI's are categorised as: B2 – probationary; B1 – Average; A2 – Above Average, and A1 – Exceptional, the latter being found about as frequently as frog's feathers! Everyone passed out from CFS as a B2 and had six months to obtain a recategorisation to B1. I achieved this on 25th January 1958 and, as a reward, was allowed to go over to RAF Strubby to have a couple of days recreational flying in the Meteor 7 and 8's I had flown during my jet conversion. It made a nice change to be able to swan about the skies <u>without</u> having to talk all the time, and to enjoy the sensation of being a free spirit whilst zooming in and out of the clouds.

Over the months I flew with a number of students, including several who had joined the RAF as graduates from various universities. My particular student was Brian Stead, a B.Sc in aerodynamics and I also flew with 'Berny' Jackson, a B.A in oriental studies who later became an Air Vice Marshal and whose obituary I read in The Times only recently.

In April 1958 a new course started which included a young man of about my own age. He had just graduated as a doctor and I was to get to know him quite well over the next five months of instruction up to 'wings' standard. He was Pilot Officer Whittle, one of the sons of Sir Frank Whittle, the inventor of the jet engine. When he graduated with his wings, PO Whittle told me that as he had now finished his National Service, he was going to emigrate to Australia. Not unnaturally I assumed he was going to become a Flying Doctor, for which he seemed eminently well qualified, but no, he informed me he was going to take up engineering like his illustrious father. How well he got on I never found out as we lost touch once he left Swinderby.

During the five-month-long course to get their wings, the students were set a 'project' to keep them occupied whenever the weather was unfit for flying. The course prior to Whittle's was set the task of building a coffee bar in the crewroom. This they did with considerable ingenuity, obtaining the cockpit of a wrecked Vampire Mk5 and fitting this out with dispensers for coffee, sugar, milk and hot water. It looked quite splendid when it was completed. Unfortunately the cup of coffee it dispensed tasted absolutely foul. The reason for this was that the method of construction called for many parts to be glued together and to achieve this with a degree of permanence they had used Bostik. The upshot of all this labour was that young Whittle and his colleagues were given a 'project' to dismantle the Vampire cockpit bar and construct something that produced a drinkable cup of coffee! Their result was less spectacular but the coffee was really good.

The spinning characteristics of the Vampire are worthy of a mention in this narrative. In the first place orders stipulated that a spin should not be initiated below 25,000 feet and that if recovery was not complete by 10,000 feet the crew should immediately eject. The reason for this was that the rate of descent in a fully developed spin was in excess of 30,000 feet per minute – quite the fastest method of descent I've ever heard of in any aeroplane.

To get into a spin you have to get the speed down to stalling and then apply full rudder in either direction at which point the aircraft does two flick rolls before the nose drops and the spin proper develops. When instructing students it was normal to start recovery after four turns by applying full opposite rudder and pushing the stick forward to get out of the stall and as soon as the rotation had stopped, centralise the rudder and recover from the ensuing dive. It was all very exciting and took much less time to do than to write about. Every three months instructors were required during Staff Continuation Training (SCT) to do an eight-turn spin, the maximum allowed. This was not at all popular among the majority of the QFI's, who always seemed to manage to count to eight long before the aircraft had done more than about five turns! Also there was always considerable debate as to whether the two flick rolls counted towards the eight turns or not.

Pilots and students of aerodynamics will know that for any given altitude and power setting an aircraft will fly at two speeds, one slow the other fast. This is easy to prove on paper, but less easy in practice. Quite by accident I discovered that these two speeds could be demonstrated in a very convincing manner. The trick was to reduce to stalling speed and just as the aircraft was about to stall gently feed in power until the throttle was fully open, at the same time constantly bringing the nose of the aircraft up. Eventually one finished with full power and an indicated speed of around 50/60 knots, well below the stalling speed. Then by just lowering the nose the aircraft would accelerate to the maximum speed for the altitude, somewhere around 400+ knots. I don't think any of the other QFI's used this demonstration, which I found great fun to do and impressed my students no end!

Towards the end of October 1958 I was allowed to go down to RAF Kemble near Cirencester for five days' flying in a Hawker Hunter F4. This was the only aircraft I ever flew without the benefit of instruction

MACH 1·0 CLUB

This is to certify that

Flt. Lt. "Hoppy" Hopkins

IS A MEMBER IN GOOD STANDING AND
HAS EXCEEDED THE SPEED OF SOUND

in A

HAWKER HUNTER MARK 4

O.C. HUNTER FLIGHT
Central Flying School

in a dual control version, as the two-seat T7 had yet to come into service. Monday morning was spent being briefed on the aircraft and its systems, controls and procedures, then after lunch you were strapped into a Mk4 with a series of crib cards strapped to your leg and away you went.

Because the Hunter had power controls, you could always tell a 'first solo' as the wings wobbled from side to side until you got used to the idea of holding the control column with thumb and forefinger instead of with the entire fist, as was necessary in a Vampire. On the second flight I was briefed to do a sonic run over the Bristol Channel and so became a member of what was then a fairly exclusive group – The Mach 1.0 Club – and my certificate of membership, permanently pasted into my log-book, is shown above.

Flying supersonic sounds quite dramatic, but in reality it is something of an anticlimax, since you can't hear the sonic boom inside the aircraft and the only way you know you are travelling faster than the speed of sound is by looking at the Mach meter! In the five days at Kemble I did a total of seven trips, the last two being formation flying, which gave me a very good insight into how easy it was to fly very accurate formation with power controls and understand how the 'Black Arrows' of 111 Squadron did such wonderful displays. All great fun but the flights were all too short as the fuel consumption was such that about 45 minutes was the maximum you could stay aloft. In fact I think the Hunter was the only aircraft I've ever flown where you could actually see the needle on the fuel gauge moving!

After all the excitement of Hunter flying, it seemed somewhat pedestrian to be flying the Vampire again the following week, but in December, the 5th to be precise, things got very exciting indeed! In the morning I led a formation of students and in the afternoon I took up a student, Pilot Officer Stewart, as a favour for our next-door flight, who were an instructor short due to sickness. The exercise was practice instrument flying for P/O Stewart, who took off, entirely on instruments, and a few seconds after the undercarriage had retracted at about 600 feet above the runway there was a tremendous 'bang' accompanied by a complete cessation of power. The impression I got was that we had run into a brick wall, somewhat unlikely at that height, but that was how it felt. I can do no better than quote from my logbook and the Green Endorsement therein:

'Flight Lieutenant Hopkins was engaged on an instructional instrument flying exercise in Vampire T11 WZ457 on 5th December 1958 with Pilot Officer Stewart as his pupil. At a height of approximately 600 feet above ground level, after an instrument take-off, and at a speed of 180 knots there was a loud bang from the engine and a complete loss of power. Flight Lieutenant Hopkins immediately took control of the aircraft and turned left to position himself for a landing on the disused runway, the only runway he could hope to reach from such a low altitude. He then lowered the undercarriage and flaps and obtained clearance for his landing. The undercarriage and one third flap came down at once, but unfortunately the remainder of the flap had to be pumped down by Pilot Officer Stewart and was slow to come down fully. Flight Lieutenant Hopkins managed to land the aircraft on the disused runway, which was only 1200 yards long. He realised that, because of the slowness of flap movement, he would not be able to stop. After touchdown, therefore, he endeavoured to retract the undercarriage. Only one leg retracted and, after the hood had been jettisoned, the aircraft came to rest about 150 yards off the end of the runway. Technical examination showed that the engine compressor had failed shortly after take-off. Flight Lieutenant Hopkins, who was ably assisted by Pilot Officer Stewart, handled this hazardous and difficult emergency with commendable skill and coolness. His showing was in keeping with the best traditions of the QFI. The Air Officer Commanding No. 23 Group has ordered that this Green Endorsement be placed in his log book.'

The picture (on the right) of the compressor shows that the cross webs in both intakes had fractured, allowing the front bearing to move. The compressor, which was about 3 feet in diameter, stopped from the maximum 10,600 rpm in 8 inches of travel around the periphery. Quite a jerk! And I think this demonstrates most impressively how robust the whole engine was and why we both thought we had hit a brick wall.

Fortunately neither of us was hurt in any way, but there was one funny incident that the official reports do not tell. After we leapt out of the cockpit into the field of stubble, in which we had come to rest, we both got about 4 feet from the aircraft before we were drawn inexorably back by the rubber emergency oxygen pipes that we had both forgotten to undo in our haste to get away in case a fire ensued. All the other QFI's and students who watched our landing said it was quite spectacular as we went through two fences and a hedge with a huge bow wave of pieces of both. The other funny happening was when we were careering down the runway trying to stop I said to P/O Stewart, 'Pump', meaning for him to pump the hydraulics and try to retract the undercarriage. Afterwards he told me that he though I had said, 'Jump!'

I seem to remember that the only 'counselling' either of us received was a cup of tea in Station Sick Quarters, where we were taken for a check-up. Counselling was a word that was seldom heard in 1958 outside legal circles. The accident happened on a Friday afternoon and both of us were flying again the following Monday with no untoward effects! When I got home, Mella wasn't in the least bit surprised when I told her what had happened, as she had known somehow that 'something' had occurred. Telepathy between two who are close maybe!

When the weather was unfit for flying, some of the instructors had a bridge school going and one day the Station Commander came round while a hand was in progress. He asked, 'What's this?' and I replied, 'Three no trumps, Sir.' He didn't say anything at the time, but a few days later an edict was issued to the effect that card games were not to be played in the crew room until all the instructors had passed their A2 recategorisation test! It will therefore come as no surprise to the reader to learn that I became an A2 QFI on 16th March 1959 during a visit from 'The Trappers'. The latter's official name was the CFS Examining team and they came around every year to test a sample of pilots, both QFI's and students, to check on the quality of both. Little did I know that one day I would be privileged to join their ranks! This examining system is one of the reasons why the standard of RAF pilots is second to none and in case you think I am biased, I should mention that many Air Forces around the world, to this day, invite the CFS Examining wing to test their pilots on a regular basis. I shall mention more on this subject in a later chapter.

In July Mella and I took Trevor for a week's holiday in Tenby or 'Little England beyond Wales', as it is known. A great spot for a seaside holiday with young children, where the sandy beach is ideal for excavating your way to Australia!

At this point I need to mention two things. Firstly that some of the staff occupied married quarters at an old wartime RAF base just outside Newark called Winthorpe and secondly that the Nottinghamshire police had a habit of sitting on the county boundary at night and stopping traffic.

It was after the Mess had held a fancy dress ball that one of my colleagues, Steve Edmondson, was driving home with his wife to Winthorpe at around 2am and was stopped by the police. They asked Steve where they had been before they looked properly into the car and when they spotted Steve's attire, which in no way went with his jet black hair and handlebar moustache, they suggested in no uncertain terms that he and his wife should go home at top speed! And what had Steve been dressed in? A complete Fairy's outfit with gossamer wings, tutu skirt and magic wand! His wife was wearing something equally ludicrous. I know they both dined out on this incident for many months, probably years!

I too had a brush with the law at the same location on one occasion just after I had finished reconditioning the engine and gearbox of the Mark V Jaguar that we had swapped for the Hillman Minx. I was coming home to Collingham (also in Nottinghamshire) at about 2am after a somewhat alcoholic formal dinner in the Mess.

The Notts boundary was at the top of a small rise and as I approached at a very stately 30mph, I was aware of a red light moving up and down. This turned out to be a board covered with red reflective studs which said, 'Police, Stop.' So I stopped and after the bobby had inquired where I was going and what had I been doing, the latter being fairly obvious as I was dressed in mess kit and breathing brandy fumes, he wanted to know how far away I was when I could see their sign. I indicated that I could see it as soon as I came over the brow of the hill. He then wanted to know how far away I was from them when I could read what it said. I reckoned about 100 yards and said so. He thanked me for being so helpful and said, 'You are the first one that has stopped tonight, we've had to jump out of the way of everyone else!' I didn't have the heart to tell him that had it not been for the fact that I was running-in my new engine and gearbox, they would probably had to do the same for me!

The next few months were uneventful from the flying point of view, but by now Mella was pregnant again. When she was pregnant with Trevor she had a constant yearning for nuts, which I seemed to spend my spare time either fetching or cracking. This time life was easier as her craving was for unripe gooseberries and fortunately we had a ready supply of these at the end of our small garden.

By this time we had become firm friends with Brian and Nancy Challand, who owned the garage in the village and also had a son, Ian, of about the same age as Trevor. Because I was often engaged in night flying, Brian had volunteered to take Mella to Nocton Hall RAF Hospital where the baby was to be delivered if I was absent when she

*An Autobiography
by Captain
D.B. Hopkins*

went into labour. Mella and Nancy kept winding Brian up whenever there was fog about as he was sure that he would be the one to have to drive over to Nocton Hall.

In the event he was let off the hook as I had some leave and on the 20th October 1959 our second son, Christopher Mark, was born. (Curiously I am writing this on his 41st birthday!) Trevor was really pleased to have a brother and one day when the health visitor called, he was so protective that he wouldn't let her go upstairs to see the baby. Jumping ahead slightly, Trevor was with Mella who was pushing Christopher in his pram some six months later, so Trevor would be about 3 years old, when he asked, 'Mummy, what is the universe?' I think the answer was something along the lines of asking Daddy when he got home. I cannot remember how I got out of this one, but I should mention that Trevor is now a PhD in computer science and a senior consultant in object technology practice for IBM, so I suppose one could regard his question as being along the lines of 'writing on the wall' for him!

In January 1960 I was asked to take on a student from the Royal Jordanian Air Force who was having trouble passing his IRT. This normally took place about half way through the course, but Officer Cadet Zaza was nowhere near ready to take his test.

In these types of circumstances a student was usually passed on to a more experienced QFI to see if an improvement was possible. After the first flight with him I could see why he was having trouble. He was basically bone-idle and had not attempted to learn all the procedures he should have known off by heart at this stage in his training. I could see that I needed to take a strong line with him and whilst I was debriefing him in one of the cubicles in the student's crew room, the noise level from the rest of the students decreased from cacophony to the point where you could hear a pin drop. At the end of around half an hour he was in tears, but he now knew what was required from him if he was not to be 'scrubbed' from the course. Being an Arab, this would have been a considerable loss of face, consequently he rapidly 'extracted the digit' and passed his IRT. I continued as his instructor until he eventually got his wings and returned to Jordan. Many years later I heard that he had been piloting the helicopter in which the Queen of Jordan was killed when it flew into a large thunderstorm. I have since wondered if I might have done the Jordanian Royal family a considerable disservice by taking so much trouble with O/C Zaza. YCNSTWLEM!

One member of the officer's mess was a Major who ran a weekend practice unit for the TA near Ollerton. He was accommodated in our mess, as there wasn't an army mess in the vicinity. One Wednesday he arranged for a few of us to go over to Ollerton and have a go at driving his tanks. The tanks in question were Centurions, which were powered by Rolls-Royce Meteor engines (no connection with the aircraft of the same name). Each of us was assigned an Army corporal to show us the ropes and explain the controls. You sat with the gear lever in between your legs and on each side were the 'steering sticks'. Pull the left one and the left track slowed or stopped and you turned left and vice versa, all controlled by the epicyclic gearbox. There were the normal foot pedals, clutch, brake and throttle, but the main problem was the gearbox, which had five forward and two reverse gears and required double de-clutching when changing gear.

I had no problem with this when changing into a lower gear, as I had learnt to drive on an old Wolseley, identical to the police cars of the time, with the same sort of 'crash' gearbox, but the corporal explained that a better result could be achieved when changing into a higher gear by simultaneously pulling the left steering stick and selecting the next gear. The tank didn't turn, as the gearbox was not in the power train when you had the clutch pedal down. I tried these 'stick changes' but I was continually managing to create distinctly nasty noises from the gearbox. 'You're bein' too gentle, Sir. Bang it in!' said the corporal. So the next time I changed up I did exactly that – and the gear knob came off in my hand! 'Now look what you've done,' he said, 'You've broken it!' In spite of my partially wrecking some of Her Majesty's equipment, the afternoon was thoroughly enjoyable and I soon got a taste for knocking down small trees and driving up seemingly impossible slopes. Great fun I must say, but if you ever get the chance to do the same, take my advice and beg, borrow or steal a set of goggles. I didn't have any such luxury and finished my tank driving with my eyes full of grit!

Every year we had the pleasure of the AOC's Inspection, if one can call it a pleasure, but be that as it may, it meant loads of 'bull'. You know the sort of thing – 'If you find something lying around salute it, if it doesn't salute back, pick it up and if it won't move, paint it!' In addition to all this in 1960 the Station Commander decided that it would be a great idea to have a mass formation display and on the right you can get an idea of what this particular 'Balbo' looked like. Why Balbo? Because the chap who pioneered large formations of aircraft such as this was an Italian, General Balbo.

Of course you can't just get 12 aircraft airborne and achieve the perfection demonstrated – it takes a lot of practice, so over the weeks before the big day in May, we had eight sessions of formation flying, which is one of the best methods of losing weight yet invented, as you sweat pounds off each time you get airborne.

The only better method of losing weight is to become a member of a formation aerobatic team, which I did at the beginning of 1961 and what this would have led to I don't know but while I was away on leave, my replacement in the team was unfortunately killed when his aircraft failed to pull out of a loop. The reason for this was never fully explained, but the result was that the powers that be decided that the team should be wound up. However the little bit that I did do flying at number 4, 'in the box' convinced me that I would lose weight at a fairly rapid rate if we had continued into the summer.

Just to give you some idea of what it was like to do formation aerobatics, I can tell you that I used to fly with my nose about six feet from the leaders tail. This requires considerable concentration and a lot of hard physical effort to stay in the same place regardless of ones attitude, be it a loop or some sort of rolling manoeuvre. Nevertheless it is great fun and we were all very disappointed not to be able to continue and put on displays for the public.

One morning the station Padre expressed a desire to have a trip, so it being a lovely clear day I took him up to 40,000 feet from where we could see for miles. It is not very often that you get really clear visibility, but when you do one can see large sections of the British Isles as though one were looking at a map. I can quite see how the astronauts felt looking down on the Earth from space! In fact from 55,000 feet you can see the curvature of the earth very clearly. Anyway after we had had our fill of sightseeing, we descended back to base for a few circuits and landings before retiring to the Mess for lunch. Whilst we were eating, someone asked the Padre what he had been doing that morning and he replied, 'I've been flying – went up to 40,000 feet for a quick interview!'

In October 1960 my three-year tour at Swinderby should have finished, but as several new instructors had been posted in at the same time as myself, it would have meant a severe dilution of the overall level of instructional experience had we all been posted out at the same time. Consequently two of us were asked if we would each extend our tours by a year. As an incentive to say 'yes' I was told I could go into 'standards flight', who were responsible for the standard of instruction on the AFTS, and also told that I could have a choice of posting in a year's time. A further carrot was another week at RAF Kemble flying the Hunter, which I thoroughly enjoyed. This seemed to be a good deal so I agreed and moved office so to speak.

Thereafter I became one of a team responsible for checking new instructors when they arrived fresh from CFS, maintaining the high standards of the instructors already at Swinderby and I also became an Instrument Rating Examiner (IRE). By now I had a 'Master Green' rating, meaning that I could fly in any weather.

My new post also meant that I got a number of what you might call odd jobs. The first of these was to take up a journalist from *The Times*, who was writing a series of articles on training in the RAF right from initial selection up to arriving on a front line squadron as a fully qualified military pilot. I decided that a suitable instructional exercise for this purpose would be stalling.

Having briefed Mr Charles just as if he were a real student, we got airborne and climbed to about 15,000 feet ready to start the stalling demonstration. Now because an aircraft can virtually 'drop out of the sky' when it stalls, it is vital for one's longevity to see that no other aircraft is in the vicinity, particularly below. To do this you performed a 'clearing turn' in each direction. This required a pull of about 2 'g'. As I was doing this rather gentle manoeuvre there was a sort of groan from Mr Charles. I immediately levelled out and inquired as to the problem. It seemed that he was totally unprepared for his body weight to double and I was thankful I hadn't decided to demonstrate steep turns at 6 ⅔ 'g'! Not that I would even have considered this as most students who were partially inured to the effects of 'g' blacked out during their first experience of a steep turn.

My next 'odd job' was in April 1961, when I had the pleasure of flying with Flying Officer R.T. Simpson, one time captain of the Nottinghamshire cricket team. He was then a pilot in the RAF Reserve and thus had to keep in flying practice. I think the last time I had seen him was at Lords during a test match. The other odd job I can remember was standing in for the Flying Wing Adjutant while he went on three weeks' leave.

Now I already had a theory about office work of this sort. My maxim was − 1. Write it down and − 2. Do it now. This seemed to work admirably well and after only a few days I had emptied my in-tray as well as that of the Wing Commander Flying. After about ten days the 'Wingco' told me that he had so little to do and he couldn't understand it! I hardly dared to tell him I had been taking 'executive' decisions on his behalf, but he seemed happy about the whole affair.

You may remember I mentioned the trilby hat I never wore − here on the right you can see it doing sterling service with our rapidly growing boys, seen in the garden at Collingham.

One chore that came around from time to time was that of 'Duty Pilot'. As such, one had to spend the whole day or night in the control tower supervising the flying and coping with any emergencies that might occur. One day there was a minor emergency, which I dealt with. However I forgot to inform the Group Captain and later I got a minor bollocking for my omission. A week or two later, when I was again 'Duty Pilot', there was a genuine emergency when an aircraft called for the arrester barrier to be raised as the take-off was abandoned. I got the Group Captain on the line very quickly and just in time to be able to say, 'Sir, there is an aircraft going into the barrier, NOW!' Revenge is sweet, they do say.

All books, forms, passes, etc. in the RAF have a number. For instance one's identity card is F.1250, while F.700 is an aircraft's technical log into which all servicing, modifications etc are recorded throughout the life of the machine. It has a section for a pilot to report any fault that he has found, and another to record what has been done to rectify the fault, and so on.

Occasionally some odd entries were noted. A pilot reported 'something loose in wing'. This was cleared by 'something tightened in wing'! On another occasion I sent a student to fly solo, but he came back soon after I had briefed him to say that the aircraft was U/S (unserviceable). A few minutes later the technicians reported that it was now serviceable, so I followed the student out to the line to see what had been the matter. He had reported, 'E2 compass missing'. (The E2 compass was for emergencies and was on the coaming and had a cover so that it could be hidden when a pilot was doing practice instrument flying). The clearing entry read, 'E2 compass cover raised, E2 compass found'!

As I mentioned earlier I was to have a choice of posting when my year in 'Standards' came to an end and I had opted to move to Transport Command and fly the Armstrong Whitworth Argosy, which was then due into service. Like many other aircraft before and since, the due date for entering service was put back, in this case by six months, and so I never even got to see the aircraft. YCNSTWLEM!

CHAPTER 8

Meteorological Reconaissance

AS CREW TRAINING ON THE ARGOSY couldn't start until the aircraft came into service, I was posted, at the beginning of October 1961, to Number 242 Operational Conversion Unit (OCU) at RAF Dishforth to learn to fly the Handley Page Hastings.

This was not at all what I had in mind as the Hastings had been around for about 13 years and I had set my sights on flying a new and modern aeroplane. However I was somewhat mollified by being selected to fly as a Captain without first having to spend three years in the right hand seat. I was the first pilot ever to do this and was looked upon as something of a freak when I arrived at the OCU, as well as gaining for myself a place in the record books! I achieved another record when, after some weeks in ground school, I became the first person ever to achieve 100% in the final exam, something that surprised me, as I found the exam was quite easy, but then all exams are easy if you know the answers!

On 23rd November I did my first flight, and what a shock to the system that was! The elevator control was so heavy that you needed to be built like the world's strongest man to be able to fly the thing. Apparently the reason for this was that the test pilot responsible for allowing the aircraft into service had the physique of a gorilla, and when someone mentioned the shortcoming to him, observed that he found it was no problem. The fact that practically everyone else <u>did</u> find it a problem was shown when the mark II version came into service with a lowered and bigger tailplane, which I'm told made a tremendous difference, although I never got to fly one.

The net result of this requirement for pilots to be built like the proverbial brick outhouse was that on landing the flight engineer handled the throttles in response to the pilot calling for power changes. Consequently a good landing was very much a team effort, helped by the fact that the flight engineer could see the starboard main wheel from his seat, so that when you called for a 'slow cut' just as you were about to touch down he could use his judgement as to how slow the cut was. I found this method of flying entirely alien after all the previous

An Autobiography by Captain D.B. Hopkins

aircraft I had flown, nonetheless I managed to 'go solo' after some 6 hours of dual instruction. I also learnt pretty quickly that pilots must not upset flight engineers if they wanted to achieve good landings!

Dishforth is east of the Pennines near Ripon and under certain westerly wind conditions a 'standing wave' can be set up. This can lead to an extremely severe wind shear over a very short horizontal distance. While doing a circuit one day I ran into just this and had it not been for prompt action by my instructor, we might well have stalled. I learnt another valuable lesson that day!

Dishforth was also the home of the OCU for the Blackburn Beverley troop transport. This was apocryphally known as the only aircraft in the world to do everything – taxi, take-off, climb, cruise and descend – at the same speed. The cockpit was about the height of a two-storey building and had a red anti-collision beacon right over the top of it. Once I asked a friend who was in the middle of learning to fly the beast what it was like. His reply has remained with me ever since – 'Like flying a brothel from the bedroom window!'

Mella and the two boys had remained in Collingham during the course at Dishforth and I managed to get home quite frequently at weekends and for Christmas. At the beginning of February I got an urgent call from 'Auntie' Willis to say Mella was very ill. I immediately got leave and drove down to Collingham at high speed over very treacherous roads covered in frozen snow. The doctor thought she might have polio, but the true cause of her sickness was never properly established. However after two weeks she had recovered sufficiently to be able to look after the boys and for me to be able to go back to the course, that by now was down south as the OCU had moved from Dishforth to Thorney Island in Sussex. The course finished at the end of February and after two cancelled postings, one to Cyprus and the other to Colerne, Wiltshire, I was sent to join Number 202 Meteorological Squadron at Aldergrove (now Belfast Airport).

By this time we had exchanged the mark V Jaguar for a mark X and in this we all travelled to Stranraer to catch the ferry to Larne and make our way to Lisburn in County Antrim, where we stayed in an hotel for a couple of weeks. During this time I found a house for us to rent, a married quarter not being available. It was in the course of this stay we became acquainted with an Ulster 'delicacy' called soda bread. Probably the less I say about this the better, but if you have to go out in a strong wind then a belly-full of soda bread will undoubtedly stop you being blown into the nearest lough!

We eventually found, and moved into, a house on an estate in Newtonbreda in south Belfast. Upon moving in, one of the first things Mella found was the remains of the previous occupants' mixed grill still in the grill pan! As both Mella and I have always prided ourselves on the cleanliness that we left behind when moving out of accommodation, this revelation was somewhat upsetting, although it was more than offset by the kindness of our neighbour, Rosemary Conn, who appeared at the adjoining fence at lunchtime on the day of our move holding a big pot of wonderful stew. The four of us devoured this with some relish, remarking how nice and friendly the neighbours were. Quite often when moving house, new neighbours have met us with offers such as: 'If there's anything you need, give us a call,' but this was the first time practical help had been forthcoming, unasked, during our many home-moves.

We made friends with our neighbours on all sides, Catholic and Protestant alike, and when some six months later we moved to a married quarter at Aldergrove, we held a party to say thank you to all these good friends. For a lot of them this was the first time they had met socially since 'Papists' and 'Prods' didn't normally speak to one another. (How small-minded and bigoted can you get!) We felt at the time that we might have done something to improve relations between the two sides, but when we visited Rosemary and her husband some months later, we were understandably disappointed to hear that the normal 'standoffishness' had resumed. I have travelled extensively in many parts of the world during my life and I can honestly say that Northern Ireland is the only place where religion is a factor deter-mining whether one person speaks to another! Puerile isn't it?

Since the weather was still quite cold, one of the next things I needed to do was to organise a supply of coal for our fires. Having ascertained the whereabouts of the local coal merchant, I went to see him. Yes he could deliver coal straight away and how much would I like? I said I would have five hundredweights, but he told me he didn't sell it by the hundredweight, but by the 'baag'! Asked how much was in a baag, he replied, 'A hundredweight and a quarter!' Whether a baag is still the unit for coal measurement I don't know, but it was then just one of the strange habits of Ulster. Lord knows how they might get on with kilos! The coal duly arrived and when I asked, 'How much?' he said to pay him next time. Next time came a few weeks later and once more I had four 'baags' delivered and once more I asked, 'How much?' and once more he said to pay him next time! By the time 'next time' arrived I felt sure I must owe him something approaching the national debt, but I still found it very difficult to get him to accept any money, although he reluctantly did after much cajoling.

Very soon I was doing my first 'Bismuth' flights. Perhaps I should explain 'Bismuth'. This was nothing to do with the element, but a codeword, something the RAF was particularly fond of using, and pre-sumably the use of a codeword was a hangover from wartime, since there seemed to be little valid reason for its continued use in peacetime.

*An Autobiography
by Captain
D.B. Hopkins*

The whole raison d'etre for the existence of No. 202 Squadron was to provide the Meteorological Office at Bracknell with information on the weather systems approaching the British Isles and to back up information provided by the Atlantic Weather Ships. All this was, of course, long before the arrival of satellites that have replaced both the ships and the meteorological squadron.

Our contract with the Met. Office required the squadron to fly five 'Bismuth' flights per week and these were usually completed on Monday to Friday. Now and again we would fly one at weekends if we had fallen short of our weekday target for some reason or another. The Bismuth tracks were identified by a letter, 'A' went down into the Bay of Biscay, 'B' went south-west into the Atlantic and so on until 'G' which went up past the Faroes. There was also a Bismuth 'O' that went round the North Sea and lasted a mere 7–8 hours compared with 10 hours for the others. We occasionally flew a probe such as 'K' shown on the map below. I've shown track 'E' because it was while we were flying this in October 1962 that I spotted what I thought was an upturned trawler somewhere near point B up by Iceland. Whilst navigator John Washington and I discussed whether we should divert from track to investigate, the 'trawler' spouted and disappeared! It must have been a grey whale, but from a distance it was easily mistaken for a ship turned turtle.

The format of each Bismuth was the same. We flew from Aldergrove to a point near Tory Island off the northeast coast of Ulster and then set off on whichever track the Met Office had asked for that day. We flew at 1,500 feet above sea level, which was pretty uncomfortable if the weather was rough and since we were specifically looking for 'weather', this was usually the case. There were eight members of the crew: captain; first officer;

navigator; flight engineer; two signallers and two met. observers. In my crew this was, in order, myself; Terry Mills; John Washington; Don Crawford, 'Sully' Sullivan, John Webb, Jeff Earnshaw and 'Steve' Stevenson. Once we were down to 1,500 feet, one of the met. observers sat in the right hand seat, from where he could take readings of temperature and pressure from instruments just outside the starboard window.

All met. observers were checked out to fly the aircraft straight and level so that Terry and myself could swap seats every two hours. This was necessary, as the aircraft had no useable autopilot and we had to fly it manually for the entire 9 or 10-hour trip! Hard labour, you might think, and you'd be right! Once at point A we would descend to 'sea level', in practice about 200 feet ASL so that the met. observer could get a reading of 'sea level' pressure and temperature. Then back up to 1,500 feet and on to point B where the routine changed. We would descend to 'sea level' and then climb to 500 millibars (18,000 feet approx.), levelling at each 50 mbs for readings to be taken. Having spiralled up to 18,000 feet, we would fly to point C at this height and then spiral down taking readings at every 50 mbs down to 'sea level', then return to base via point D at 1,500 feet. None of the crew particularly liked the 2-hour high level leg as we all had to wear oxygen masks because the Hastings was not pressurised.

In February 1963 I flew a probe 'K' as shown in the diagram above, to find the centre of a hurricane that was moving west from the Caribbean towards the British Isles. The winds were extremely strong, so strong in fact that the tops of the considerable waves were being blown off. The north Atlantic that day was at its most threatening and we were all heartily glad that we were not riding out the storm in one of the weather ships! The profile of a 'probe' was different to that of the regular Bismuth in that we returned from 30° west at 10,000 feet. At this height we had a tremendous tailwind giving us a groundspeed in excess of 300 knots, a record for a Hastings, which compared most favourably with our groundspeed on the outward leg of 120 knots!

On Boxing Day, 1961 one of the Captains had the misfortune to crash a Hastings on take-off. The subsequent board of inquiry ruled that he had been negligent and when I arrived on the squadron he was awaiting a court martial. When an officer is court martialled he has the choice of being defended by a professional lawyer or by a brother officer. In this particular case, Flying Officer Bloggs (not his real name) decided that he would be better off with the second choice and he asked me to defend him. I had had absolutely no training for, or experience of, being a defence counsel and I asked him why he had picked on me. He indicated that as I was a QFI I had to be clever, a non sequitur if ever I heard one, and because I was new on the squadron I was not likely to

*An Autobiography
by Captain
D.B. Hopkins*

be biased, which was fair comment. Somewhat against my better judgement I agreed to help him and so, for three weeks until the day of his trial, I was to be found studying the Manual of Air Force Law with great enthusiasm and considerable depth.

I was, as you can imagine, extremely nervous when the trial started, but I soon got into my stride trying to get various witnesses to agree that Flg. Off. Bloggs was totally justified in continuing the take-off after allowing a swing to develop. After browbeating three or four witnesses to my way of thinking I was about to start on the next witness when I was advised by the kindly Judge Advocate to 'quit while I was ahead'. I took his advice and then suggested to the court that there was no prima facie case to answer. I was somewhat taken aback when the court decided after some deliberation that there was a case to answer, and so the trial was adjourned to the following day for me to present the case for the defence. (I learnt after the trial finished that the court just wanted to hear what the defence was!)

The following day I brought in two 'expert' witnesses in the form of two very experienced Hastings pilots, who agreed with my submission that Flg. Off. Bloggs was entirely justified in continuing the take-off, which so unfortunately led to the crash. I was more than amazed,

and as relieved as my 'client', when the verdict of not guilty was announced. I was also most gratified to be congratulated by the prosecuting officer, a professional lawyer, on my conduct of the defence case. For some time after this I was known on the squadron as 'Perry Mason Hopkins'!

Although by modern standards the Hastings was not particularly large, it was still a fairly big collection of metal and rivets as can be seen in the picture of myself checking the propeller of one of the four engines. This was taken just as I was about to fly a 'Bismuth' taking with me the RAF's chief photographer, Mike Chase. Mike was responsible for most of the superb pictures of various aircraft to be seen adorning the walls of offices and headquarters throughout the RAF.

The fact that the Hastings had a tail wheel in an era when most aircraft had nose wheels (even the Hermes, the civil version of the Hastings was thus equipped) led occasionally to some ribald comments from casual observers.

Once, one of our aircraft had diverted to Lajes, in the Azores, for some technical reason and was parked at the end of a long line of ultra modern USAF B47's. A crewman from one of these came wandering past and inquired from the signaller, who was standing by his aircraft, 'Say, what's this goddam thing?' The signaller, six foot four if he was an inch and appropriately built to scale, drew himself up to his full height and replied, 'It is a Royal Air Force Handley Page Hastings!' The American responded with, 'Goddam it's even got a tail wheel!' This was too much for our signaller who grabbed the Yank by the front of his shirt and lifted him up to his own eye level and said, "Ere, you ain't never seen a bird land on its bleeding beak 'ave you?' Exit American suitably abashed!

Just behind the cockpit was a small plastic dome. The navigator used this for taking sextant, or 'sun gun' readings on the sun, moon or stars. Immediately behind the dome was an open tube through which a Verey signalling pistol could be fired. Since the aircraft was not pressurised and the tube was open there was always a considerable suction through it.

Each member of the crew was given an allowance of one shilling and eleven and a half pence (just under 10p!) for each flight with which to purchase food etc. What we did was to send one of the Met. Observers down to the NAAFI with all our money to buy tea, coffee, milk, bread, tinned pilchards and a Birds Eye 'dinner-for-one' for each of us. Any few pence surplus was usually spent on a few hard-boiled eggs. Now and again we had a few of these eggs left over and it just happened that the Very pistol tube was just the right size to allow an egg offered up to it to be sucked out of the aircraft. An egg sucked out thus would zigzag its way back towards the fin and we had an ongoing competition to see if anyone could hit the fin with an egg. Of course no one ever did because the air pressure round the fin always deflected the egg. I have often wondered since what life form, if any, benefited from our largesse, or perhaps I should issue a warning to operators of mini-submarines to alert them to the presence of hens eggs on the floor of the Atlantic Ocean!

On another occasion one of the Met Observers made me a pilchard sandwich, something that I normally ate with relish. This day though I didn't feel in the mood for such a delicacy and not wishing to hurt the fellow's feelings I decided to throw it out of the side window of the cockpit. It went out all right, but immediately came back and plastered itself all over the rear side window. I told the groundcrew who had to

An Autobiography
by Captain
D.B. Hopkins

clean off the remains that we had been low flying and hit a flying fish, but I don't think they believed me!

In July 1962 I flew a full complement of 38 service passengers from Aldergrove to Gibraltar. As I mentioned in chapter six, I had a fairly dodgy experience the first time I went to Gibraltar and this time confirmed my opinion that landing there was not to be treated lightly. This time two things were making life difficult. First, the runway was being resurfaced, which meant that we had to land on the taxiway whose edge was perilously close to the sea, and second the wind was in that awkward direction well known to aviators who have flown into the place, where it flows around the Rock in such a way that you land <u>downwind</u> no matter which runway you choose! Also about half way along the runway there is considerable turbulence where the direction changes by 180°. The net result of all this was that I had considerable difficulty in keeping the aircraft on the substitute runway, very nearly putting one wheel over the edge into the sea!

I could see that Terry was not impressed by the ashen colour of his face as I finally brought the aircraft to a standstill. It was undoubtedly what we in the flying profession describe as a sixpence, half-crown, dustbin lid landing! Still, we also say that if you walk away from a landing it must have been a good one!

By this time Trevor had started school in Newtonbreda and I must say that he got an excellent grounding in the 3 R's that has undoubtedly stood him in good stead. The boys played for many a happy hour in their wigwam and cowboy suits and in the picture below some 'car repairs' are in progress. In Christopher's case this turned out to be as

prophetic as the picture in Chapter 1 of me in a similar position, as he has since become a skilled mechanic in his spare time.

As I was already a QFI, the Squadron Commander decided that the Transport Command Standardisation unit should check me out to become an Instrument Rating Examiner (IRE) on the Hastings. This involved flying across to Benson in Oxfordshire. I duly went across with the CO, who had decided that he too would get qualified as an IRE. He was given a very thorough grilling by the examiner, both on technical subjects and in the air. By the time my turn came I had lost interest in the whole proceedings since there was absolutely no requirement for two more IRE's on the squadron, but to my total surprise the examiner asked me just one technical question, got me to fly one approach and then told me I had passed! Later on I became a full QFI on the type and thereafter did quite a lot of training and checking of the other pilots on the squadron.

At this time Belfast Airport was still at Nutts Corner, Aldergrove Civil Airport being under construction. Because Aldergrove is built over some form of magnetic rock, it was impossible to do an accurate compass swing on the airfield, so we used to take the aircraft over to Nutts Corner, an extremely arduous flight of 5 minutes! On one occasion, after the compass swing was complete, I was in the control tower getting clearance to fly back to Aldergrove and the controller, whom I knew, told me of a hilarious incident that had recently occurred.

Nutts Corner was what you could describe as a 'country airport', with the public car park quite close to the runway. Every night a Dakota flew in from London at about 0300 with the newspapers for the province. On the night in question the pilot of the Dakota had been most indignant to find a car driving up the runway towards his aircraft as he completed his landing. After the offending driver was apprehended he was asked whether he had seen the Dakota, to which he replied in an unmistakably Irish accent, 'Sure I did – I blew my horn!'

The next remarkable occasion was during the winter of 1962/3 when we had a severe snowfall, to the extent that many roads became impassable. One day I was asked to take some volunteers and an ambulance and try to reach an isolated farmhouse where the farmer had fallen down stairs and supposedly broken his leg. We got to within about a mile of the farm in the ambulance and then had to take to our feet and by walking along the top of the snow covered hedgerows we eventually got to the farmhouse, to find the farmer with his leg all colours of the rainbow. He seemed in a pretty poor way so we loaded him onto the stretcher we had brought along and struggled back the way we had come along the tops of the hedgerows. After an exhausting period of stumbling along we finally got him into the ambulance and drove him to hospital in Belfast. The next day I went in to see if he was

*An Autobiography
by Captain
D.B. Hopkins*

recovering and was amazed to find he had already been discharged after treatment for just a bad bruise. YCNSTWLEM!

Another result of the severe winter that year was that we got involved in supply dropping to the sheep and cattle cut off from their food supplies. We did a number of sorties throwing out bales of hay from the back of the aircraft and you would be surprised at the amount of loose hay we had to clean out of our machines after the emergency was over!

About the end of February I left 202 Squadron and became Station Adjutant. This was to be a short posting lasting about a year, during which time a couple of amusing incidents occurred. The first was the occasion when I caught sight of the new Station Commander poking the bottom of the flagstaff on the parade ground with his swagger stick. I enquired as to the reason for this odd behaviour and he told me that on his last station he was in the middle of the final rehearsal for the annual AOC's parade when on the command 'Present Arms', the flagstaff crashed to the ground, narrowly missing him. It transpired that the thing was completely rotten and so he was checking to make sure there would be no repeat on the parade ground at Aldergrove.

The second memorable episode was the bayonet find. Going into the Group Captain's office one morning, I noticed he had a very old bayonet lying on his desk. He explained that he had been inspecting the station armoury a few days previously and had noticed a trapdoor in the ceiling. He instructed the Station Warrant Officer who was with him to get a ladder so that they could see what was in the loft. Apart from the collection of dust and cobwebs one would expect, the only thing of note was a large chest. This was found to contain a considerable number of 18-inch bayonets in leather scabbards dating back to 1907. Most of them were in a very sorry state but the CO had had the SWO clean up one of the better ones for him to keep as a trophy. I asked permission to get the SWO to clean one up for me and I have it to this day hanging in my hall, where it would be quite handy for seeing off any intruder. 'They don't like it up them!'

Just after the stretcher incident, Mella was taken ill with hepatitis and was confined to bed for some two months. As she had also recently become pregnant, you can imagine how sick she was and how worried that her illness might affect our unborn child. You can imagine our relief when Austen James was born on 9th November quite unaffected by the hepatitis. However fate had yet more in store that year, for on 20th December on our way to a party Mella slipped on some ice and broke her ankle. This was a major headache for both of us as Austen was only a few weeks old and after having her ankle set *and* reset, Mella was in a full-length plaster and having to sleep downstairs. I had to do all the cooking, something I'm not particularly good at, although I did manage a goose and all the trimmings for Christmas with expert guidance from Mella from her sickbed.

Fortunately we did have the luxury of a batman, Sean, who kept the house clean, but we had to keep an eye on him when he wielded the brasso. He was so liberal in the use of this that on one occasion we were unable to get our key into the front door Yale lock, as the hole was completely full! YNCSTWLEM!

Thus came to an end a not particularly happy episode in the lives of the Hopkins clan, and we were all happy to return to England and sanity.

*An Autobiography
by Captain
D.B. Hopkins*

CHAPTER 9

Bassingbourn – Again!

TOWARDS THE END OF JANUARY 1964 I was posted back to the mainland to do a refresher course on Canberras. By this time Mella was in a walking plaster, but it was still with some reluctance that I left her coping with two small boys and a baby while I went off to Bassingbourn for the second time. It was a great relief to get back to flying jet aircraft and I was crewed with a Squadron Leader navigator who was going to a B(I)8 Interdictor squadron in Germany as their Navigation Leader. This suited me fine as I had always had a yen to fly the B(I)8 version, which could be fitted with an under belly gun pack and wing pylons for carrying external stores. It also had a bubble canopy that gave the pilot a much-enhanced view, very much like the Mark 8 Meteor .

However my dream of flying this magnificent version of the Canberra was soon shattered when I was told that I would not be going to Germany, as the squadron did not need my services. YCNST-WLEM!! Instead I was given the chance to stay at Bassingbourn as an instructor on the OCU and I must say that in many ways this was a better option as moving the family to Germany would have been a major upheaval with Mella's ankle still less than perfect.

I resolved to find us a suitable place to set up home and in this I was lucky to find, through a colleague, a builder who was erecting two bungalows on the site of an old farmhouse in Meldreth only four miles from the airfield. I hastily went to see him and put my name on one of them with little idea how I was going to finance the deal. Nowadays the price, of less than £4,000, would be something one could find in petty cash, so to speak, but in 1964 it was a major amount of money. However I soon arranged a mortgage and was able to let Mella know the good news. At first she thought I was barking mad as my salary was only about £2,000 per annum and we had little or no furniture, but my mother gave us some that I was able to renovate over the next few months while the bungalow was completed.

In the meantime I found an old thatched cottage in Shepreth, close enough to Meldreth to allow Trevor and Christopher to go to the village primary school and not have to change schools when we finally moved to Meldreth. This cottage was an amalgamation of two small cottages and as a result had two sets of stairs, one at each end, that the boys found great fun, although Mella found them somewhat difficult, as they were very narrow and winding. I had been able to take a week's leave at the end of March to go back to Northern Ireland and collect the boys and Mella, who by now was out of plaster and on the road back to normality. Fortunately the summer was exceptionally sunny, so I was able to work on the furniture renovation in the back garden.

At the end of May I started my standardisation as a Canberra QFI and IRE and by the end of June I was ready to start instructing students, some of whom were 'ab initio' on the Canberra while others were doing a 'retread' as I had recently done. All were interesting to teach and I, as in my previous instructing, was learning more about the Canberra and flying in general.

On 20th September I flew to Malta to take part in a formation fly-past to celebrate Malta's independence and this photo, taken during a practice, shows how close our formation was. In fact the distance between the nose of my aircraft and the tail of the leader was about ten feet. As I mentioned in earlier chapters, the closer you get the easier it is to spot when you get out of position.

*An Autobiography
by Captain
D.B. Hopkins*

In January 1965 I took a B2 on a 'Lone Ranger' to Luqa (Malta), El Adem (Libya) and Akrotiri (Cyprus), with two navigators, flight lieutenants Cook and Williamson. Whilst at El Adem I did a low-level cross-country flight over the Sahara Desert. This was my first opportunity to try some 'real' low level flying. In the UK the minimum height for low flying is 250 feet above the ground, but over the desert there is no restriction other than safety considerations. In wartime one would need to fly as low as possible to avoid being seen by enemy radar, so an opportunity to do some practice at a realistically low level was not to be missed.

One valuable lesson I learnt was that over featureless terrain it is very difficult to judge your exact height above the ground, especially when it is all sand coloured. I was thoroughly enjoying myself whizzing along at 450 knots (520 mph) about six to ten feet above the sand when there was a yell from Williamson who was lying in the nose on the bomb-aimers couch, 'Didn't you see it?' 'See what?' I replied. 'That bloody camel – you nearly hit it!' I really hadn't seen the animal, so well was it camouflaged against the desert. Still they say a miss is as good as a mile!

At the end of January I was summoned to the Wing Commander Flying's office to be told I had been selected to instruct a senior officer who was going to Akrotiri as the Station Commander. I was partly flattered to be selected and partly nervous as to what my new student might be like. I needn't have worried, as Air Commodore North-Lewis was both a very good pilot and a splendid person to be with. His letter to me after his course says it all.

The Air Commodore had said to me before he left Bassingbourn that should I find myself in Akrotiri at any time I should look him up. It so happened that in September I was given the task of ferrying a T4 from Bassingbourn to Akrotiri, so I took the opportunity to go and see him. When I arrived at his office I told his PA who I was and what I had come for, but she told me that the Air Commodore was busy handing out Long Service and Good Conduct medals. However his door was open and he must have heard me speak and recognised my voice for he instructed his PA to send me in. We had a chat for 15 minutes during which time he apologised that he was unable to entertain me that evening as he had a prior engagement, but somewhat to my embarrassment he instructed one of his Wing Commanders to look after me. I was treated right royally and had a splendid meal in a local restaurant. For the non-service reader I should perhaps explain that a Wing Commander entertaining a mere Flight Lieutenant was a pretty unusual circumstance and certainly outside my previous experience! More significantly, though, it does demonstrate the sincerity of the words in the letter.

Also in his letter the Air Commodore wished me luck in my new job. This was a transfer to the Bomber Command Standardisation Flight (BCSF), also at Bassingbourn, and meant I was again part of a team responsible for the standard of all the QFI's at Bassingbourn. In the meantime in June I was busy taking my recategorisation as an A1 QFI. This was a much more extensive test, or rather set of tests, involving two flying tests, a lecture and an oral.

The subject of my lecture was 'Probable Developments in Automatic Landings'. To research this I went over to RAF Bedford, where the Automatic Landing Development Unit was based, and spent a day with them during which I flew in the Comet 3 that they used for their experimental work. It was all very interesting and one of the 'probable' developments I forecast was the use of a cassette with an entire flight profile written on it to be used in conjunction with a suitably modified autopilot that would mean an aircraft flying, say, from Heathrow to New York entirely automatically. Although I never actually saw the system working, Gordon Corps told me that something like this was in use in Concorde. YCNSTWLEM!

About this time I had the opportunity to buy a 12-bore double-barrelled shotgun from a colleague who was being posted to Germany where he would be unable to use it. I had never used such a gun before, but by good fortune my student at the time, Lieutenant Eagle RN, was something of an ace and he kindly took me pigeon shooting a few times and gave me many useful hints. There was a four-gun rough-shoot at Bassingbourn that I joined and I enjoyed many a Saturday morning walk around the airfield letting fly at the occasional pheasant or hare. I kept that gun until 1998, when I moved from country to town and sold it at a profit of 400%! I had a lot of fun with it and did my bit to keep down the rabbit population of Sussex.

Coincident with my transfer to the BCSF in September, I became a member of the CFS Examining Wing responsible for examining Canberra pilots throughout the RAF. At this time there were 22 RAF units operating Canberras in such diverse places as Laarbruch, Geilenkirchen, Wildenrath, Bruggen, (all in Germany), Binbrook, Pershore, Strubby, Watton (UK), Luqa (Malta), Akrotiri (Cyprus) and Tengah (Singapore). The units in Germany and UK we visited each year, the others every other year.

The result of all this was that I was away from home a lot, about three months of each year, so Mella had to look after the three boys and their education to a very large extent. In this regard we were very lucky with the primary school in Meldreth, run by headmaster Ron Harding, who had previously run the school on Tristan da Cunha. He was what I would call an ideal teacher who took great interest in all his pupils and not only did he teach them academic subjects, but practical ones as well.

For instance he had most of the pupils involved in building a swimming pool for the benefit of the entire school. Early on during his time at the school he contacted us to tell us that Trevor, who was about seven at the time and sat at the back of the classroom, kept walking up to the front of the class to look at what was written on the blackboard. This seemed so odd that I immediately took Trevor to see our MO, who tested his eyesight. It turned out that he was very short-sighted, so much so that when we had got him fitted out with spectacles he observed that, 'that's much better I can see the bus at the end of the street now!' It is difficult to know when one's offspring have poor eyesight and they just think what they see is normal, so it's just as well an incident like this drew our attention to Trevor's problem.

One of the benefits of being a CFS Examiner or 'trapper', as we were universally known, was to be able to fly the particular type of Canberra that the examinee squadron operated. Over my time on Canberras I had the pleasure of flying B2's; PR3's; T4's; B6's; PR7's; B(I)8's; PR9's; B15's; and T17's, the latter being used at the time for training Air Electronic Officers in the art of radar jamming and similar techniques.

Usually as trappers we would fly a typical operational sortie that the squadron did, so for instance one of my trips in a B(I)8 was a low level bombing sortie over Germany, finishing by dropping a practice bomb at the range at Nordhorn, using a then new technique. I was teased when I got back to the Mess by the members of the squadron trying to get me to believe that I had dropped an ODA (outside the danger area), whereas in reality it had been a 10 yard error, which for most munitions is as good as a direct hit!

Another interesting sortie was photographing a part of Borneo from a PR7 as part of an aerial survey of the country that had been going on since 1948. The reason why this survey took such an incredibly long time was the cloud conditions over Borneo. I suppose today infra-red photography would have cut the whole procedure short, but in 1967 such technology didn't exist. One PR3 I flew was the one, WE139, that won the London to New Zealand Air Race in 1953 and which is now on display in the RAF Museum at Hendon.

While I was visiting the B(I)8 squadron mentioned above, I heard an amusing tale about a non-constituted crew doing a 'pundit crawl' around Germany one night. I must first explain that a non-constituted crew is one of pilot and navigator who don't normally fly together and a 'pundit crawl' is a map-reading navigational exercise flying from one airfield to another, on to a third and back to base. Its pundit, i.e. a coloured light flashing the two identity letters for that airfield in Morse code, red for military airfields and green for civilian, identifies each airfield. It seems that both the pilot and navigator had allowed their knowledge of Morse to get rusty, so when the pilot spotted a pundit flashing 'dah dah dit, dah dit dah' he couldn't remember what it was, so he asked the navigator who couldn't remember either. 'Shall I look it up?' says the Nav. 'No, don't bother' replied the pilot, 'I'll ask someone.' So he pressed the tit and said, 'Wildenrath, this is Alpha Delta, what is dah dah dit, dah dit dah?' Back from the darkness came the most helpful reply, 'Morse clot!'

Also on a light note, we had a visit to Bassingbourn by some officers of one of the Guards regiments. I was showing two subalterns the 'business' end of a Canberra, i.e. where the pilot and navigator sat. One of these two chinless wonders turned to me to ask where I sat. I pointed to the pilot's seat, whereupon he asked, 'Oh, don't you have a driver?' I suppose he thought it was like a tank with the commander sticking his head out of the top. YCNSTWLEM!

To give an idea of our workload as trappers, in 1967 I was in Geilenkirchen for a week in April, Laarbruch and Bruggen a week each in May, Binbrook and Laarbruch a week each in June, Bruggen a week in July, Tengah for three weeks in October/ November, Watton three weeks in November/December. For each test the pilot had to be briefed before the flight, debriefed after the flight and then a report was written up for submission to CFS Examining Wing. So although the average length of a test flight was about one and a half hours, we could only do a maximum of three per day, and that was jolly hard work and meant a working day from 0900 to 2100! Between times I would be testing students and staff at Bassingbourn, doing air tests and so on.

Speaking of air tests, there was one occasion when a student reported a B2 unserviceable, as the critical speed on the port engine was way above the correct figure. Without getting too technical, the critical speed is that speed below which directional control cannot be

*An Autobiography
by Captain
D.B. Hopkins*

maintained with full rudder and full power on one engine, the other engine being at idle. It is important to know what these speeds are and to be able to fly the aircraft in such a configuration without losing control.

Consequently I was sent up to verify the student's figures. Sure enough, the crit. speed for the starboard engine was normal, but that for the port was much too high. The aircraft was taken out of service for examination by the engineers, who surprisingly could find nothing wrong with it, so I was asked to test it again. This I did with the same results as previously. Back to the hangar it went for further and more detailed examination that eventually revealed a curious and hitherto unheard-of fault.

The rudder on a Canberra has a device to prevent too much rudder being applied at high speeds and causing undue stress on the airframe. The main component of this device is a torque-tube that is progressively loaded by the pilot applying rudder. In this instance the torque-tube had suffered a spiral crack down its entire length, so that in one direction the crack was being compressed and working normally and in the other opened, with the consequent differences in crit. speeds. As far as I'm aware this was the only occasion that a fault like this was ever experienced.

During this era the role of the Canberra as a high level bomber had become obsolete and had been changed to a new role delivering nuclear weapons at high speed and low level using a system called LABS (Low Altitude Bombing System). As the Canberra had never been considered for this type of flying at its inception, nobody had written a suitable chapter on 'low flying' either for the Instructor's Guide or Pilot's Notes. The omission was given to me to rectify. (See Annex 'A'). Most of it was simple common sense, but when I came to write about minimum radius turns, I could not find any source for the information I needed. Neither the manufacturers nor the test pilots at Boscombe Down could help, so I set about working it out from basics.

I needed to know what the radius of turn was at sea level at full power on both engines and pulling the maximum allowed '4g'. I set to with pen, paper and slide rule and came up with a figure of about 150 yards. 'This is ridiculous,' I thought, 'I must have made an error with the decimal point somewhere and the result should be x 10!' However no matter how many times I reworked my figures I kept getting essentially the same result. The answer, I felt, was to go and try it in practice. So with a suitably hardy navigator, who didn't mind being subjected to repeated turns at 4g, I took off and went over to East Anglia to find a disused airfield to test my theoretical result. To my total surprise I found my results to be pretty accurate. Looking back, I suppose I shouldn't have been all that surprised at the Canberra's low-level performance as it had a very low wing loading.

It is interesting to surmise that as long as one's fuel held out one could avoid being shot down by any fighter in the world at that time simply by doing a 4g turn. The frustrated fighter pilot would just not have been able to 'get a bead' on you! YCNSTWLEM! (For the benefit of technical types and other aviators I have included my treatise on Low Flying as well as that on Braking as annexes at the end of my book.)

I've occasionally been asked how the 'standardisers' standardised themselves. Quite simply by what the government today would call self-regulation, only in our case it worked and worked extremely well. There were three examiners at any given time and we spent quite a lot of time flying with each other, either travelling to a squadron or for revalidating each other's CIRE (Command Instrument Rating Examiner) qualifications. When testing pilots, we gave them a mark out of ten, although this was only for our own purposes and was not recorded anywhere. Every so often two of us would each fly with a particular pilot for some reason and in every case the mark we gave was the same. Another method we adopted was to obey one of Socrates' tenets, i.e. to be critical of each other, but to be particularly self-critical and analyse what one had just done. I did this throughout my flying career and found it very useful indeed.

Whilst I am on the subject of standards, I must mention a visit we did to a squadron in Germany whose result the previous year had been quite satisfactory. This year it was a completely different story, even though the majority of the pilots were the same ones whom we had tested only 12 months before. By the Wednesday of our visit I had the AOC on the phone asking me what I thought of them. When told that their standard was pretty dire, he expressed the opinion that he expected as much. The next day the C in C Germany rang me with exactly the same comments. We didn't have too far to look for the cause of this sudden and grave lowering of standards. As in any other organisation, the fault lay at the top, i.e. with the squadron CO, but because he was a Navigator his competence was outside our remit. Nevertheless my comments to the C in C bore fruit as the CO was sacked and replaced by a pilot Wing Commander. The following year all the pilots had regained their previous standards, proving my long-held theory that the man at the top is usually to blame in these sorts of circumstances.

Similarly I once had to deal with a Wing Commander pilot doing a refresher course prior to going to Germany to become CO of a squadron. I had cause to take him off flying altogether. This might seem pretty drastic, but not only was this man's flying ability totally unacceptable, he also refused to believe me when I told him of his shortcomings. A bad pilot is dangerous, but a pilot who won't acknowledge this is lethal, not only to himself but also to his crew!

One of my colleagues, Jim Rutter, and I spent some time flying

*An Autobiography
by Captain
D.B. Hopkins*

together in a T4 doing 'blind' landings using the ILS (Instrument Landing System) and we found that on a calm day we could both fly completely blind down the ILS right on to the runway. Of course we were not allowed to do this for real, but the lessons I learnt from these experiments saved my bacon on a couple of occasions when I was flying commercially, as I shall relate in another chapter.

Some time in 1966 I was informed by MOD that I could, if I wished, extend my service until the age of 55 instead of retiring at the age of 38. In order to make an informed decision, I had an interview with a Wing Commander at MOD to ascertain my career prospects. I was told that I was unlikely to get promotion beyond my present rank of Flight Lieutenant, notwithstanding the fact that I had passed my promotion examination, which meant that my salary would not rise much in the next few years. I was also told that my next posting would be to Air Traffic Control.

To say that I was astounded at the latter idea would be the understatement of the century. Considering that I was at that time one of the best qualified pilots in the entire Air Force, it seemed to me to be a total waste of my talents to shunt me into a ground job, and in any case I didn't join the RAF to fly a 'mahogany bomber'. If I'd wanted to do that I would have joined a bank or building society! Anyway I was so disgusted that I came home from the interview and immediately booked a correspondence course to get an Airline Transport Pilot's Licence (ATPL). I also informed MOD that I would not be remaining in the RAF beyond my 38th birthday.

Judging by the fact that the RAF today seems to be short of experienced pilots, it would seem that the 'faceless wonders' at MOD still haven't learnt the value of giving top quality people a sensible career. In fairness I should mention that I and Jim Rutter had been chosen to be the first QFI's on the cancelled TSR2 and once we had got the initial pilots trained, we were to be the 'trappers' for the type. I only found out about this just before I left the RAF on 8th December 1968.

In late 1967 I spent a very interesting day at Dunlop's factory gleaning information to help me write another chapter for the Canberra Instructor's Guide regarding braking techniques. (See Annex 'B'). As with so much in life, there is more to the subject than meets the eye! Whilst at the factory, I saw the brakes for the Concord under development testing to destruction. Quite an awe-inspiring sight, with flames shooting out all over the place and demonstrating very vividly the amount of energy that needs to be dissipated whilst stopping an aircraft.

As an illustration of this I was once told that the amount of heat energy dissipated through the brakes of a Victor bomber during stopping was sufficient to raise six elephants a hundred feet in the air and cook them. And they would be overdone! An amusing way of bringing home to pilots the nature of the problem.

This chapter would not be complete without a picture of the ill-fated TSR2. I was fortunate enough to attend a lecture given by Roland Beamont about his time flying this magnificent aircraft. One thing I learnt was that the TSR2 would carry a bigger load, further than the equivalent aircraft of today, the Tornado. Imagine what the TSR2 would have been able to do 35 years on, with uprated engines and enhanced lightweight systems!

I also learnt in later years that the main reason for cancelling TSR2 was so that the Americans could sell their vastly inferior Phantom around the world. But for Harold Wilson our aviation industry would have had a world-beater and had the TSR2 not been the subject of political sleaze, I probably would have stayed in the service until 1985!! YCNSTWLEM!!!

Although the powers that be at the MOD did not seem to value my talents enough either to promote me or to give me a worthwhile career, it would appear that somebody had other ideas, for in the New Years Honours list in 1969 I was the very proud recipient of a Queen's Commendation. This was a singularly pleasant and totally unexpected honour and the certificate on next page serves as a constant reminder of just over sixteen very enjoyable years serving Her Majesty in the Royal Air Force. I would recommend any young man wishing to become a pilot to follow in my footsteps.

*An Autobiography
by Captain
D.B. Hopkins*

By the QUEEN'S Order the name of

Flight Lieutenant D.B.Hopkins,

Royal Air Force (Retired),

was published in the London Gazette on

1st January, 1969,

as commended for valuable service in the air.
I am charged to record
Her Majesty's high appreciation.

Denis Healey

Secretary of State for Defence.

Chapter Nine

CHAPTER 10

'Elmgate'

WHEN OUR NEW BUNGALOW WAS FINALLY FINISHED in October 1964, we moved in straight away and my spare time became very busy indeed with decorating and fixing the garden. The site of the latter had at one time been a farmyard, in the days when ploughing engines were used. Hence amongst heaps of general rubbish I dug up remains of coils of wire rope that was used to pull the seven-share ploughs back and forth across the fields. The other 'artefacts' I found were coins (pennies mostly) dating back to the mid 19th century, so they were most likely to have been dropped by the navvies who were building the railway line that ran along the back of the garden.

In the picture, 'Elmgate' is on the right, in the middle is the elm tree after which we named the bungalow, and on the left the 'Flying Scotsman' is just coming into view with the then owner, Alan Pegler,

on the footplate. I mention him as he was at one time married to my cousin Pam Marshall, daughter of Uncle Nelson and Aunt Dorothy. We did think that the trains going past at regular intervals might detract from the peace and quiet of living in the country, but the only time we really noticed them was when they stopped running due to engineering work on the line.

We lived at Elmgate for a total of 12 years, over which period we made many changes both to the house and the garden. One of the first major alterations was the conservatory that I built from a kit. This was the first building I had ever done, so I was very pleased when it was completed without any problems. I even got the whole building square to within a quarter of an inch on the diagonals, which the building inspector told me was quite a rare achievement even among professional builders.

This addition gave us some really useful extra space as well as somewhere to sit in cold but sunny weather. I also built the patio seen in the picture. The dog looking at the camera was Mitzi 2, who was unfortunately killed by a passing goods train one day when I was away. We had taught her to sit at the edge of the line before crossing, but she sat just an inch or two too close and was struck by a protruding piece of a truck and killed instantaneously. Very sad as she was a lovely dog, who used to sulk the moment I put on my uniform to go away again, and when I returned from a trip it was a case of greet the dog, the children and Mella in that order, before I could get out of the car!

One Christmas Trevor was given a 'Boy Electronics' set. He soon exhausted the scope of this but it certainly lit his enthusiasm for building things electronic. This was all well and good, but it resulted in his bedroom carpet being constantly full of solder. Not wishing to deter his enthusiasm and to give all three boys space to do 'their thing', whatever it was, I decided to build them a playroom in the garden. This I did with a summerhouse kit I bought. It was fitted out with a bench each, an intercom to the kitchen so that Mella could call them in for meals, and electric light and power. It was a very successful addition to the 'estate' with the added benefit that it kept Trevor's carpet solder free!

The garden came in for a lot of attention and gradually over the years had pretty much everything one could want – two greenhouses, a water feature, a compost heap, a fruit cage with raspberries, strawberries etc., a vegetable patch and a chicken run. For the latter's nest boxes I needed a supply of straw that I got from a farm I passed on my way to work at Bassingbourn. The farmer was a Mr Conningsby, who looked every bit the part with his ruddy complexion. He was an archetypal farmer, but also he was a man of very few words. I used to visit him about every three months or so to get a new bale of straw and the conversation was usually along the following lines: 'Morning Mr Conningsby, are you well?' 'Yus.' 'Could I have a bale of straw?' 'Yus.' 'Thank you, goodbye.' I would pay him and load the straw into my car and that was that.

However, one day in about mid-July I went to him for yet another bale. The usual conversation took place at the end of which he said, ''Ave yer got a minute?' I said I had. 'Come and look at this,' he said leading me into his vegetable garden. In the middle of his row of magnificent runner beans there was a weird looking plant about ten feet high, the like of which I had never seen before or since. However knowing that I was a keen gardener he said, 'Do yer know what that is, it just growd there?' I indicated that I had no idea what it was, but that I would look it up in my gardening reference books when I got home and let him know if I could identify the plant. I did and I couldn't, so it was another three months before I saw him again for more straw. The habitual conversation ensued and then I asked if he ever found out what his rogue plant was. 'Oh yus,' he said, 'The village constable came by on his bike and saw it and they came and took it away and burnt it!' It turned out that it was a cannabis plant and I couldn't help falling about laughing as Mr Conningsby was about the most unlikely man to grow 'pot' in his back garden as any in the entire world. YCNSTWLEM!

Another major construction that involved the three boys and myself was our model railway up in the attic. This was 00 scale and a very comprehensive layout with stations, bridges, tunnels, roads etc, etc.

It lead, on one occasion, to a rather amusing incident with Helen, the wife of one of our friends, Michael, in the village. One of the boys' birthdays was approaching and I had popped into Royston during my lunch hour, still in my RAF uniform, to visit the toyshop with the intention of purchasing another engine for the layout. As I entered the shop I saw Helen and greeted her, 'Hello Helen', but was somewhat taken aback when she ignored me totally. So I tried again, 'Hello Helen.' This time she looked at me and said with conversation-stopping loudness, 'Hello Derek, I'm sorry I didn't recognise you with your clothes on!'

To say that Helen was a little absent-minded is something of an understatement. On another occasion she popped in to see Mella, who

*An Autobiography
by Captain
D.B. Hopkins*

was pressing a pair of my trousers at the time, and asked her if she had seen Michael's trousers anywhere! There is really no answer to a question like that, but we teased her unmercifully ever after, although I think she found the offending pair of breeks at the cleaners, where she had taken them.

Elmgate was up a drive that led to a level crossing over the railway to an orchard on the other side. We shared this drive with the occupants of the other bungalow, one of my navigator colleagues from Bassingbourn, Roly and his wife Molly Bee. The two bungalows were so situated that Elmgate and Roly's garage formed a sort of venturi and when the wind blew from a certain direction it could fairly whistle between the two buildings.

One day Roly bought a garden shed of the sort that looked rather like one of those old discarded railway trucks that one occasionally sees on allotments masquerading as a shed. He decided to erect this in his garden right alongside the drive, where it filled the view from our living room window and, more importantly, right in the path of the venturi enhanced wind. I told him that I didn't think much of his choice for siting this monstrosity, and that, as he hadn't fastened it down it might well blow away, but to no avail as he insisted on leaving it there.

The shed had been in position for around six months when we had a strong wind from 'the' direction. Mella, the boys and I were sitting having lunch when Roly's shed got airborne, rather like the Tardis of Dr Who, drifted slowly up his garden and collapsed on the ground like a pack of cards. Miraculously not a pane of glass was broken, as I found when I went across after lunch to help Roly move it across his garden to a more suitable site. Quite how I refrained from saying 'I told you so' I do not know!

My first greenhouse, shown left with Austen, Trevor and

Christopher in respective school uniforms, was an Alton and specially designed for growing tomatoes. The first year I had it, I filled it with tomato plants and sold the resulting fruit to friends and neighbours, the proceeds of which paid for the entire cost of the greenhouse. Thereafter I grew all my bedding plants, house plants as well as tomatoes for our own consumption.

When Trevor was about fourteen and attending Cambridge Grammar School together with Christopher, he had developed a very great interest in electronics. To get more information about things like computers that were then just in their infancy, so to speak, he was writing to companies and asking for their brochures. Some companies refused to send their brochures to individuals, so Trevor invented a couple of companies of his own to overcome this problem. One, I remember, was 'The Hopkins Repair Company' and our daily postal delivery was soon getting quite large.

One day after I had recently told him to exercise some discretion about sending for brochures, I was standing in the greenhouse, from which I could see right down the drive. I noticed a car drive up with the driver obviously looking for something, so I went out to see if I could help. He turned out to be a salesman from some computer company or other and said he had come in response to my expressed interest in their product of a computer costing around £600 (a lot of money in 1971!). When I told him rather apologetically that the person he wanted to see was at school and only 14 I was quite prepared for him to get very upset for having his time wasted. To my surprise and relief he said he was pleased to think that a boy of Trevor's age was sufficiently interested in the subject to ask for information.

Lest I give the impression that Trevor's talents only extended to matters electronic, I am including a poem he wrote at the age of nine.

MIGRATION

The birds fly away for the winter,
And they always make me bitter,
Over the fields and treetops they fly,
Always so graceful, always so high,
Over the ocean dark and deep,
To their course they always keep,
Over to Africa they fly
And back again, unless they die.

The advice I received when I bought my first greenhouse was to decide what size one needs, then to buy the next size up. Good advice because as soon as one gets a greenhouse, 'Parkinson's Law' comes into effect and the contents rapidly expand to fill the available space. So much so that I had to get a second one, another Alton, this time a plastic-covered aluminium one. The original red cedar one was excellent, but it needed painting with preservative at regular intervals, whereas the new one needed practically no maintenance other than cleaning the glass.

On the right of the path leading to the new greenhouse was the chicken shed with the nest boxes that one could open from outside to collect the eggs without going into the run and getting ones feet muddy. Mella and I always vied with each other as to who could collect

*An Autobiography
by Captain
D.B. Hopkins*

the most eggs on any one day. Quite silly really when one considers it is the chickens that are doing the laying. However we had a competition going and I was determined to win. To do this I closed off the outside of one of the nest boxes and when it had got several days worth of eggs in it, 'lo and behold' I *found* them and won the competition. That is until Mella found out what I had done and she still hasn't forgiven me 30 years later!

Several years during the May half-term holiday the three boys, the dog and myself would take to the canals in a narrow-boat. Mella preferred to stay at home and have a rest and keep well away from water, with which she has never been comfortable since she was immersed in the Medway during our courtship.

In the pictures left to right are Trevor, Austen and myself; Austen and Christopher opening a lock gate and Trevor sitting on a gate beam after we had all had a good laugh at the dyslexic '6' on it. Travelling the canals is a wonderful way of seeing parts of Britain that are not accessible any other way and because you are always close to the tow-path, it is possible for boys and dogs to run alongside and get some exercise

when they get fed up with boating. The other benefit is being able to buy provisions from canal-side house owners, who provide such delicacies as home-made pies, cooked chickens, home-baked bread and so on. All these things were much appreciated by our three boys, who all suffered from' Hollow Leg Syndrome'!

One of our neighbours in Meldreth was a retired Major, who had had the misfortune to be involved in the evacuation of the BEF from Dunkirk. Like so many things in life it had its funny side, certainly in retrospect if not at the time. He had been on the beach for several days and his time for rescue had eventually arrived. Up to his chest in the water he was somewhat surprised to see his batman wading through the waves towards him and even more astonished when the man got to him, saluted smartly and said, 'I wish to give three months notice, Sir!'

After 1969 when I had joined Tradewinds, I was commuting to work at Gatwick by car through London, a journey of anything between two and four hours (the motorways were not yet built). This was not quite as onerous as it might seem, because being a long haul operation, I only went to work three or four times a month on average, although it did mean that extra journeys to and from Gatwick were to be avoided whenever possible.

One day I was called by the crewing officer to go down for some training. Before I could leave she rang back to say I was not needed, but soon after that she rang yet again asking me to go. I set off in my Jaguar XJ6 but, approaching Ware, I saw a police car going in the opposite direction with the two officers looking intently at me. I thought it was just idle curiosity until a mile or so further on they came up behind me and flagged me down. When I had stopped and got out of the car they said, 'Captain Hopkins?' I thought it was frightfully clever of them to know my name, but all became clear when they explained that they had had a message to stop me and tell me to ring Gatwick. It seems that Crewing had decided that I was not required after all but had rung too late to stop me. Mella was very quick thinking and rang the police in Ware and asked if they would mind stopping me, something they were delighted to do, to save me a wasted journey all the way down to Gatwick and back. I found a public telephone, rang Crewing, and would you believe it, they had changed their minds yet again and so Mella's enterprise and the police's co-operation was somewhat wasted. YNCSTWLEM!!

In April one year we were sitting in the garden with friends when a swarm of bees appeared. We all rushed inside and closed the windows and then I went out to see where the swarm had gone. Most appropriately, they had taken up residence about 30 feet up a tree in Roly Bee's garden. As Roly and Molly were away on holiday, I contacted a local beekeeper to come and collect the swarm and when he arrived he asked me to help him get them into his straw skep.

*An Autobiography
by Captain
D.B. Hopkins*

I had by this time put a ladder up against the tree and followed the beekeeper up. He assured me that there was little danger of being stung unless it rained, when bees tend to get bad tempered. Fortunately it was a nice sunny day so I felt slightly reassured. I was instructed to hold the skep just under the swarm while the beekeeper tapped the branch so that the swarm would fall into the skep. So there I was 30 feet up a tree, precariously balanced on a ladder wearing only shorts and shirt, with my face inches from a buzzing swarm of bees, a buzzing that seemed to me to be getting angrier by the second, caused no doubt by a passing thunderstorm starting to deposit large drops of rain. To say that I was mightily relieved when the bees obligingly dropped into the skep and the lid was put in place was a considerable understatement, but I was also amazed at how little 60,000 bees weigh!

We got back to terra firma without getting stung and with only slightly wet clothes and the beekeeper went off highly delighted with his newly acquired trophies! From my point of view, it was a useful lesson in catching bees as later we had six beehives in our garden in Sussex and I was able to collect swarms on several occasions and so save the beekeeper from losing a valuable resource. Nowadays, so I understand, a swarm is worth around £50 and it is a case of 'finders keepers'.

During my time off between flights around the world with Tradewinds, I built a small fishpond in the garden. This was the first of three water features I have constructed and it is quite true that a garden is incomplete without 'water'. It is also true that a pond is a 'time waster' as one can sit and watch the fish, or just the water, for hours on end.

One of the boys, Christopher I think, caught a trout in the stream at the bottom of the orchard and we put this in the pond, but it quite soon leapt out in a bid to return to its natural habitat, and unfortunately perished before we discovered it.

CHAPTER 11

Commercial Flying

I HAD NO TROUBLE PASSING the first part of the exams for my ATPL, but the second part required flying lessons and a test by an examiner from the Civil Aviation Flying Unit (CAFU) at Stansted Airport. It might seem strange at first sight that I should need instruction, but it was absolutely necessary to prepare for a totally different type of flying environment to that I had experienced in the RAF.

The first problem to overcome was to get flying lessons without having the funds to pay for them! Fortunately I came across Captain Eric Thurston, who ran a flying school at Stapleford Tawney which you can see nowadays as you travel west towards the M11 along the M25. Eric was very understanding and knowing that I was going to receive a terminal grant at the end of my service, allowed me to have flying lessons on the fly now – pay later scheme. Not only that but I did a lot of flying with him for nothing by accompanying him on commercial flights around the country. This was not entirely altruistic since he was always in danger of exceeding the maximum hours he was allowed to fly each month and by putting me down as 'Captain' he didn't need to log the hours!

I flew the Piper PA23 Apache and a lot of my instruction came from a female instructor, which along with the new environment was something of a shock to the system. Her name was Deli Gray-Fisk and I believe she later became the first woman captain with BEA. She was an excellent instructor from whom I learnt a great deal.

I did all this flying during my terminal leave in September and October 1968 and I eventually passed my IRT with CAFU, thus gaining my ATPL, which I still keep for old times sake, although it is no longer valid for several reasons, not the least of which is the fact that I'm now too old!

Getting an ATPL was one thing, but finding a job was quite another matter. I had had another frustrating interview with a nebulous prat at MOD as part of the resettlement scheme for officers leaving the service. This chap was about as much use as an ashtray on a motorbike,

*An Autobiography
by Captain
D.B. Hopkins*

since he told me that it was most unlikely that I would get a job as a civilian pilot!

Thankfully I took no notice of this idiot and as luck would have it I became aware of a new airline starting up at Gatwick from the 'ashes' of Transglobe, which had just folded and which had been flying the Canadair CL44 swingtail shown in the next picture. Transglobe had flown IT (Inclusive Tour) passengers, but the new airline, Tradewinds, was to be all cargo.

Having been on the dole for ten weeks since leaving the RAF, I was more than glad to be taken on by Tradewinds as a First Officer at a salary in excess of that which I had received in the service of Her Majesty.

I started the course at Gatwick towards the end of February 1969, and what an eye-opener this was for me, being used to the structured and disciplined courses in the RAF! I found life in the world of commercial flying much more relaxed and it was very much left to the individual to make sure that he, or she, passed the appropriate examinations. In this case the exam was the ARB (Air Registration Board) type test for the CL44 and until one had passed it, one was not allowed to fly the aircraft.

During the course I had a call to go for an interview with Shell for a post as one of their executive jet pilots. I didn't get the job, which in retrospect I was thankful for, but at Shell I was treated like a VIP and given the most generous expenses for coming to see them. This was not at all what I was used to and I felt that I was going to enjoy civil flying in great measure!

The CL44 was very much like a Brittania to look at, but there the similarity ended as the CL44 had Rolls-Royce Tyne engines and, as can be seen, the tail opened to allow cargo to loaded much more easily than

through the side door, though it also had one of these on the port side. It could carry a load of 27.5 tonnes some 2,700 statute miles. When I joined Tradewinds the company was operating six aircraft, three on their own behalf and three for Trans Mediterranean Airways (TMA), based in Beirut. More about them later.

My first flight in a CL44 was partly at night and the pre-flight briefing from the training captain consisted of, 'Get in!' This was quite definitely not what I was used to in the RAF, but as it was 1st April I thought it might not be the norm! (By the time I became a training captain in February 1973, training of new pilots became much more organised.) I completed my basic training as a first officer in just a week, considerably less than I expected, and went on my first flight down the route from 15th to 21st April. This took me to Istanbul, Bombay, Kuala Lumpur, Singapore, Darwin, Brisbane, Singapore, Bahrain and then back to UK at Stansted, where we had our engineering base. Quite an introduction to long haul flying, I think you will agree!

While in Singapore I bought a record player, a cassette player, an amplifier and two records. Quite how I managed to carry all this home I can't remember, but it has been with us ever since and we still have it set up in our sitting room in our present house. One of the other first officers, Pete Button, was an avid Hi Fi enthusiast and he gave me the plans for a set of four speakers that I set to and made as soon as I could. These too still provide us with some excellent listening to music when the mood strikes us.

After a swift trip to Beirut and back to Frankfurt, my next trip took me to Brussels, Fort Lamy (Chad), Kinshasa (Congo), Fort Lamy, Kinshasa and back to Gatwick, so you can see that I was rapidly getting experience of operating in some very different parts of the world. Fort Lamy was the hottest place I had ever been to at the time and walking the streets in the city I could feel the heat of the ground through my shoes.

TMA operated a regular return service from London Heathrow to Tokyo via Frankfurt, Beirut, Karachi, Bangkok, Manila and Osaka and sometimes to various parts of the Gulf, Hong Kong and Taipei. For this service we had crews detached to Beirut and Bangkok for a fortnight at a time, plus one crew stationed in Tokyo for a month and operating between there and Manila with occasional visits to Osaka and Taipei.

On what was known as the 'Beirut fortnight' we stayed in Beirut and operated to Bangkok via Karachi and back twice before returning to UK. I flew the route from Frankfurt to Beirut and back so much that at one time I could reel off all the reporting points on the route, together with the frequencies and callsigns of the beacons, no mean feat as there were quite a number of them! In 1969 Beirut was a splendid place to be,

*An Autobiography
by Captain
D.B. Hopkins*

the weather was usually pleasant and allowed us to swim in the Mediterranean and the hotels, people and food were all most agreeable. An additional benefit was the allowances we received and usually didn't need to spend, so that with my enhanced salary life became quite luxurious compared to my time in the RAF.

At the end of October 1969 I was posted to Tokyo for a month. I flew to Tokyo by courtesy of BOAC (known to all aircrew as Better On A Camel!) in a Boeing 707 over Iceland, Greenland, the North Pole, with a stop at Anchorage, Alaska to refuel. On the trip I was fortunate enough to sit next to a Japanese businessman from whom I learned a few basic words of Japanese, a little about their customs and how they write the date. When I arrived in Tokyo the date was 45.30.10 in the era called Showa. The 45 referred to the number of years since the death of the last Emperor.

When we arrived at Tokyo International airport, the first thing that happened was an illustration of how small the world has become since the invention of the aeroplane – I ran into an old acquaintance from my days in the RAF. YCNSTWLEM!

I was to share an apartment with the flight engineer and had been given an address to go to by taxi from the airport. The taxi ride started well enough, but as soon as we got downtown the driver kept getting out of the cab and dashing into shops apparently to ask the way. I thought, not unreasonably, that I was getting the 'bums rush' and would have to pay accordingly. Not so. I arrived at the flat for a totally reasonable fare, no tip as they won't accept them, and all was well. I eventually discovered the reason for the taxi driver's strange behaviour – it seems that when the first house is built on a road its address is number 1. When the second house is built it becomes, logically, number 2 and so on. The fact that numbers 1 and 2 may be a mile or so apart, and in between are several hundred other houses, explains the confusion.

Whilst there I visited the Tokyo Tower to enjoy the view from the top, which is quite spectacular as the tower is a few feet higher than Paris's Eiffel Tower. During my time in Japan I operated to Osaka, Taipei and Manila; Manila to Tokyo and Tokyo to Osaka finishing in Manila.

As I had at one point some spare time between flights, I became a tourist to see as much as I could of the country and the people. I went on a day tour starting with a coach trip through Yokohama to see the Great Buddha at Kamakura, which was built in 1252 and was originally housed in a big hall until this was washed away by a typhoon and tsunami. From here I went across Lake Hakone by ferry to see Mount Fuji, which I was lucky actually to see, as more often than not it cannot be seen from any distance due to poor visibility. Then I travelled on a cable car, passing high above Owakidani with its fissures emitting steam and sulphur that give it its name, meaning Boiling Hell. From here a coach took me to the Kowakien Hotel in Kowakidani for some refreshments before boarding a 'bullet train' back to Tokyo.

One of the delights offered by the hotel was mixed bathing in the nude in the traditional Japanese style. Unfortunately I wasn't there long enough to take advantage of this, but I did have time to read the large notice displayed in the hotel foyer advertising the facility. This particularly amused me with its exhortation to guests, 'Please to take towel in lieu of fig leaf!'

Travelling about Tokyo was not only easy but also cheap using the tube, where the approach of the next station was heralded by an announcement on the public address system. Using this method of transport, I went to see the Meiji Jingu shrine on 15th November. This is an important day in the Shinto calendar, called Shichi-go-san. It is a festival when children aged 7, 5 and 3 are taken to the shrine to pray for their future happiness. It was most intriguing to see all the children dressed in highly colourful traditional costume with their parents also dressed up for the occasion.

Travelling by bullet train is quite an experience – firstly your ticket has your coach and seat number on it. You stand on the platform by the painted number of your coach and when the train stops, the door is right in front of you. Having found the correct seat, you then discover it is just like that in an aircraft with a table in front. All very civilised and I do believe British trains will soon have similar arrangements some 32 years on. There's progress for you!

On another free day I took the train to Kofu, a small town not far outside Tokyo, where I was able to see what life was like outside the city. At an auction of Bonsai trees I was invited inside, but I dared not move a muscle in case I bought one! A lot of the scenery reminded me in many ways of England except that it was much more mountainous and because of this, I tend to say that Japan is where I would like to live if I was exiled from home.

Soon after my arrival in Japan I needed to get a haircut before my ears disappeared under my hair, so I walked down to where I had previously seen a barbers shop and sat down in the queue to await my turn. As soon as it came, I was led to a chair very much as in my local barber's at home, but the first difference was that I was set upon by a nice young lady and given a head massage with a hot towel. My hair was then cut by the barber, after which he enquired if I would like a shampoo. I said 'no thank you' in my best Japanese and promptly had a shampoo! I had forgotten what I had been told on the flight over, that in Japan questions are phrased in such a way that to answer in the negative you have to say 'yes', and vice versa. All very confusing when you first get there and haven't got used to the idea.

*An Autobiography
by Captain
D.B. Hopkins*

Towards the end of November I did my last Tokyo, Osaka, Manila trip, but this time we didn't go to our apartment in Manila. Instead the three of us stayed on board our aircraft for the next leg to Bangkok, from where we were to catch our JAL flight back to UK. The flight from Manila to Bangkok was different, to say the least, as the captain elected to approach Bangkok airport at about 50 feet above the ground from around 40 miles. This was most unconventional although not particularly dangerous, since the land is as flat as a pancake in that area, but it was not unexpected from the particular captain we were flying with, who was well known for his eccentricities. Only a few months later he was diagnosed as having a brain tumour, which explained his bizarre behaviour and from which he sadly died soon after.

We arrived in Bangkok in time to witness the festival of Loy Krathong that takes place on the night of the 12th full moon of the year. A Krathong is a basket made from banana leaves, decorated with flowers, candles and joss sticks. Buddhists put all their sins of the past year into this basket and let them sail away down the Chao Phraya River, thus ridding themselves of their sins and at the same time rewarding onlookers with a spectacular sight: all the little baskets lit by the candles floating down the river with the perfume of the joss sticks wafting across the waters. According to the Buddhist calendar 1969 was 2511, i.e. 2511 years since the death of the Buddha.

Because of my previous RAF flying experience, I was promoted to Senior First Officer in the comparatively short time of only 18 months and to Captain five months later in November 1970. Thus I was following in my father's footsteps both by becoming a captain and by travelling all over the Far East as he had done, albeit by sea, some 50 years earlier.

Incidentally my father also started to write his autobiography, entitled *You Can't Eat Lavender*, but sadly he died before he had got very far with it and what he had written has unfortunately been lost. I did, though, discover why he picked on that particular title for his book – during the First World War he was a cadet on HMS *Mercury*, which was a shore-based establishment training young men intent on careers at sea. It was situated in Hampshire at a large country house that had a very large vegetable garden to keep the cadets supplied with fresh food. The cadets were assigned for duties in the garden to help with the cultivation and this was very popular, as there is usually something edible in a kitchen garden. Being in his mid-teens at the time and perpetually hungry in a period of severe food shortages, father was looking forward to his turn to help in the garden. Being an old garden, the vegetable plots were divided by low hedges of lavender, so it was with a considerable degree of disappointment that father found himself 'helping' in the garden during the winter months when the only thing growing was the lavender, and, as father put it – 'You Can't Eat Lavender!'

Father did, however write one book, something that has been the standard work on the subject ever since it was first published in 1961, although it has been revised many times in order to keep it up to date with the changes in law etc. It is entitled *Business and Law for the Shipmaster* and it can be found in the library of any ship operating in British waters. However I digress.

My first trip in command was to Khartoum with a cargo of 27.5 tonnes of cigarettes for BAT (British American Tobacco), for whom we did a lot of work. Over the years we were contracted to BAT we took cigarettes to several places other than Khartoum, e.g. Cairo, Mogadishu in Somalia, Djakarta and Djibouti in Afars and Issas. On the right is a cargo of cigarettes being offloaded in Mogadishu.

At one time it was found that there was a small amount of pilfering taking place, usually amounting to maybe 10 cartons of 200. It was assumed at first that this was happening at the point of unloading but because the practice was increasing the company employed a security agency to try to catch the pilferers. Eventually the culprits were found to be the loaders at Gatwick, or 'Gatnick', as it had become known, along with the other major London Airport, 'Thiefrow'. Eventually the miscreants were caught and sacked and the problem was resolved.

This leads me on to the subject of cargo security. Generally, if a loaded aircraft had to be left unattended at night, the best security was achieved by not telling anyone what was on board and by removing the boarding steps, making it more or less impossible to gain entry. This might seem a somewhat casual approach, but as far as I'm aware we never lost any cargo other than the cigarettes. In fact we fairly often used to pick up 25 tonnes of silver from Dubai to bring to the UK for refining and this was usually loaded and the aircraft shut up for the night while the crew rested before departing the following day. No problem with this highly valuable cargo was ever encountered.

The first time I flew a load of silver, I walked on board the aircraft, looked around and thought it had yet to be loaded. This was because the

*An Autobiography
by Captain
D.B. Hopkins*

load was spread all over the cargo deck and was only a few inches deep, due of the density of silver. It was all in different shapes, some like soup plates, some in the shape of WW II American army helmets, some had been poured directly into a small depression in the ground, and there were many other weird and wonderful shapes and sizes. When I enquired as to the reason, I was told that it all came from India, where extraction of silver from the local ores was something of a cottage industry and where they poured the molten metal into more or less anything they could lay their hands on.

So how did it get to Dubai? It seems that Arab fishing dhows used to collect it from India in exchange for gold in what was, apparently, an illegal trade. Once it got to Dubai it suddenly became all above board! One of my colleagues once asked a piratical looking skipper of one of these dhows if he could go with them on one of their trips. He was told in no uncertain terms that although he was welcome to go with them, he would not come back!

Mogadishu was not one of my favourite destinations as the hotel accommodation left much to be desired. The route we used was from Gatwick to Cairo, where we refuelled and then on to Mogadishu, all of which took about 15 hours or so. Once there the first thing I wanted to do was have a bath or shower to rid myself of the accumulated grime. Imagine how I felt when I turned on the tap in the bath nothing came out for quite some time until eventually there was a sort of gurgling and from the tap emerged several million tiny ants! However I waited patiently for several more minutes and was finally rewarded with water, with which I was able to get rid of the ants and then have my bath.

Another destination that I found not particularly agreeable was Djibouti. The hotel we were usually put up in was the Croce Del Sud, again very basic, but normal for that part of Africa. A thing I particularly liked to do at the end of a long duty day was to clean my teeth, so on my first visit to Djibouti I dived into the so called bathroom of the Croce Del Sud, where I noticed a small basin in the corner with a single tap. Under the basin there were a number of bottles, which I ignored. This turned out to be a mistake for when I had laced my toothbrush with paste I turned on the single tap and proceeded to brush my teeth and got a very nasty shock. The water was straight from the sea. Ugh! The fresh water was in the bottles under the basin, but it wasn't much better, so after that I used to take a can of 7-UP with me from the aircraft to use for teeth cleaning. I knew it was sterile and certainly it tasted better.

I mention these little incidents lest anyone should get the idea that life down the route was all sitting around swimming pools with glamorous hostesses. Our catering on board was taken care of by the loadmasters, who, to a man, were definitely not glamorous!

Quite frequently we went to Jeddah in Saudi Arabia. Here one was obliged to hand one's passport to the police on entry and collect it on departure. The system we used on departure was for the flight engineer to go and refuel the aircraft, the first officer would file the flight plan, the loadmaster would check the load and catering, while the captain paid the landing and handling fees and collected the passports of all the crew.

On one occasion we had taken off and were 10 minutes into the climb to cruising height on the way to Cairo when the first officer said to me, 'Can I have my passport please skipper?' After turning the air blue for a moment or two, I had to admit that I had forgotten to collect them! So I called the controller and asked if we could return for them. He said that was OK, but that I would have to pay another landing fee of around £700. I didn't think this would be terribly popular with my boss, so after enquiring as to our destination, the controller said he would put them on another aircraft going to Cairo and we could collect them there. Ten minutes later he informed us that there weren't any aircraft going to Cairo that day, but that he had put them on an aircraft bound for Beirut, from where there were always lots of aircraft going to Cairo.

Knowing that passports are worth a lot of money on the black-market in Beirut, I thought that would be the last we would ever see of them and I would have to fork out for four new ones. Having landed at Cairo, we could not get off the airport without passports and the Airport Hotel, within the airport area, was full, so we had to spend the night on what was euphemistically known as 'The Tradewinds Hilton', i.e. sleep on the seats and bunks aboard our aircraft. Imagine then my total disbelief when at about four o'clock in the morning I was roused from a fitful sleep on a seat by a knock on the door of the aircraft. On opening it revealed an Arab standing on the steps holding our four passports with an elastic band round them. YCNSTWLEM!

I wouldn't want to give the impression that all flights with Tradewinds were epics of one sort or another. Usually they went quite smoothly without anything extraordinary happening, but because the company was to all intents and purposes operating like the tramp steamers of old, we quite often found ourselves going to places that were not on the itinerary we were given before leaving base.

In November 1971 I took off from Manston with a load for Kano and Lagos, expecting to return direct to Gatwick. While in Lagos, I received a telex from the Operations Director, Ted Parker, instructing us to go to Buenos Aires. These sorts of telexes were known to all crews as 'Regards Parker' messages as he always signed them thus, and they were usually telling one to go somewhere unexpected. As we didn't have the necessary charts and airfield information, I replied asking where I could obtain the relevant data, to which I got a terse telex

*An Autobiography
by Captain
D.B. Hopkins*

telling me to 'obtain locally'. This was a joke, since nobody on the airport at Lagos had ever heard of Buenos Aires, let alone had any information on the place. Fortunately the navigator with me, Ginger Adams, was an old RAF hand at the game and by furkling in his nav bag for a moment, came up with a South Atlantic chart he had used some ten years previously.

After erasing the lines on it, we set off for Recife in Brazil and from there, after a stopover, we made our way to Buenos Aires. Of course it was dark when we arrived at Recife (it always seems to be dark when landing at some new destination), but fortunately the weather was clear. Not having any airfield information with us, I was blissfully unaware that quite close to the airfield are some fairly high mountains. I was able to see them the next morning and they gave me a bit of a surprise. Again it was fortunate Ginger was with me since he spoke a smattering of Spanish and this made it possible for us to communicate with the Argentineans, none of whom spoke any English. We returned to UK via Recife and Sal in the Cape Verde Islands with a load of formula 1 racing cars. Sal is pretty close to what I imagine a moonscape looks like – totally barren volcanic rock and definitely not on my list of holiday destinations.

On another occasion I flew direct from Lagos to Buenos Aires, which, at 14¼ hours, all of it over the sea, was pretty boring. One part of the South Atlantic looks very much like the next. It is flights like this that give rise to the saying that long-haul flying is two ten-minute periods of sheer terror divided by hour upon hour of unmitigated boredom. This is particularly true in some parts of the world where you are pretty much the only aircraft there.

On one occasion we were flying from Colombo to Perth at night. The route took us over the Cocos Islands, where Australians run air traffic control. As you may or may not know, everything said on RT is recorded both in the aircraft and by ATC for use in case of accidents. It just happened that somebody on the crew had brought with them a book of limericks, several of which began, 'There was a young man of Australia'. They were quite unsuitable for repetition in polite society, but I thought it might brighten up what was a fairly dull night, so I asked the controller if he would like to hear some. He said he would, but after hearing several of them and nearly cracking up laughing, he said, 'For Christ's sake no more, no more!' About an hour later we heard him calling Perth on the HF radio to say, 'Perth, I'm going off the air for half an hour. I've got to change a tape!'

A couple of months later I chanced to fly the same route again with a different crew, one of whom had been stationed in the Cocos Islands and knew the three controllers there. While he was passing the time of day with one of them I recognised his voice as that of the recipient of the limericks. I cheekily asked him, 'have you heard any good limericks lately?' To which he replied, 'For heavens sake, not you again. I've got a tape here – I can't use it and I can't lose it!' I wonder if it is still lurking about in the tower gathering dust?

In May 1972 I flew down to Lusaka to collect some ostriches and other exotic birds to bring back to Birmingham for the zoo there. When we got to Lusaka, we found the 36 ostriches all ready in individual boxes, as we had been told to expect, for loading on to the aircraft in a double row along the entire length of the cargo bay. Owing to an error on somebody's part, the boxes had been built about two inches too high, which meant that we could only load a single row. The charterer was most unhappy with the idea of having only half his load transported, so after some head scratching and discussion it was agreed that we should hire some scaffolding and build pens in the aircraft and load the ostriches into these. This was done and <u>all</u> the birds were loaded successfully. The ostriches were absolutely no trouble at all, but it was really fascinating to come out of the flight deck during the flight and see 36 pairs of long eyelashes fluttering at you. The exotic birds consisted of things like secretary birds and others whose diet was dead meat, the smell of which was not nearly so fascinating or pleasant!

At one point we were carrying live cows from Nairobi to Addis Ababa and we used the scaffolding pens for this, as it was the only way to get the beasts on board successfully. Cows were also no problem, but horses – that's quite a different story that I'll come to in a while!

On another occasion I was taking a mixed cargo, which included some half grown pigs, to Lagos. Whilst crossing the Sahara at about 3 o'clock in the morning, I was somewhat surprised to be disturbed from my crossword by grunting. The pigs were at the rear of the cargo deck. I looked around just in time to see one of the pigs push his way on to the flight deck. It seems that one small pig had been able to turn round in his box and lift the slot at the back and gain his freedom. Another case of YCNSTWLEM!

Talking of smelly cargoes – we did a series of flights at one time from Nairobi to Tripoli with chilled carcasses of sheep. These were chilled when put on board and we kept the temperature in the cargo hold as low as possible, but the drawback was the temperature in Tripoli. This soon warmed the meat and attracted swarms of flies so that after we had closed the tail on departure, we had to spray the entire aircraft to avoid bringing flies back to the UK. As the flow of air in the CL44 was from the rear, forwards to the flight deck, the routine was to spray from the back forwards with the aircraft very slightly pressurised and then, when we literally could not see through the windows for flies, to open a window on the flight deck. The flies were then ejected very rapidly indeed in a big black cloud, which gives

*An Autobiography
by Captain
D.B. Hopkins*

rise to the riddle: What has four engines and flies? Answer – A Tradewinds meat flight!

My one and only experience of flying horses was a load of 35 race-horses from Melbourne to Hong Kong via Darwin. All 35 had their own individual boxes and all were tranquillised by the handlers who accompanied them, before leaving Melbourne and again at Darwin while we refuelled. Notwithstanding this, I have never heard so much noise from the back of the aircraft caused by these thoroughbreds stamping about in their boxes. Also they urinated a tremendous amount and this tended to vaporise and move with the flow of air to the flight deck. Here it condensed on the bare metal around the windows and dropped on us two pilots. To avoid smelling like a horse when we arrived at Hong Kong, we both swapped our uniforms for bathing trunks for the entire flight. Ah, the joys of flying livestock!

I've often been asked if I was ever afraid that the swing-tail of the CL44 might open in flight. To answer this I've included the diagram below of what is a very clever piece of engineering. The two halves were locked together by 12 hydraulically operated bolts and to make it impossible for these to open in flight, the hydraulic pipe that provided the power for locking/unlocking was disconnected in flight. The only problem encountered occasionally was if dirt got into one of the 12 micro switches fitted to let the pilots know that all 12 bolts were locked. In these circumstances a warning light would come on on the annunciator panel, but since we were used to this happening it was not a cause for concern. The tail took 90 seconds to open and close and this could be done in winds up to 30mph. Once locked open, the system would hold it open even in winds of 60mph.

One had to be careful not to put an excessive weight onto the back of the aircraft or it could tip on its tail. This was not a concern when

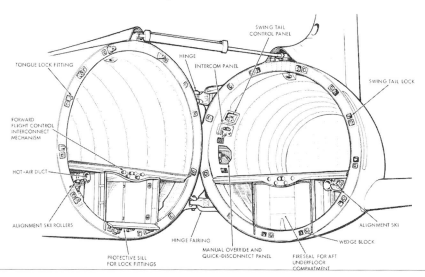

we were loading cargo on palettes, but on a couple of occasions it was quite a problem. The first was when the company undertook a series of flights from Manchester to Vancouver carrying huge parts of gear wheels for an ore crushing plant. I cannot remember how much these parts weighed, but suffice it to say we could only get three on board at a time. These trips were routed through Frobisher, on Baffin Island on the Arctic Circle, where the temperature was −40°C. As there was a strong wind blowing when we arrived, it meant that we had just 20 seconds to get from aircraft into the bus to take us to the transit lounge before our extremities suffered from frostbite. In one way these flights were very disappointing – it was dark flying over Canada in both directions so I never got to see the Rockies!

The other occasion when loading and off-loading had to be done very carefully was when I flew the heaviest piece of cargo ever loaded onto an aircraft in one piece. This was a steam turbine rotor for a power station at Wyalla, near Adelaide, which weighed 16 tonnes including the 'sledge' of huge timbers it was sitting on to spread the load. Before any attempt was made to load this, the nose of the aircraft was secured with ropes to some heavy pieces of ground equipment and two tonnes of ballast was placed at the front of the cargo deck, just behind the flight deck. When all this had been done, a crane hoisted the load up to the level of the floor at the rear of the aircraft and it was gently slid into place somewhere near the centre of gravity, before the ballast, etc. was removed. The whole process took place in reverse once we got to Adelaide and this was featured prominently in the local press. The picture below shows our CL44 parked at Adelaide just before we left to go to Hong Kong via Darwin. We loaded at HK and flew back to Amsterdam, the destination for the cargo, via Bombay and Ankara.

Whilst in Bombay an amusing incident took place. In places where the wind is light or non-existent, aircraft are sometimes given a choice of runway so that they don't waste fuel and time by setting off in the 'wrong' direction. In this case two aircraft called for taxi clearance at

*An Autobiography
by Captain
D.B. Hopkins*

the same time and one was cleared for one runway and the other for the same runway, but in the opposite direction. Perfectly normal procedure except that both aircraft got lined up at opposite ends of the runway <u>at the same time</u>. This was pointed out to ATC whose comment was one of the best, 'Oh dear, not another day like yesterday!'

At one point some Arabs from The Gulf invested money in the company and this led to the formation of 'Tradewinds Gulf'. Together with Captain Parker (Operations Director) and Captain Jones (Chief Pilot), I was on the inaugural flight to Sharjah. Upon landing we were met by the Sheikh (brother of the Ruler), who was in charge of Airports and Seaports (one of each). He said he would drive me to the hotel. He invited me to jump into his large American car, which I did with alacrity, only to jump out even more quickly after sitting on his Sten gun! He apologised for his oversight and threw the ancient piece of weaponry

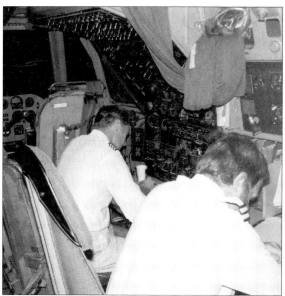

into the boot while I tried to take shelter, knowing that it takes very little to make a Sten gun go off of its own accord. YCNSTWLEM!

Having made it to the hotel in one piece, we were then treated to a very substantial Arab-type feast with lashings of alcoholic drinks of every sort imaginable. It seems that this particular Sheikh was well known for his love of Scotch and ancient guns. It would also appear that although the official Muslim policy is one of total abstinence, in those days not everyone kept to the rules!

Tradewinds Gulf didn't stay in operation for very long, although I'm unsure of the reason, but it may have had something to do with the fact that we became part of the Lonrho Empire not long afterwards.

In the CL44 the flight engineer and navigator sat side-by-side sharing a desk, as in the picture, F/E on the left and Nav on the right. This was a perfectly normal arrangement, but on Tradewinds there was a particularly 'bolshie' navigator called Jim.

As we were about to set off on a voyage lasting several days, I saw Jim draw a line with a chinagraph pencil marking the dividing line between his and the flight engineer's halves of the desk. He indicated in no uncertain terms that he would not tolerate the latter's paperwork straying on to his half under any circumstances. The flight engineer, a stoic Scot, said nothing and away we went.

A few days later I heard sounds of an altercation from their area and turned round just in time to see the Nav's paperwork that had drifted on to the flight engineer's half being handed back to him, having been neatly sliced off along the chinagraph dividing line with a razor blade. Never a dull moment!

One of the more unusual places I ever got to was Kufra Oasis in the Libyan part of the Sahara desert. Apparently there is an almost inexhaustible supply of water only 100 feet under the surface in this area. It is so pure that it is drinkable just as it emerges from beneath the ground. The Libyans were taking advantage of this to sink boreholes and bring water to the surface, where it was fed into a kilometre-long pipe on wheels that travelled in a circle with the water spraying out and irrigating a huge area every few hours. Here they could grow wheat and alfalfa for feeding to sheep. We were taking some of the pumping equipment ready to be used on the next borehole. Although there was a brand new runway being built, we were unable to use it and had to land on the old wartime desert strip. This was no problem until we put on reverse thrust to stop the aircraft, at which point we disappeared in a sandstorm of our own making. Mind you, it gave all the turbine blades a thorough cleaning by sand blasting!

Another unusual place was Fort Lamy and, in particular, Lake Chad. As you fly over the lake, it changes from a series of what might be called puddles in the desert to a series of desert islands in the lake. I have never seen another place anything like it. At the time Fort Lamy was the hottest place I had ever been to and I mentioned earlier my feet burning through the soles of my shoes as I walked along the roads in the city. I think the temperature was in the high 40's, but that was nothing to what I experienced in Baghdad during a six-day stopover there in 1975.

By this time the company was flying regular routes and had introduced the slip-crew system, whereby you flew to a destination and a new crew took the aircraft onwards while you waited for the next one to arrive. I and most of my colleagues did not find this much to our liking as most of the places at which we 'slipped' were not exactly tourist traps. The period I speak of was definitely the hottest I have experienced anywhere on earth. The daily temperature got up to 54°C, making it quite impossible to go outside during the hours of daylight. At this time we just had to stay in our hotel which, in spite of so called air-conditioning, was extremely uncomfortable. It was something of a relief from both temperature and boredom to be able to go out in the evening, walk along the banks of the Tigris, and watch the local populace doing the same thing.

On our way to and from Hong Kong we often flew over Da Nang during the Vietnam War. This was a very active area militarily. We had a minimum height at which to fly, but even at this height one could see

*An Autobiography
by Captain
D.B. Hopkins*

the path of tracer ammunition passing below like a sinister firework display.

Sometimes we flew empty direct to HK from Australia, and it was during one of these trips that I was forced to land at Manila. The reason for this unscheduled landing was an oversight by our operations department in failing to get overflight diplomatic clearance for us. The authorities were quite stroppy when I met them on landing, so I rang the British Embassy to enlist their help to resolve the situation. Bad idea! I should have known that trying to get anything done by our embassies at teatime was a non-starter. The best advice the duty officer to whom I spoke could come up with was, 'If you think of anything give me a ring!' I really don't know why the Foreign Office employs such incompetent idiots – must be something to do with the 'old boy' network!

Anyway I could see which way the wind was blowing so after I had written an apology to the military commander of the airport and paid 'compensation', we continued on our way. We got away from Manila just in the nick of time to avoid a massive typhoon that was about to strike, and looking at the ominous and incredibly black clouds, I was thankful we didn't have to fly through it!

You may remember that in chapter nine I described how my colleague Jim and I trained ourselves to be able to land in fog by use of the ILS. This came in extremely handy one day going into Ras al Khaimah in the Gulf. The Gulf area is notorious for all the airports becoming fog bound at the same time, leaving one with nowhere to go and looking for a 'skyhook' on which to park until the fog clears! Unfortunately in real life 'skyhooks' are as scarce as frogs feathers, so when I arrived at Ras al Khaimah to find the visibility at around 300 yards and all the other Gulf airports in the same condition, I was left no option but to put my previous training into practice. I am happy to say that it worked perfectly and it is very hard to describe the feeling of wonderment one gets when runway lights become visible through the fog exactly where they are supposed to be, unless you have had the experience. Although you know from the instruments in the cockpit that they are there, it still comes as a sense of considerable relief to find them.

I imagine I am not alone in thinking that one of the main areas of the world in which one expects to find fog is Europe in general and the UK in particular. Curiously, though, the only times I have *had* to land in fog have been elsewhere. Apart from the experience in the Gulf, I was extremely thankful to have my RAF training to fall back on when encountering fog in Karachi a couple of times at first light, before the sun has had time to burn the stuff off. Quite what I would have done if a landing had not been possible I'm not sure. YCNSTWLEM!

CHAPTER 12

More Adventures with Tradewinds

T HE FOLLOWING 'ADVENTURES' are not in any particular order, certainly not chronologically speaking, but just as I remember them and I include them here to illustrate further what life was like flying for a charter, all-cargo, airline.

As a captain, one was given a bag of money, usually travellers cheques, but sometimes quite a lot of cash in dollars or sterling and sent on one's way to whatever destination a cargo had to be delivered. Cash was needed in abundance when sent to Mogadishu, for instance, where we had to pay for the fuel in cash, because, for some reason they would not accept our fuel carnet, with which we paid for fuel more or less everywhere else. It was quite normal to leave Gatwick with up to £40,000 in one's briefcase, and remember I'm talking about the seventies. In fact when I first got my command, in 1970, currency restrictions were still in force and all the captains had to have special dispensation to leave the UK with such large amounts of money.

As a captain with a company like Tradewinds, one had to be more than just a good pilot. In fact one's skill as a pilot was fairly low on the list of attributes needed to make a good commander. More than a smattering of knowledge of accountancy was definitely needed, as was the ability to deal with unexpected situations like the one I related in the last chapter, in which we were forced to land in Manila. Also required was the ability to write sensible reports of situations that had caused delays etc.

One such happened in Lagos when we arrived during a strike by the ground engineers. Because of the way in which the engines were started on the CL44, an 'air start' truck had to be used. These provided a large volume of air at moderate pressure to get the propeller and turbine rotating. With the strike in progress, such assistance was not forthcoming so we were grounded. I enlisted the help of the Pan American Airways station manager, who did his best to provide equipment to get

An Autobiography by Captain D.B. Hopkins

the engines started. We tried high-pressure air bottles and all sorts of other ingenious methods to get the necessary volume and pressure of air, but it was all to no avail, so we had to sit out the strike for the next three days. To show my gratitude to the PAA station manager I suggested that he might like to bring his wife to the hotel one evening so that I could buy them both a drink. They accepted my invitation, but when I asked them what drink they would like, they said that neither of them touched alcohol – nor soft drinks like Coca Cola, nor tea, nor coffee. I eventually discovered that they were Mormons and so the most I could do was to get them a drink of water. Never before or since have I met a couple that lived their religion quite like them.

Speaking of Lagos, after the Biafran civil war we were chartered by one of the aid agencies to fly relief to Lagos. This took the form of seven Land Rovers, donated by the Rover Company and specially painted white with red crosses, plus a very large amount of medical supplies. After unloading at Lagos, all the latter were stored in what was euphemistically known as the 'cargo shed'. It was actually a series of lean-to sheds with corrugated iron roofs of great age that allowed the rain to leak in. When it rains in Lagos it really comes down by the bucketful, consequently by the time I got there again some three weeks later the medical supplies were not only still in the 'cargo shed' but also soaked with water and completely useless. I also learned that of the seven Land Rovers we had brought three weeks ago only one was still serviceable. So much for giving aid to third world countries without proper supervision as to its use.

Going into Cairo one day, we had to divert to Luxor due to bad visibility. Not having been there before, I was apprehensive as to whether they had the correct facilities for handling a CL44, but I was assured by ATC at Cairo that all would be well. It was not! Next day when we came to start the engines, we found that they did not have an air-start truck so we were forced to kick our heels in Luxor while one was driven by road from Cairo, a journey of 24 hours. I think something was lost in our communications because the people in Luxor who had assured us that they had an air-start truck thought that the ground power truck was, as they put it, an 'electric air start'.

Whilst staying in Cairo for a day or two during one stopover, I took the opportunity to see the Great Pyramid at Giza that was visible from our rooms at the Mena House Hotel, at that time one of the better hotels in Cairo. The inside of the pyramid is quite amazing not only for the sheer amount of masonry involved, but also for the accuracy with which each individual block has been finished. I didn't have one with me to try, but I'm certain a 10 thou feeler gauge wouldn't fit between the blocks. Whoever the masons were they certainly knew a thing or two about their trade!

I also visited the Cairo Museum, which at that time was appallingly badly cared for. Very few of the exhibits had any sort of labelling and those that did were a leftover from the days of British/French influence. However I did find one exhibit that was labelled, this being a case full of stone tablets dating back thousands of years, several of which had a translation of the hieroglyphics that were engraved upon them. One particularly caught my eye – it was from one king to another complaining that not only had he not had a reply to the message he sent seven years ago, but also that he had not yet had his messenger returned and he would like both! I've often wondered what happened to the messenger – did he fall by the wayside, did he perhaps find the other kingdom more to his taste and decide to stay there? The possibilities seem endless.

Most people have heard of Poona, usually in connection with the British rule in India, in the days when it was used as a refuge for the women and children in summer from the unbearable heat in Bombay. I never expected to go there nor did I ever expect to pick up such an unlikely cargo. I was sent there to collect 27 tonnes of small petrol-driven engines for forklift trucks. It seems that these were manufactured locally and a great deal more cheaply than anything available in the West.

The airfield at Poona is run by the IAF (Indian Air Force) and they had a squadron of Canberra B(I)8's stationed there. I felt quite at home and we were right royally treated by the officers, including the Station Commander, a Group Captain, who was fascinated to learn that I had been a 'trapper' on the Canberra. In fact I was able to tell him that we had had a visit by two of his aircraft while I was serving at Bassingbourn.

Another interesting series of flights the company undertook was the transportation of the formula 1 racing cars to all their races around the world. When we first started this contract, we were able to get 18 cars and several tonnes of spares into the aircraft, but by the second year the formula 1 had changed, making each car just a few inches wider. This meant that henceforth we could only get 12 cars plus spares into the CL44.

One destination I went to with the cars was Long Beach, California, where we stayed for the duration of the race. Whilst there, I was being driven with my crew to our hotel in a large American 'people-mover'. At that time I had recently bought my first Rolls-Royce Silver Shadow and I fell into a conversation with the driver, in the course of which we touched on the subject of fuel consumption. He asked me how many miles to the gallon my Rolls did, and when I said about 12 or 13, he said quite seriously, 'Oh, an economy car!' It was the first time I've heard a Rolls-Royce called by such a name, but I suppose it is a matter of relativity, as the people-mover only did 8 mpg.

*An Autobiography
by Captain
D.B. Hopkins*

During the period when President Idi Amin was expelling all the Asians from Uganda, we were involved in transporting their possessions from Entebbe to Heathrow. Not only was it a terribly sad sight to see all these refugees' three-piece suites and so on stored on the tarmac out in the open and totally ruined by the rain, but also there was a considerable problem with the rats that were concealed among them. So much so that on one occasion I went up to Heathrow to fly one of our aircraft after it had just been to Entebbe, to find that it had been impounded by the authorities until it had been fumigated with cyanide because a rat had been seen running about inside. YCNSTWLEM!

On the subject of authorities, I must mention our Customs and Excise. Because aircrew go in and out of the country with such regularity, we did not enjoy the same allowances in the way of duty free alcohol, cigarettes, etc. as passengers did. However we had a concession whereby we could bring in part of a bottle of spirits – say half to two-thirds full – when we had been out of the country for a few days. Returning to UK, we all filled in a Declaration Form saying how much alcohol, how many cigars or cigarettes we had and so on. The form was such that the space for each entry was only about half an inch square, so that to declare our alcohol there was just about room to write 'part bot'. When we got to the stand at Gatwick, Stansted or Heathrow, the duty Customs Officer would come on board and collect the form along with the other paperwork.

Usually they would take our word that we had got only what was declared on the form, but occasionally they would ask the crew to report to Concord House with their bags to have them inspected. It was on one such occasion that I was flying with another captain, who shall be nameless to avoid embarrassment should he ever read this, and who was well known for stretching the rules somewhat. When we got to Concord House and opened our bags the Customs Officer expressed surprise that Captain X had got not only a bottle of whisky about half full but also a full, unopened bottle. The customs officer said, 'What's this, Captain? You've declared a part bot!' 'Yes,' says the captain, 'There's the part,' pointing to the half full one and 'There's the bot,' pointing to the full one. The customs officer fell about laughing, but told Captain X not to try it on again!

Customs abroad were quite a different matter. For instance in Lagos it was normal to put a currency note on top of the contents of one's case if one didn't want them to rifle through it and confiscate anything that took their fancy. In India it was not permitted to take alcoholic drinks into the country at all, but as long as one didn't declare them, it was a case of 'what the eye doesn't see … etc.'

Going into Delhi on one occasion I was with another captain who was rather religious and therefore would insist on declaring the one and only bottle of beer he had in his case. The customs officer said that he could not take it into the country unless he deleted it from the declaration form. He would not do this and the resulting argument got more and more acrimonious over the next hour or so until the Chief Customs Officer was summoned from his office. He wanted to know from me what was the matter with the other captain to make him so obstreperous. I could see that he just wanted to get us out of his hair, so I put my finger to my temple and made a screwing motion with it, indicating that he was slightly mad, whereupon we were all allowed to get into taxis and go to the hotel. There are quite definitely circumstances when it pays to be economical with the truth. The trick is knowing when!

One place we went to with monotonous regularity was Asmara, the capital of Eritrea, now part of Ethiopia. The city was very pleasant and the people very friendly. To illustrate this, I am recalling the day the crew and I were looking for a suitable restaurant to have a meal. We stopped outside one from which were coming sounds of some sort of celebration. Through the open door we could see there was a wedding reception in progress, so not wishing to intrude we started to walk off to look for another watering hole. As we did so one of the restaurant staff rushed after us and insisted we come in and join the celebrations. It was fascinating and as far as I could see very much like a wedding reception at home, with the bride in a lovely white dress and the groom in a smart DJ. The only real difference I could see was the line of women sitting along one side of the room ululating very loudly every few minutes after each dance finished.

The airport in Asmara is just less than 8000 feet above sea level and because of this we had to take off with only sufficient fuel to get to Jeddah, across the other side of the Red Sea, with our load of 27.5 tonnes of fresh produce destined for various places in Europe. Because the temperature in Jeddah rises very quickly after dawn we used to leave Asmara as soon as it was light enough to see, which meant that we had to leave our hotel very early indeed. In order to have some breakfast before we left the night porter would provide us with toast and coffee and usually some hard-boiled eggs that must have come from very small chickens or probably bantams. Anyway they were most welcome for I have always liked to start the day with a hearty breakfast so you can imagine how I felt one day when after eating three of these miniscule eggs I was hammering the shell of the fourth and as it broke the contents trickled slowly through my fingers. Somehow it had missed the attentions of the chef the previous evening. YCNSTWLEM!

The filigree brooch probably has the reader wondering what it has to do with Asmara. Wandering around some of the lanes in the city one day, I came across a series of tiny roadside workshops where very

*An Autobiography
by Captain
D.B. Hopkins*

skilled craftsmen were making all sorts of filigree work in gold and silver. I discovered that each craftsman had an apprentice, who made identical articles to those produced by his master, but in silver not gold. One they had completed their apprenticeships, they were allowed to start making gold pieces. The gold one in the picture I brought back for Mella and I have shown it to illustrate the incredibly intricate workmanship.

As I say, we had to get to Jeddah quickly so as to be able to get airborne with enough fuel to reach our destination in Europe while the vegetables were still fresh. The vegetables were usually either green beans (delicious with white sauce!) or green peppers. The latter had a very strong odour in bulk, strong enough to make one's eyes water even though the temperature in the cargo bay was kept just above freezing. The places to which we delivered these included Frankfurt, Munich, Stuttgart, Amsterdam and, of course, Gatwick. One rather pleasant advantage of carrying fruit and vegetables – and something my family missed when I gave up flying – was the fact that almost always the charterer would give each of the crew a box of whatever produce we were carrying. Inevitably this was much fresher than any that one could buy, even from the best stores.

Flowers were another fresh product we brought in quite often, usually from Nairobi, and once again this necessitated keeping the cargo bay at a low temperature to ensure that the contents arrived in tip-top condition. The drawback, from the crew's point of view, of a low-temperature cargo bay was that it meant the flight deck also got uncomfortably cold during a long voyage, to the extent that most us could be seen wearing our raincoats on top of our uniforms, and this leads me neatly into another true incident.

Tradewinds bought our uniforms from British Airways, the only difference being that we had buttons, wings and cap badges to our own company design. When in hot climes, we wore 'shirt sleeve order' and that meant that we were indistinguishable from BA crews except for our cap badges.

After a night stop in the BA Hotel in Bahrain, I came down to pay the bill for the crew and having done so, I sat down in the lobby to await my crew before getting a taxi to the airport. I hadn't been sitting long when a BA stewardess came along and after wishing me a respectful 'Good Morning Captain', sat down beside me. It was not long before another joined us, then another and so on until I had the entire cabin crew from a 747 around me. By the time there were five or six around me, I realised that they thought I was the captain for their next leg. This is not particularly surprising as BA cabin and flight crews often slip at different places. Anyway, I thought the situation might lead to some amusement, so I said nothing until the 'real' captain appeared. His face was a picture of disbelief when he saw me sitting there with all 'his' crew – he had obviously been stuck in Bahrain for too long and was dying to move on. He said to me, 'I thought I was taking the Frankfurt flight.' 'Oh, I'm on a different aircraft,' I replied to which his answer is ever etched on my memory: 'Oh, you're Concorde are you?' I just smiled and sauntered off, collected my crew and went my way chuckling to myself.

The forerunner of BA was BOAC and before that Empire Airways. It was during the latter's heyday that they were forced to build secure accommodation for their passengers at each stop. In those leisurely days, the trip to the Far East in the Empire Flying Boats had many stops, one of which was at Sharjah.

One day going in to Dubai, which is very close to Sharjah, I was informed by ATC that there was no hotel accommodation available due to some conference or other. Sharjah ATC, who were on the same frequency, chipped in to say that we could stay in 'The Fort' if we cared to. I agreed that I would like this, not knowing what 'The Fort' was. When we got there, we found it was one of the old, fortified hotels built by Empire Airways to protect their passengers from marauding bands of Arabs.

Whilst there I heard a wonderful story, no doubt apocryphal, about the famous Captain O.P.Jones, who was well known as being a martinet. It was said that he never spoke directly to a First Officer, only through a Senior First Officer and was a stickler for etiquette and discipline. Apparently every time he climbed into the left hand seat on the flight deck, he had a routine he carried out religiously before doing the pre-flight checks and getting airborne. He would produce a gold key on a chain from his pocket to unlock a very small attaché case, open it and stare at its contents for a few seconds before closing and locking it. After putting away the key, he would call for the checks and get on with the business of flying. Being such a martinet with a short temper, nobody had ever had the temerity to ask him what the case could possibly contain that was the subject of such intense scrutiny before each flight. That is until his very last flight before retirement.

On this occasion he had with him a particularly brash First Officer who was determined to find out his secret. The young man asked what was in the case and to his surprise OPJ agreed to show him as it was his last flight. So out came the gold key, the case was unlocked and

*An Autobiography
by Captain
D.B. Hopkins*

passed to the brash young man for his inspection. Inside the case was a single piece of paper on which was written in capital letters, 'PORT IS LEFT'. Not many personalities like that around these days, which is, I think, a great pity.

Tradewinds undertook a series of flights to Muscat carrying fittings and furnishings for the palace being built for the young Sultan after he deposed his father. Until then Muscat had been positively medieval in that the gates to the city were closed from six o'clock at night to six o'clock in the morning. There was only one small hotel of 12 rooms that always seemed to be full. Because of this, we had, after unloading, to fly to Dubai to take our statutory rest. The head of the firm of architects who were overseeing the building of the palace was based in Dubai and on one flight he met us at the airport to express his thanks for our efforts and invited the whole crew to a meal at his house in Dubai that evening.

At this dinner I found myself sitting next to an Englishman who had recently arrived in the Gulf for a three-year stint and who told me that he had just been to his first proper Arab feast. This took place out in the desert in a very large tent with carpets decorating the walls and lit by oil lamps. Before going to this 'do', he had been briefed by his colleagues as to the correct etiquette, for instance always eat with your right hand and whilst sitting on the floor cross-legged avoid pointing the soles of your shoes at anyone as it is considered very rude to do so. He was also advised that the enormous mound of boiled rice upon which a cooked whole sheep is brought on a vast brass tray stays hot or at least warm for a considerable time. As the evening wears on, a handful of palatable rice can still be obtained by putting one's hand well into the pile. After some three hours or so sitting in the dim light on crossed legs he was taking this advice only to feel his fingers touch something wriggling in the centre of the mound! He immediately withdrew his hand very rapidly only to see the man sitting opposite do the same thing with an equally pained expression on his face. YCNSTWLEM!

We were stuck for accommodation on another occasion in Muscat and were helped out by some geologists working for the Seismic Survey group. In exchange for a bottle of scotch, they offered us the use of a couple of their huts for the night. These huts were of the Nissan variety with a removable partition in the middle dividing them into two decent sized rooms. In the one I used the partition had been taken out and leant against the other half behind my bed in which, after a couple of scotches, I slept very soundly all night.

In the morning there was a knock at the door and in came an Arab servant with a nice hot cup of tea. Looking at him, I immediately sensed that not all was well as he was not looking at, but behind, me. He took off his flip-flop and proceeded to hit something just behind and above my head a tremendous blow. With a grin he showed me what he had just killed – a fawn and white coloured camel spider about the size of my hand with, he told me, a very nasty bite. If I had known it was lurking behind my bed all night I would most definitely not have slept so soundly. He spent the next few minutes looking for and despatching the male half of the pair. Two things about flying: 'It's a great life if you don't weaken!' AND 'If you can't take a joke you shouldn't have joined!'

During the period of Idi Amin's rule in Uganda the coffee plantations in neighbouring Rwanda could not get their beans out of the country as the roads/railways were sealed off. In consequence I spent almost two months in the summer of 1977 shuttling between Mombasa and Kigali with 27 tonnes of coffee beans destined to be taken to Europe by ship. This was very a pleasant interlude from our normal flying as we only flew by day, Kigali not being open at night, and stayed in a hotel on the beach in Mombasa, which these days is a much favoured holiday resort.

It goes to show that not all our stopover places were bad. The down side to this episode was the death of one of my colleagues as he was being driven from Nairobi to Mombasa along what is well known to be a very dangerous road. It is used by heavy trucks whose drivers work very long hours and frequently drop asleep at the wheel, as happened in this case when the truck hit my colleague's car head on. In twenty-nine years of flying I think I lost more colleagues in road accidents than in flying accidents, which says a lot about the relative safety of both forms of transport.

I had always had a yen to go to Indonesia, so you can imagine how pleased I was to be briefed to take a load of cigarettes to Djakarta in October 1974, routeing via Istanbul, Karachi and Singapore. The last was to be just a refuelling stop and after paying the landing and handling fees, I arrived back at the aircraft anxious to get airborne only to find all the crew lounging around with resigned looks on their faces. To my suggestion that they pulled their fingers out and got the show on the road they replied that one of the engines had seized, hence the looks of resignation. After consultations with 'Company Operations' at Gatwick it was decided that we should off-load the cargo and put it in bond, then when we had taken rest at a hotel in the city, ferry the aircraft to Hong Kong, where a spare engine could be fitted to replace our failed one.

A great advantage of the CL44 was that it could be ferried with only three engines operative, provided that no cargo was carried and that the captain was suitably qualified. It was just as well that this facility existed, as we went through a period when the rear bearings of the Tyne engine seized with monotonous regularity. The cause of these

*An Autobiography
by Captain
D.B. Hopkins*

failures took some finding, but it was eventually discovered that a sub-contractor in Canada who was responsible for reconditioning the engines and who was supposed to replace old bearings with new, was in fact just exchanging the rollers without renewing the inner and outer races. False economy in every sense and the Tradewinds eventually obtained redress for the lost revenue that this poor standard of engineering caused.

The next day we set off for HK on three engines and we had got to about 100 feet above the ground when the fire warning went off for the other engine on the same side as the failed one. The flight engineer wanted to shut the engine down, but I forbade him to do this, since I was certain that it was a spurious warning. A check through the window proved this to be the case as no smoke or flames were visible and so we continued to HK without further trouble.

How was I so certain that it was a spurious warning? Well, this was one of those situations where intuition based on previous experience proved invaluable. The engine fire warning system of the CL44/Tyne installation consisted of a 'fire-wire' that went around the engine bay, held in place at strategic points by clips. If a fire occurred the wire would burn through and trigger the alarm bells/lights. The problem with the system was that the wire passing through the clips sometimes chafed on parts of the engine, resulting in a spurious warning. This had happened often enough to me to allow me to make the decision I did without endangering the aircraft or crew. In fact shutting the engine down leaving me to control the aircraft on two engines on one side was the more hazardous of the options available. After a three night stop-over in HK while the new engine was fitted and a new load taken aboard, we flew back to Gatwick via Karachi and Istanbul without further incident. Experience is something that money cannot buy, but when you have it the result can be a great saviour!

I've already mentioned meat flights to Tripoli and the swarms of flies one encountered on these occasions, but there was another problem with going to Tripoli that was much more infuriating. The Libyan authorities would not allow the bills to be paid direct to the recipients in case anybody took advantage of the black market in their very much overvalued currency. As if we would! Consequently captains were obliged to collect the various bills from the handling agent, ATC and the Met office, take them to the National Bank of Libya in the main airport building and pay all of them in hard currency, i.e. dollars or sterling, then return the receipted bills to the correct office. This was bad enough and took a long time, making a one-hour turnaround an impossibility, but every now and then a captain's worst nightmare would occur when you got to the bank. A shift change!!

As the bank was open 24 hours a day, it was only reasonable that the tellers had to change over every so often. The problem was their method of handover! The teller handing over would count by hand all, and I do mean <u>all</u>, the money in the bank. Then the teller taking over would do the same. If their totals did not agree, which was always, then the whole process would be repeated until they did concur. For me the record time for standing in the queue was, incredibly, two hours!

Another irritant was that Colonel Gadaffi had decreed that all signs and notices were to be in Arabic *only*, and since I, and the rest of my colleagues did not read the language, this could cause further delays while we found our way around. No wonder we all hated going to Libya!

The only other destination I went to in Libya other than Tripoli and Kufra Oasis was Sebha. This was a strange place indeed and reputed to be the site for the Libyan's production of chemical and biological weapons. I never discovered whether this was the case, but there was a whole collection of what appeared to be houses such as one might see in any town. The curious thing was that the whole area seemed to be devoid of human habitation, so my guess is that the houses were some sort of camouflage for nefarious activity. To my suspicious mind the place looked decidedly 'iffy'!

From Sebha we flew to Pisa where I saw the famous Leaning Tower for the one and only time in my life. The next day we went to Delhi via Shiraz in Iran, where we stayed the night. I was most impressed by the roses that adorned the beds in the middle of the dual carriageway roads in the city. In my ignorance I thought it rather strange that roses should be found in great profusion in such a place, and it was only much later that I learned that many roses were introduced into Europe from Shiraz. YCNSTWLEM!

When I was in the RAF somebody once remarked to me that 'once an instructor, always an instructor' and I can confirm that this is entirely true as in January 1973, only two years after I was promoted to captain, I was sent to Stansted to do a two-week course at the Civil Aviation Flying Unit (CAFU) to become once again, an IRE. I thoroughly enjoyed the course, as I knew several of the instructors on the staff from my RAF days. Oddly, you might think, there is no record in my logbook of the flying I did in the twin-engined De Havilland Dove while on the course. The reason for this apparent omission is the fact I was not qualified on the type so I could not legally log the hours. In common with most other pilots who have done the course, I had never before flown the Dove. The system was to put one in the left hand seat on day one and get one to fly an instrument rating test, which, like everyone else one inevitably failed. Then one spent the rest of the time conducting mock IRT's on fellow students and the staff pilots and also conducting mock oral tests. After two weeks of this, I was authorised to conduct IRT's for the company and thus I became once again a QFI or, in civil airlines parlance, a training captain.

It was not long after I was appointed to this post that I was acting as guinea pig for another training captain who was being tested by a CAFU examiner. I was doing a two-engined night approach on the ILS (instrument landing system) into Gatwick and after I had landed I lowered the nosewheel onto the runway and there was a tremendous vibration caused by the nosewheel shimmying. Realising that all was not well, I stopped and suggested that we should ask to be towed off the runway. However the decision by the commander was to continue taxying very slowly off the fast turn-off, stop and investigate the situation further.

Once stopped the flight engineer opened the door and hung out with the aid of a rope. By the light of a torch he was able to see that we had only one nosewheel instead of two! The missing one was eventually found about half a mile further on down the airfield, where it had come to rest, fortunately without damaging anything or anybody. Investigation revealed that the four bolts that held it in place on the splined axle had all come adrift, allowing the wheel to get free during the landing run. The incompetent engineer responsible for using bolts that were too short was, I believe, instantly sacked. And quite right too!

Now that I had a training role again, I found myself commuting between 'Elmgate' and Gatwick rather more than hitherto and it was during this period that the incident with the police in Ware took place. By 1976 I was beginning to tire of all this travel through London and also because both my parents were getting on in years (Mella's parents had died in 1974), we decided to look for a house nearer to Gatwick. We eventually settled in Wivelsfield Green during the long hot summer of 1976, but all that is the subject of a later chapter.

Flying between Muscat and Khartoum on one occasion I crossed the so-called 'Empty Quarter' of Saudi Arabia and saw a sight to rival the changing landscape of Lake Chad. It looked from our height like a rock plateau on which there were hundreds of conical piles of sand arranged in neat lines with almost mathematical precision, just as though it had been done by human hand. Quite unique, but I never had a second opportunity to see it and observe whether the wind had changed it.

And speaking of sand and Khartoum, where we went very frequently, I must mention 'haboobs'. A haboob is the local name for a sandstorm that occurs quite frequently and without warning during a particular season of the year. The sand in this part of Africa is rather like brown talcum powder, so that a comparatively light wind can get

sufficient of it airborne to reduce visibility to the point where landing at Khartoum becomes impossible.

Khartoum is a very long way from the nearest airport suitable for diversion purposes and in cases like these the diversion fuel carried by law consists of what is known as 'Island Hold'. This is sufficient fuel for the aircraft to hold overhead a destination for 2½ hours, during which time the weather conditions almost always get better, allowing a successful approach to be made. As a 'haboob' can blow up very quickly, you can imagine that pilots keep a very close watch on the weather while on the way to Khartoum during the 'haboob' season.

On one such an occasion we had kept asking ATC at Khartoum for the visibility about every half hour all the way from Cairo. Every time we got the welcome news that visibility was 'unlimited'. However when we got overhead Shendi where it was normal to ask for clearance to descend from the usual flight level 170, we were given clearance to descend to 4000 feet and almost as an afterthought, ATC mentioned the fact that the visibility was now down to 300 yards! Needless to say we did not descend, but stayed at FL170 to conserve fuel. Once we got overhead Khartoum, we could see the airport through the dust but we could not legally make an attempt to land until the visibility rose above the limits for our type of aircraft, which after all these years I have forgotten.

Nowadays I understand the airport is equipped with ILS that makes a successful approach possible with much, much lower visibilities, but at the time this incident took place the only aid was a radio beacon. Fortunately, however, the road bridge over the Nile had some very bright sodium lighting and the road was more or less aligned with the runway. Consequently, after we had held at FL170 for quite a while and when the visibility had improved somewhat, I was able to land using the sodiums to find the runway, much to the relief of all on board including myself. This was an occasion when some local knowledge was worth a lot! The other problem with a haboob was that while the aircraft was being unloaded of the 27 tonnes of cigarettes we had brought, everything became smothered in a fine brown dust that got on to ones uniform making all the crew look like 'dusty miller' on a day when he was grinding brown flour!

Using Bombay as a refuelling stop on the way to the Far East was looked upon favourably by the company, as the landing and handling charges were very reasonable, so we often found ourselves transiting the place. The main drawback from the crew's point of view was the time it took to get Air India officials to prepare a bill. They had a vast office with many tables, most of which were presided over by some official shuffling mountains of paperwork, and most of whom were determined to ignore both us and our requests for some action to speed us on our way. In fact the Indians are extremely good at 'red tape', but then who am I to complain when you consider that it was the British that taught them!

*An Autobiography
by Captain
D.B. Hopkins*

One day, going through with an experienced captain, I learned how to deal with the situation in a somewhat unorthodox manner. Captain Nigel's solution was to march into the office without speaking to anyone, find an empty table and sit on it swinging his legs until finally somebody came and asked what he wanted. This usually happened quickly and I can only suppose it was so effective as the officials objected to his presence, which could be likened to that of a vulture waiting beside a kill for the tiger to move away.

Once when going into Bombay, I decided to practice my *Indian Type Talking*. It's not possible to imitate this on paper, so the reader must imagine the effect perhaps comparing it with the TV programme *Goodness Gracious Me*. I started off as soon as I called Bombay ATC about half an hour out and kept up the pretence all the way in. After I had parked the aircraft, ATC called me to say, 'Will the captain please report to the tower, and by God he'd better be Indian!' Needless to say I didn't go anywhere near the tower and since I heard no more about it, I am confident that they saw it as just as amusing as the rest of us.

In pursuit of good international relations I have always tried to greet foreign air traffic controllers in their own language, notwithstanding that English is <u>the</u> language of air traffic control worldwide. At one time I could do this in American, Texan, Australian, French, Italian, Arabic, Japanese, Greek, German and Spanish.

There is, however a time and place for everything so when I was once doing a sub-charter for Al Italia taking off from Rome, I checked in with my callsign and a suitable greeting in Italian. The controller responded with a stream of instructions in Italian that I had to ask him to repeat in English – most embarrassing and served me right for being too clever! However, when going into Cairo, it was a definite benefit to be able to greet them with 'Salaam Alekoum', since the controller didn't know whether I spoke Arabic fluently or just a few words, as was the true situation. It would have meant a loss of face for them to ask me and the net result was that I usually got preferential treatment when I asked for clearance to descend! But I am digressing from my Italian story.

Going into Rome for this sub-charter, we were handled most efficiently until we arrived at crew customs, at which point the system broke down completely. I was trying to find somebody to tell me which hotel had been booked for us, but not only could nobody help, nobody could provide me with the slotted coins that are needed to be able to use the public telephones in Italy. Finally I found an Italian employee of BEA who tried to assist, only to become a victim of the favourite Italian 'momento' trick. You've not heard of this? Well, if you have not been at the receiving end of this annoying habit you will not know how frustrating it is.

What happens is this – you ring a number and the person at the other end answers with 'Prego?' You say to whom you wish to speak and the answerer says 'momento', puts down the phone, goes away *and never comes back*! It is absolutely infuriating and especially so when you don't speak the language. After about an hour and a half of this treatment the kindly fellow who was doing his best to help me finally turned to me and said, 'No wonder we lost the last war!' I replied, 'Well you said it!' Eventually we did get to the hotel for a much needed rest and recuperation.

Hong Kong was a 'fun' place to land at, especially when approaching on the landward side that meant a right hand circuit and a last minute turn at the 'chequer board'. At this point you were lower than the skyscrapers and I'm sure if you had had the time for sightseeing, you would have been able to see in through the windows of the hundreds of flats.

Because we were not a scheduled operator, we had to land at Hong Kong during off-peak hours. It was on one such occasion, when I was training a senior first officer for promotion to captain, that SFO John had landed after an approach round the chequer board, which meant a very long taxi back to the cargo area for parking and loading. John was taxying extremely slowly for some reason or another when we got a call from the Australian controller in the tower, 'I don't want to worry you Tradewinds, but you're just about to be overtaken by a snail!' So I said to John, 'What have you got to say to that?' he replied, 'Ask him if he knows I'm a black belt at karate!' When I did the Aussie came back with, 'In that case I'll shut up!!' Curiously I never did discover the reason for John's snail-like taxying. YCNSTWLEM!

*An Autobiography
by Captain
D.B. Hopkins*

CHAPTER 13

Positioning

I F I DISAPPOINT THE READER, AT THIS POINT, I apologise. This chapter has nothing to do with the Kama Sutra, only with flying around the world as a passenger. Every now and again it would be necessary to fly to some place or other to replace another pilot who had to return to base for some reason – sickness, leave or some other cause. Sometimes this 'positioning' was done on a company aircraft and sometimes as a regular passenger.

My first experience of positioning is mentioned briefly in chapter 10, when I flew to Tokyo to spend a month operating between there and Manila. This trip was by courtesy of BOAC or 'Better On A Camel', as they were known throughout the world of aviation, in a Boeing 707 like the one below.

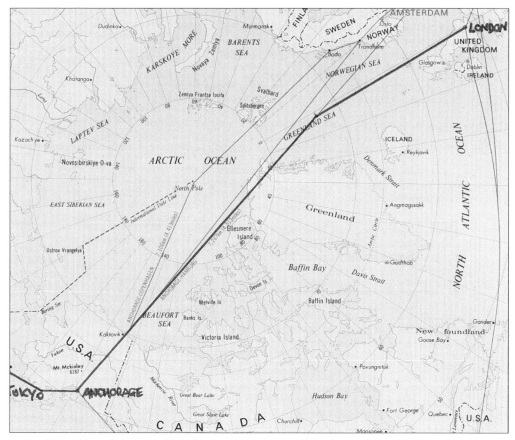

Incidentally, a lot of airlines have pet names and here are just a few that I can remember: Danair = Dandare; Pan American Airways = Pandemonium Scareways; Pakistan International Airways (PIA) = Perhaps It'll Arrive; Sabena = Such A Bloody Experience Never Again; Air France = Air Chance; British Airways = British Aeroflop; TWA = Teeny Weeny Airlines; Aer Lingus = Air Fungus; Lufthansa = Let Us Fornicate The Hostesses And Not Say Anything; Qantas = Queers And Nymphomaniacs Travelling As Stewards. (Not very PC, but then what the hell!)

However, to get back to my trip across the Arctic regions, which was more or less along the route shown in black on the map. All this was very exciting as I had not previously flown over the pole and looking down on the ice sheets made me realise what epic journeys have been undertaken by the explorers of the last century.

I spent some of the trip on the flight deck talking to the crew, whose conversation was centred around the forthcoming introduction into service with BOAC of the new Boeing 747 Jumbo Jet. At the time BALPA, the pilot's trade union, was in dispute with management over various aspects of the pay and conditions for the crews who were to

An Autobiography by Captain D.B. Hopkins

operate the new fleet. I was absolutely amazed, having only recently left the RAF, at the attitude of these very highly paid pilots, who, it seemed, were not going to agree to fly the 747 until they got the rate of pay they thought they deserved. Personally I would have given my right arm to be able to fly the aircraft and I found it very hard to understand their attitude.

I've often heard people discussing the relative merits of flying with different airlines, but what they don't seem to realise is that the quality of a particular flight is usually due to the crew who are operating it. For instance, I had reason to fly with Pan American on two occasions. The first, in a 747, was absolutely diabolical. The service was dreadful, the food inedible and the whole experience one that I would like to forget. On the other hand, the second was one of the nicest flights I've ever made as a passenger. The difference between the two was entirely due to the cabin attendants, who in the first instance were insufficiently motivated to look after their passengers, while in the second they could not do enough for them. Standards should be the same, but human nature being what it is, it is almost impossible to ensure that the same high standards are universally employed.

I found another instance of the difference a really good crew can make on a flight with Air Canada from London to Gander. As usual we were booked in economy, but as soon as the chief hostess discovered that we were aircrew, she upgraded the three of us into first class. Here the service was second to none and the food out of this world, with a piece of hake that just melted in the mouth. When asked what I would like to drink with it, I said I would have a glass of white wine, where-upon I was presented with a whole bottle! When we arrived at Gander the hostess came along with about half a dozen bottles of wine that had had their corks pulled ready for use and then partly replaced, and asked us if we would take them off the aircraft with us as she couldn't use them for the next set of passengers. Needless to say we were only too happy to oblige, and as we had a couple of days to wait at Gander for our own aircraft, we managed to put them to very good use!

On another occasion I had to fly down to Nairobi to replace one of our captains who had to return home to be at his wife's side at the birth of their first baby. I flew British Airways, as it had just become, in a B747 from Heathrow and I was in mufti, as was our custom when positioning by means other than that the company aircraft. Departure time came and went without any sign of engines being started and shortly thereafter the captain announced over the PA system that they were having trouble closing one of the underbelly cargo doors. This was a fairly common fault with doors on most aircraft, and is usually caused by dirt getting in the door runners during the loading and unloading of cargo.

Some ten minutes later, during which time I could hear the ground crew making noises under where I was sitting, the captain apologised for the delay and said that he was sending the flight engineer down to assist in closing the door. I remarked to the man sitting next to me that shortly we would hear a bang under us, caused by the F/E hitting the door in a certain place with the fire axe, and all would be well. Sure enough, there was the bang, shortly followed by the captain's announcement that all was well and that we would now be leaving. My fellow traveller looked at me as though I was psychic until I explained that I too was an airline captain and that hitting these cargo doors with the fire axe was standard practice for closing recalcitrant ones. Known in the trade as a 'technical tap'!

The next tale of positioning illustrates a couple of points. Firstly that management have a naïve belief that all airlines around the world operate to the same high standards as those in Europe, and secondly that if you look official and act as though you own the place, you can get away with murder!

I had to get to Lagos to replace one of our captains who was sick. There was a company aircraft going to Kano, so operations put me on that and told me to make my own way from Kano to Lagos (both in Nigeria). What our operations staff chose to ignore, even if they actually knew, was that all internal flights in Nigeria are greatly over-subscribed and that even though one might have a ticket, it was necessary to bribe the right person in order to obtain a boarding card and even the possession of a boarding card doesn't guarantee you a seat. I have witnessed flights in Nigeria that were overloaded to the point where some passengers were standing in the aisles. With previous experience of trying to get from Kano to Lagos, I could see that my flight was bound to be an adventure!

When we arrived in Kano there was a Nigerian Airways Boeing 707 standing on the tarmac next to where we were parked. I made my way over to it and asked the Nigerian ground staff standing at the bottom of the steps what their destination was. 'Lagos' came the reply. 'Wonderful', I thought, 'I'll see if I can cadge a lift with them'. With this in mind, I went up to the flight deck to speak to the captain. I assumed the Nigerian pilot in the left seat was the captain, but it turned out that the Indian sitting in the jump seat was the commander. I asked if I could possibly have a lift with them as I had to get to Lagos quickly, but my request was met with a lot of humming and ha-ing and sucking of teeth. After some minutes of this indecision, I was told by the commander that, 'We will not be knowing if you are on board!' (Said in that 'goodness gracious me' type of voice.)

I took this as a 'yes' and immediately fetched my luggage from our CL44, in which I had come from Gatwick, climbed the steps and

An Autobiography by Captain D.B. Hopkins

marched into the first class section of the plane, threw my suitcase onto one seat and sat in the one next to it. Almost immediately a very, very large Nigerian airhostess came up and I thought that I was about to get asked for my ticket. Since I had none, and although I was in my captain's uniform, she didn't know me from Adam, so I fully expected to get chucked off. But no – all she wanted to know was whether I would like tea or coffee with my breakfast. Somewhat relieved, we took off for Lagos with me enjoying my breakfast, but there was still a major problem to overcome.

Having arrived in Kano and not gone through immigration or customs, I was in the country illegally so I had to decide what to do when I arrived in Lagos. I felt the best plan of action was to leave the aircraft by the steps provided for the crew and depart the airport through the crew facility, marching smartly past the bevy of customs officers wishing them 'Good Morning!' Amazingly this worked a treat and within ten minutes of arriving on the stand, I was in a taxi bound for the Hilton hotel in the city where we normally stayed – quite definitely the quickest entry into Nigeria I ever made. Aha, you ask, how did I leave the country without anything in my passport to say I had entered? No problem as it happened, because our Station Manager, a Nigerian Chief, always drove us straight to the plane in the crew bus without going through the official channels.

Speaking of station managers, when Tradewinds started 'slipping' crews down the route, they appointed a station manager and deputy to look after our interests in Cairo. When I was first told the manager's name, I thought somebody must have been pulling my leg. Mustapha Kamel was a very tall Egyptian who had previously been with BOAC, and although I had been assured his name was genuine, I had difficulty in not laughing the first time I met him. He was indeed a gentleman and on one occasion he invited the Chief Pilot and myself to his palatial house for a meal and to meet his wife. On arrival we were greeted most hospitably and plied with delicious food and drink. By the time dinner was served, both Ted and I had indulged ourselves much too heartily on the 'nibbles', thinking that this was the meal, that we had to make a real effort to do the excellent dinner justice. YCNSTWLEM!

My final tale of positioning took place when I had to get back from Larnaca to London in a hurry. I arranged a lift on a B707 of Cyprus Airways that was flying empty to Heathrow to collect a charter group. Being the only 'passenger' on board, I was looked after right royally and had the run of the whole aircraft to myself. This gave me an opportunity to do something I had always wanted to do, namely use the public address system. As I normally only flew cargo and one doesn't usually bother with, 'Good Morning Oil Drums, this is your captain speaking!' I seized the opportunity for a bit of innocent fun. So when the hostesses were all looking the other way I got hold of their PA microphone and announced, 'Good Morning Crew, this is your passenger speaking.' Quite puerile really, but it got a good laugh and anything remotely funny helps to pass the time!

*An Autobiography
by Captain
D.B. Hopkins*

CHAPTER 14

Jet Propelled Again –
But Only Briefly

EARLY IN 1978 Tradewinds bought three Boeing 707-323C's from American Airlines, part of the deal being that AA would train all the crews who were to fly them. Consequently, at the end of July 1978, I did my last flights in a CL44, before I went off to Dallas/Fort Worth, Texas to start a course at the American Airlines Academy, feeling greatly excited at the prospect of flying jets once more. It was a splendid experience in all respects bar one – the temperature in Dallas in July, August and September is just too hot. Even the Texans think so and the many I've met in the years since I went there all expressed their sympathy at my badly timed visit to their State.

I flew from Gatwick to New York on a 747 of a now defunct airline, and there transferred to an American Airlines Boeing 727 for the flight to DFW. As soon as I stepped aboard this flight, I knew I was going to enjoy myself with AA when I was handed a gin and tonic practically before my bottom touched the seat and long before we took off. Refills appeared as if by magic, making the flight all too short. Soon I was installed in a motel at Arlington, half way between Dallas and Fort Worth and quite close to the Flight Academy, and from here we were shuttled to and fro by a limousine service.

During my stay I cooked for myself, except on the rare occasion when I went out for a meal. It was on one of these visits to a local 'eatery' that I made the mistake of ordering some catfish. I am particularly fond of fish and I have eaten many varieties in many different parts of the world, practically all of which have been delicious. Catfish however proved the exception to the rule – it was like having a mouthful of mud – quite disgusting. YCNSTWLEM!

For provisions I went to a local supermarket called Skaggs that was open 24 hours, 7 days a week. No matter what time of day you shopped there, even at 3am, there was always somebody to pack your goods into

The Extraordinary Story of a Very Ordinary Person

the ubiquitous American brown paper sack. I think the packers were all students paying their way through college of one sort or another.

The course was arguably the best organised and most enjoyable of any in my entire career. We were picked up at the motel each morning, or at whatever time we were going on duty, since we quite often started in the simulator at 4 o'clock in the morning or some other equally ungodly hour. On arrival at the operations desk at the academy, one first had to collect the computer sheet for the day that told one where to be and at what time.

Collecting my sheet one morning, I was suddenly aware of a tall man staring curiously at me from the other end of the counter. I looked at my zip to see if I had a problem in that direction, (you know the sort of thing XYZ – examine your zip, ABC – all been checked) but all was well, so I went to speak to him. He knew my name, which was quite a surprise, as I didn't recognise him at all, although I could tell he was English by his accent. He turned out to be an old colleague from my days at Swinderby instructing on Vampires. In those days he had been quite a tubby chap, but due to illness he had lost a vast amount of weight and that was why I had failed to recognise him. He had emigrated to the USA, was married to an American girl, and had a job with American Airlines, and of course he wanted to know what I was doing in Texas. We met later for a drink and caught up with each other's lives since we last met. It's a small world, and getting smaller all the time!

The technical part of the course was fully automated and when the instructor asked a question, all one had to do was press the button on the desk to pick the correct multi-choice answer provided. As long as one wasn't asleep this was, I found, all too easy and once we (myself, the first officer and flight engineer) had completed the initial sections of the course, we started the flying training, which was almost all in a simulator. The only time we actually got airborne in 'the real thing' was two flights to finish the course.

Our instructor, Captain Peter Singleton, was a great fan of antique cars and his pride and joy was an ancient Oldsmobile he had lovingly restored. He brought it along one day and drove the first officer and myself down to the airport in it, apologising for the fact that it only had 4/50 air conditioning. Naturally we had to ask what in the world 4/50 air conditioning was only to hear the reply, '4 windows open, 50 miles an hour!' YCNSTWLEM!

I got back to the UK in the middle of September for some welcome leave before starting my route training with a long trip from Gatwick to Athens, Djibouti, Mogadishu, Madras, Bahrain, and Rome. The landing at Rome Fiumicino was at night in the some of the most appalling weather conditions I've ever encountered, causing the training captain to make remarks along the lines of, 'if you can cope with that you can

An Autobiography
by Captain
D.B. Hopkins

cope with anything!' I'm not certain to this day how I did manage to get the thing on the ground – roughly 'by guess and by God' and an innate sense of self preservation that often gets one out of difficulty. Some people refer to it as 'experience'. That landing was certainly an 'experience'!

In November Air France were having an industrial dispute with their pilots so Tradewinds were contracted to do a series of flights from Paris, Charles de Gaulle to Point-à-Pitre. One of these flights enabled me to see at first hand the accuracy of our Inertial Navigation System (INS). From Paris to Guadeloupe was around 4000 nautical miles, practically entirely over the sea with no opportunity to update the system, and at the end of the flight the INS had only a 1-mile error! At that time this was a very accurate system of gyroscopes and accelerometers, but nowadays it has been superseded by the Global Positioning System. Below is the view from the cockpit window that we had at Point-à-Pitre.

Operating for Air France was quite delightful from the point of view of the catering they provided for their crews. In the first place they provided napkins with a buttonhole in one corner, enabling it to be attached to the top button of one's shirt, thus preventing bits of food

staining one's uniform. Secondly each crew member was given a small of a bottle red wine to wash down the excellent food. All very civilised and if you are scandalised by the thought of aircrew drinking on duty, think of the wine, always rouge, as a preventative medicine against heart disease!

I went to Chicago O'Hare for the one and only time of my life in February 1979. It was on the day after the unfortunate disaster of the DC10 crashing when one of its engines fell off. The place was covered in some three feet of snow, and although it had been cleared from runways and taxiways, the indicator boards at the side of the latter were not visible, thus making it difficult to know where you were on the airfield. At one point I had to admit to ATC that I was lost, making me feel a right idiot, but I was somewhat mollified when a pilot from United Airlines, who was presumably familiar with the place, admitted that he too was lost!

Landing at Gander one winter's day, I managed to give myself, and I daresay the rest of the crew, something of a scare when I found myself hurtling down an ice covered runway that was downhill towards the lake at the end. Even with full reverse thrust and anti-skid brakes it seemed to be touch and go whether the aircraft, with 45 tonnes of freight, would stop without sliding off the end. It did but it was definitely another of what we pilots describe as a sixpence, half-crown, dustbin lid occasions.

Speaking of going off the runway reminds me of the time when Pan American Airways, or Pandemonium Scareways as they were affectionately known in flying circles, were taxying out at Heathrow during the period when they were having financial difficulties. They had been running a prolonged advertising campaign, in which they described themselves as 'the world's most experienced airline'. On this occasion their 707 had turned too sharply and one main wheel bogie had gone off the tarmac taxiway onto the very wet grass and sunk up to its axle. Whilst they were stuck, the captain of another aircraft taxying past announced to his passengers, 'Ladies and Gentlemen, Captain speaking, if you look out of your left hand window you can see the world's most experienced airline – having one of their experiences!' It was the sort of repartee I would loved to have come out with except that I would have thought of it about a week later!

Twenty one years to the day after my contretemps with a Vampire T11 at Swinderby, I became, yet again, a training captain. Could it be that 5th December is my lucky day? Who knows, but thereafter I spent many of my trips either training new pilots or checking ones who were already qualified.

In the middle of February 1981 I did something that should qualify me for an entry in the Guinness Book of Records. One of our 707's was needed at our engineering base at Lasham, between Basingstoke and Alton, for some urgent maintenance, but due to my late arrival back from a trip to Nairobi, Djibouti and Cairo it was after dark and the regulations did not allow a 707 to land at Lasham, a gliding centre with a short runway, except in daylight. Management asked me if I would be kind enough to have a go. It was stressed that they could not authorise me to do it, but that they would be very pleased if I would. It was one of those situations that happen now and again where you're damned if you do and damned if you don't, but anyway off I went after Lasham had agreed to lay out a 'wartime' type flare path with 'goose neck' flares. The landing was no big deal, but those people I've spoken to who have done gliding courses at Lasham seemed suitably impressed!

Although I didn't know it at the time, I did my last flight in a 707 and for that matter, any aircraft, on 5th April 1981. Having got back from Khartoum and Larnaca I went for my six-monthly medical as required by the CAA and to my complete and utter surprise I was informed that I had had a heart attack during the six months since my

An Autobiography by Captain D.B. Hopkins

last medical. As I had not felt anything untoward during the past six months, I thought it must have been a mistake, but an angiogram at Kings College Hospital confirmed it and that brought my flying career to a very abrupt and unexpected halt. YCNSTWLEM! Interestingly the only ill effects I felt from my heart attack occurred after I had my angiogram, when I suffered attacks of angina for a short period. Psychosomatic?

During my 29-year flying career I amassed 11,538 hours, landed at 251 airports in some 74 different countries and travelled just under 4.5 million miles, about the same distance as 9 round trips to the moon. On looking back I realise I have had a pretty good run for my money with only one major accident in all that time, but I was still quite sad that it all had to come to an end.

The question was – what to do next?

CHAPTER 15

We Buy A Mansion

BEFORE RELATING 'what I did next', I think it appropriate to tell about our move to Sussex from Cambridgeshire. By 1973 the boys were becoming quite grown up, as can be seen in the snap below, in which Austen is sporting a plaster on his right arm. He broke it twice within the space of nine weeks, having fallen from a climbing frame the first time and getting tripped up the second, both when he was attending his primary school. Trevor and Chris were still at Cambridge Grammar School and both doing well, although Trevor seemed to make a habit of leaving his satchel on the school bus, which meant Mella having to go to the depot to retrieve it with such regularity that she became a well known visitor. It was Trevor's absent-mindedness that made us think that he might become a professor one day, and in fact I think he was nicknamed 'the professor' at school. Our prognostications turned out to be correct while he was a senior lecturer at Manchester University, when he was offered two chairs in the faculty of computer science, one at St. Andrews and the other at Hull.

In the meantime I was commuting to and from Gatwick with increasing frequency after I had become a training captain in the January, and by 1976 both Mella and I felt that a move to somewhere nearer Gatwick would be a good idea. By now Trevor had completed his gap year prior to going up to Manchester University, Christopher was thinking of studying for a qualification as a graphic designer and Austen had just started at secondary school. All in all it seemed to

be the best time to make a move, so one Saturday in April Mella, Austen and I went down to Haywards Heath in Sussex to look for a suitable house.

Why Haywards Heath? Well, we had drawn a circle of 20-mile radius around Gatwick and noted the different flight paths used by aircraft going in and out of the airport, and Haywards Heath seemed a good starting point. We visited several different estate agents with a list of our requirements and even went to look at one house in Newick that appeared to be a possibility. It was not, however, what we were looking for and bearing in mind the long journey back to Meldreth, we were about to give up for the day when the agent suggested we might like to look at a house three miles outside Haywards Heath that had been on the market for two years. We were told that it had 13/14 bedrooms and was the biggest house in Mid Sussex. It was certainly much bigger than anything we had in mind and the only reason we went to look at it was for a bit of fun.

Above is what we saw when we arrived at Wivelsfield Hall, an enormous Edwardian house built in three years from 1903 to 1906, with about four acres of lovely grounds, including some magnificent rhododendrons, of which I'm particularly fond, plus a very grand entrance hall with an oak strip floor sprung for dancing and a stained glass window with a bee motif. If you saw all this you would probably see why we thought the place had possibilities, especially as a 'Granny Flat' for my parents was one of our requirements.

The price of the house and grounds when it had come onto the market had been £62,000, but the estate agent suggested that we might be successful with an offer around £40,000, so without further ado we went home and the following Monday I got my solicitor to make an offer of £37,500. I knew I was being cheeky, but to my surprise I got a reply to say that we could have it for £40,000. After the usual formalities the deal took place, and in the August we moved in, but not before we had made several visits to negotiate buying large amounts of furniture that the sellers were not taking with them as they were moving to a bungalow, while we were moving out of one. On the day of the move Mella and Christopher went ahead in the Morris Estate, loaded to the roof with Chris's disco equipment, a bale of straw (the last from Mr Coningsby!) and our twelve hens all clucking madly.

Sadly my father, who had been seriously ill with myeloid leukaemia for a couple of years, died on 2nd June so he never saw the place, but my mother did move up from Eastbourne into her own rooms, where we had expected she would see out her remaining years. This was not to be for after being with us for only six months, she decided that she would rather be back in Eastbourne where her friends were. In some ways this was a blessing in disguise as in her final years mother needed nursing care that we would have been hard pressed to provide in house, so to speak, and in the end she died in a nursing home in Eastbourne 14 years to the day after my father passed away. YCNSTWLEM!

One of the first things we had to do to the house was to bring the electricity system up to date and make it safe. What we found was a mixture of vulcanised cable in conduits, lead covered cables, rubber cables and the modern plastic type. There were seven switch boxes fed from two meters (i.e. two phases) and no less than six distribution boards. There were no wiring diagrams and so it was impossible to tell which fuse fed what! Fortunately Joan and Eric Stanley, our friends from our Louth days, were able to step into the breach, as Eric had been an electrician with the Ministry of Public Building and Works, working for many years on RAF airfields. They came to stay for a few days and during that time he checked all the cables for soundness and safety and for some days all you could hear were shouts of, 'Is that on now?' and 'What about now?' and so on. Eventually I had a set of notes telling me what fed what and so I was able to rearrange the wiring from the switch boxes to ensure the loads were evenly spread. It was then just a matter of taking out all the old 5 and 15 amp sockets and replacing them with modern 13-amp fused outlets, and then re-equipping all the electric fires and other appliances with suitable 13-amp plugs. Twenty-two years later when we sold the house all was still in tiptop working order, which was something of a miracle when you consider I'm not an electrician.

During the first autumn I planted one area of the garden with an

*An Autobiography
by Captain
D.B. Hopkins*

orchard of pears, plums, eating apples, cooking apples and Morello cherry trees. These all produced plenty of fruit over the years and later on the area around them became a chicken run.

However the garden lacked one thing that I wanted: water. Therefore it was not long before all my spare time between flights became occupied with building a water garden. Just for the record I calculated that I moved something like a hundred tons of clay from the ten-yard diameter hole with just a shovel and wheelbarrow.

These two pictures show the completed pond, stream and waterfall, with some of the planting finished in the bog garden on the right. What they don't show are the fish, six Koi that I bought and 19 Golden Orfe that a neighbourly farmer let me catch from his lake, which contained hundreds. When we left in 1998, there were some 75 Koi, varying in size from about 12 to 24 inches. The stream on the right became a haven for all sorts of wild life, including newts, great diving beetles, leeches and grass snakes. On one occasion I saw a weird looking thing that I eventually identified as a water stick insect. We introduced some frogspawn one year and for some years after we had frogs breeding, but eventually the newts ate all the tadpoles and thereafter the frogs disappeared.

I made the pond three feet deep to ensure that herons would be unable to stand in it to fish, and also to avoid problems with ice in cold winters. After the addition of strands of wire round the edge of the pond to a height of 15 inches, the anti-heron defences worked perfectly, although I lost a couple of Koi before I added the wire. We once saw a Kingfisher sitting on the wire, but it had little luck in getting a meal as all the fish were much too big for it.

Under the square slab with the planter on top was a hollow tower made of breezeblock through which the water filtered on its way back to the sump underneath the waterfall, ready to be pumped back along

the stream. This was invaluable in keeping the water well oxygenated, particularly in hot weather, although the resulting oxygen levels did result in an annual problem with blanket weed that necessitated my wading in to remove it manually. One year, on the advice of a friend, I tried removing the weed by chemical means, but while this had no ill effects on the fish and other wild life, it killed off the water lilies most effectively, and meant replanting with some new ones.

On the subject of wild life, we saw an amazing variety in or around Wivelsfield Hall over the 22 years we were there, including weasels, stoats, foxes, deer, common lizards and a vast selection of birds. Among the latter was a pheasant we named 'Phred'. He suddenly appeared from nowhere one summer and remained with us for about 18 months. He was completely tame and would follow us about waiting for a handful of corn, which he would eat from the hand. Eventually he disappeared as suddenly as he arrived and to be realistic I imagine he finished up on someone's plate!

In July one year there was great excitement when I saw a glow-worm in the orchard as I was walking the dogs last thing before going to bed. I quickly fetched Mella and the boys to see this rare sight, which was just as well, because it was the only time we ever saw one, probably due to a combination of the use of chemicals in the garden and the constant grass mowing that was necessary to keep the orchard under control.

In Annex 'D' is a comprehensive list of the bird species we saw during the 22 years. The Alpine Swift took a long time to identify and two others are worthy of a special mention. First is the Hoopoe, which is a rare summer visitor to Sussex. Mella had been out shopping and as we all sat down to lunch, she mentioned somewhat diffidently that she was sure she had seen an exotic bird as she drove up the drive. Before anyone could say anything, the bird in question flew past two windows before our very eyes, as if it had been waiting for its cue to do so. We were all absolutely flabbergasted, but delighted to have had 'our very own' Hoopoe in the garden!

The other one I must mention was the parrot. We were having breakfast and Austen came in and announced that there was a large green parrot with some red on it sitting at the top of one of the oak trees in what we called 'the spinney'. I expressed my doubts as to his sighting, but went out to have a look. To my considerable surprise there it was, about the size of a pheasant, sitting on top of the tree as if it owned it. We guessed it had escaped from somewhere and tried making encouraging noises to coax it down, but it was having no truck with us. It screeched and flew off over the forest behind the house and we never saw it again.

It will come as no surprise to learn that we had continued keeping hens,

*An Autobiography
by Captain
D.B. Hopkins*

and at one time we had over 50 of them. The run had a gate so that they could be allowed to wander freely in the field beyond, with the farmer's permission of course, but there was one snag to this arrangement. Foxes! Contrary to what the idiots who want to ban fox hunting would like you to believe, foxes are unlike most other animals in that they kill for pleasure and are definitely to be regarded as vermin. Whilst one can put up with the loss of an occasional chicken that the fox takes for food, one cannot put up with a killing spree in which large numbers of birds are killed and left lying about. This usually happens in late May when the vixen is teaching the cubs to hunt and at this time of year it is vital the hens are protected by suitable wire netting. Even so, we lost several dozen over the 22 years we were keeping them. Such are the tribulations of country living, but having said that, I wouldn't have been without them, as there is nothing like a couple of really fresh eggs for breakfast.

The other vermin that always arrives on the premises when you keep chickens is rats. It was the same when we were at Elmgate and it was necessary to have a purge every now and again to keep the situation under control. Both Mella and I were pretty good shots with an air rifle, but I found the shotgun to be more effective when trying to shoot rats at dusk, the best time to creep up on them without them seeing you.

Early on during our tenure at Wivelsfield it was necessary to have a new central heating boiler. Access to the boiler room was outside in a small cellar and the first time we went in there we thought we had stepped into a ship's engine room by mistake. The pipes were huge and so was the Potterton 'Avon' boiler that came with the house. Eventually this developed a leak, so it had to go.

The company that installed our new one, a Seagold, assured me that they would not leave the huge cast iron sections of the Potterton lying about, and would arrange for a scrap metal dealer to take them away. Consequently I was not surprised to see a lorry arrive one afternoon while I was doing some gardening, driven by what I might describe as the archetypal scrap metal merchant. This gentleman, a rough diamond if ever I saw one, informed me that he couldn't get his lorry close enough to the five two-hundredweight sections to be able to lift them with his crane.

Whilst we were debating the best method for him to remove them, he looked up at the front of the house and asked, 'What is this place then Guv, a school?' I assured him that it was just a private house, and to emphasise why I needed such a large one, I told him that I had a very large family, three sons and eight daughters. He looked at me with considerable admiration in his eyes, clapped me on the back and said, 'Well done lad!' Of course I neglected to tell him that my eight 'daughters' were all air stewardesses whom we let use our surplus bedrooms (8), bathrooms (2) and kitchens (2). This arrangement ensured that all the rooms were kept in good condition since lack of use always tends to allow things to deteriorate rather rapidly.

In 1978 we were asked to host a charity fashion show, something we were only too pleased to do. The hall, drawing room and dining room were used to seat the audience and our bedroom for the model's changing room. The event was a great success, attended by about 200 hundred people packed like sardines into the three rooms. The models came out of our bedroom (big enough to hold two double beds and a settee), down the stairs, through the hall, drawing room and dining room, leaving by the rear door and back up the rear stairs into our bedroom via the en-suite bathroom, ready to change for the next round.

The following year we were asked to host a series of concerts to raise money to buy a piano for the Village Hall. In the first of these there were four harpists performing in front of the fireplace in the hall which was a sight to behold and the music was quite delightful. A later concert featured a children's orchestra playing ancient instruments such as the sackbut, lute and crumhorn. They were seated in two corners of the hall and another two corners of the galleried landing, thus enabling them to produce a quadraphonic effect for the first time, as all their previous venues had been two small for them. All in all we had five concerts over a period of a few months and were able to provide the necessary funds for the purchase of the piano that is in use to this day in the Wivelsfield Village Hall.

On another occasion we hosted a tea party for the local 'Good Companions' club. It was through this I learnt an interesting piece of the history of Wivelsfield Hall. In 1936 a Mr Jeffries bought the house and lived in it with his sister until they both died in 1955. By all accounts he was something of an art lover, since he covered practically all the walls with paintings of one sort or another. At the tea party an elderly man told me how he used to escort Mr Jeffries from Wivelsfield station to the house during the war when he was a special constable. I asked why he should do this and he was quite surprised to find that I didn't know that Mr Jeffries had been a Kings Messenger!

Another gentleman informed me that he used to come up to the house when he was ten years old to play with the son of the then owner, a knight of the realm whose name I have forgotten, and when the house was known locally as 'the house on the hill'. At this time all the trees around were small enough for the house to be seen from the village, but by the time we bought it, the trees had grown large enough to prevent the house being seen from practically anywhere in Wivelsfield Green.

In May 1977 I realised an ambition I had held for some time by acquiring a Rolls-Royce. I purchased a 1967 Silver Shadow from a company in Putney. It was one of the early Shadows, having a 4-speed

*An Autobiography
by Captain
D.B. Hopkins*

automatic gearbox of Rolls-Royce's own design. Later cars used a General Motors 3-speed box, the GM400. The 4-speed box in the car I bought was extremely jerky in its operation, so the company agreed to replace it. This they did three times, before I finally lost patience with the thing and changed it for a 1969 model.

It was during one of my visits to Putney, when I was parked outside their showroom right across a double yellow line, that I saw a traffic warden approaching. I immediately went out to meet her to explain my badly parked car, but before I could utter one word, she started complaining about the way she had been treated over her sickness benefit during a recent bout of illness. She sought my advice, which I was totally unqualified to give, although I made sympathetic noises regarding her misfortunes. Eventually after some ten minutes or so she departed, completely ignoring the law-breaking position of my Rolls. YCNSTWLEM!

It was not long after this incident that I began to find that having a Rolls had definite benefits in regard to parking. Soon after we moved from Meldreth to Wivelsfield, I found myself winding up the estate of an old lady who used to baby-sit for us. To this end I had to go to the probate office in Brighton and although I knew where it was, I hadn't a clue as to where I could park for half an hour or so.

As I approached the location of the office, I saw a traffic warden walking along the pavement, drew up alongside him, rolled the window down and asked, 'Can you tell me where I can park for half an hour while I visit the Probate Office?' He snapped to attention (I felt he was probably an ex-serviceman) and proceeded to give me some complicated directions. Seeing my uncomprehending look he then said, 'Follow me, Sir,' and took off along a road to the left leading to what I now know to be the Lewes Road, along which was a long line of parking meter bays. It was full to capacity and to my enquiry as to where I should park he indicated that I should leave my car at one end of the line half on the pavement. I said, 'Are you sure that will be OK?' To which he replied, 'Oh, don't worry, Sir, I'll keep an eye on it for you!'

On another occasion Mella and I went up to the Guildhall for a formal dinner to celebrate the 21st anniversary of the Guild of Air pilots and Air Navigators, wearing full fig of white tie etc. When we got to the Guildhall, I dropped Mella at the entrance and, not wishing to leave the Rolls in any of the side streets thereabouts, enquired from the man holding the door open for Mella to alight, 'Where can I park?' He said I should go down to the member's underground car park, giving me instructions how to get there. I thought to myself, 'I'm not a member, but I'll give it a try!' When I arrived below, the parking attendant showed me where to park and after backing into the space indicated, I somewhat diffidently asked if that would be all right. He

replied, 'Don't worry, Sir, I won't let anyone park either side of it!'

Sometime in 1979 I decided that YDN 7 was showing signs of its age and needed a respray. I must have been mad in deciding to do it myself and know several of my friends were definitely of that opinion, but I was convinced that I could do it, spurred on, I suppose, in the knowledge that I had done my first car, the Wolseley Hornet 'Green Goddess' some 29 years previously. Accordingly I cleared a space in what we called 'the long shed', an old house for rearing chickens, bought a small compressor and spray gun, and set to work in between my flights with Tradewinds.

The whole process of stripping it down to the bare metal, priming, undercoating, colour and finally clear varnish together with hours and hours of filling and rubbing down took well over three months of spare time, but I think the result, as pictured above in 1982 fully decorated at a wedding with me resplendent in my chauffeur's uniform (Captain's uniform with insignia removed!), was well worth the effort. I may be the only idiot to ever to attempt a complete respray of a Rolls-Royce without first practising on something less ambitious like a Mini! The fact that the result was most satisfactory was demonstrated when I won a prize with it in the early days of my membership of the Rolls-Royce Enthusiasts Club (RREC). The proof of the pudding is in the eating, I'm told! YCNSTWLEM!

I joined the RREC soon after I got a Rolls, membership of which is open to anyone who has a genuine enthusiasm for the works of Sir Henry Royce, whether or not they are lucky enough to own one. The Club is the biggest single marque motor club in the world with a current membership of around 10,000, and consequently it is divided into sections for ease of administration.

*An Autobiography
by Captain
D.B. Hopkins*

We became members of the South East Section that covers Kent and East Sussex and after a couple of years I was asked to become the Honorary Secretary for the section. This involved making arrangements for a series of meetings throughout the summer months at various places of interest in the district. I found this good fun and we used to meet practically every Sunday from the beginning of May to the end of September.

In the autumn and winter we held meetings about every three weeks at a suitable pub. By suitable I mean that it had to have a car park large enough to accommodate anything up to 15 or 20 Rolls-Royce and Bentley motorcars. On several occasions we held meetings at Wivelsfield Hall. Unfortunately I don't have any picture of what was arguably the most famous car in the section – a 1913 Silver Ghost that was used by Lord Kitchener as his staff car during the First World War.

Towards the end of my six-year tenure as secretary, the section was

awarded the annual prize for the most improved section in the Club, presented each year at the Annual Rally attended by members from all over the world, and at which it is usual to be able to inspect anything up to eight or nine hundred Rolls and Bentleys. It was a proud moment for me as I accepted the trophy on behalf of our section. The photograph above shows my current Rolls with the then Section Treasurer, Tommy Welham, Chairman Philip Francis and Committee member Jack Henley.

I have always been of the opinion that the most effective committee in terms of size is *one*, and I enjoyed good fortune in that the other members of our SE Section committee agreed with this principle, so that at our extremely rare committee meetings all that was required was for me to report what I had arranged.

As secretary my other duty was to produce a quarterly news letter to send to all our 400 or so members. Whilst I enjoyed the production of this, I was always very grateful to have Mella's help in putting it in the envelopes and attaching the self-adhesive address labels and stamps.

Contrary to what most people think, motoring in a Rolls-Royce is comparatively cheap if you consider the fact that a well looked-after Rolls will maintain its value for many years, in contrast to your average 'ordinary' car, that loses anything up to a quarter of its value the first time you take it on the road. I have had my current one for 15 years and were I to sell it today, I would probably realise 80% of what I paid for it. You have to agree that that compares extremely favourably with any other car.

One visit I arranged for members of the South East Section was to Crewe, where we were able to witness for ourselves the meticulous care put into the production of 'the best car in the world'. As you leave one of the assembly plants and cross the road to the next, you see a large notice advising you to 'BEWARE OF SILENT MOTOR CARS' and having had the pleasure and privilege of being associated with them for nearly a quarter of a century, I can assure the reader that the notice needs to be taken seriously!

One downside to our tenure of Wivelsfield Hall was the occasion when we were burgled one night in 1984. Two little 'toerags' gained entry by removing a small pane of glass from the leaded windows of the hall and notwithstanding the fact that 13 people were asleep in the house, proceeded to relieve us of most of our silver, our video and a few other items. About six months later we received a call from the police at Caterham to say that they had some items that they thought might belong to us. We went hot-foot to see and in the room into which we were shown there was a veritable Aladdin's Cave of recovered stolen goods, including most of what had been taken from us.

Having identified our property, which we had had the good sense to photograph, making it easier for the police to recognise, we had to wait a further 12 months before we got it back, as it was required as evidence in the prosecution of the two 'toerags' concerned and by the time we had our property back, these two villains had been in prison and released to carry on with their villainy. At least they had the good sense not to return to us as by this time I had installed window locks on all the openable downstairs windows.

I referred earlier to the 1987 hurricane that swept across southern England with such devastating effect on the night of 15/16th October. On the 15th I had been up to London to collect Sir Peter and Lady Hall and bring them to their house in Sussex. I noticed that the wind was quite strong as I drove down the M23 at around 1.30am on the 16th, but I thought it was fairly normal for the time of the year. I finally got to bed at around 2.30am, only to be woken at 6.30am by Austen knocking urgently on our bedroom door and saying, 'Dad, come quick and look outside!' I felt like telling him to buzz off as I was tired, but something in his voice told me that things were not right. So I tumbled out of bed and went to look and my first reaction to the devastation outside was that someone had set off a nuclear device! As I had slept very soundly, I had heard neither the sound of the wind blowing down the trees nor the clatter of the tiles that were sucked off our roof.

*An Autobiography
by Captain
D.B. Hopkins*

By the time I had dressed, the wind had abated considerably and when we went outside again, there was almost total silence. No traffic noise, no birds singing, nothing! This silence was gradually replaced in the next couple of hours by the sound of chainsaws, far and near, as people tried to clear the roads, railways, etc. I got my own chainsaw out and it is no exaggeration to say that it took ten of us some four hours before we could get a car down the quarter-mile long drive from the house. Clearing the remainder of the fallen trees took several months and we finished up with piles of logs all over the place, quite a few of which we handed on to the new owners when we sold the house in 1998.

Not all the trees that fell were killed – an English Lime some 80 feet high had been blown down with the root ball, cutting the telephone line, which was not repaired for about three weeks. The electricity supply was also cut for about a week to ten days, but fortunately I had invested in a small mobile generator during Harold Wilson's 'winter of discontent', and it saved us losing all the contents of our freezers, also enabling us to have some hot water in the evenings. Although the generator is only of 1500 watts, it has been worth its weight in gold over the years since I bought it, and I still have it in my garage ready to keep us going in the event of a power cut. In the aftermath of the hurricane it was next to impossible to get hold of a roofer, so it was indeed fortunate that we had a supply of spare tiles that were left over when the house was re-roofed a few years before we bought it. I was able therefore to get up on the roof and replace all the tiles sucked off by the terrific wind before any water had a chance to get in.

With the best part of 4 acres to tend, it was necessary to employ a gardener, especially as Bill, who sort of came with the house, soon retired. He had been taken on in 1960 on a 'temporary' basis by the Bedfords from whom we bought the house. For a short time I employed a woman, who was excellent, but unfortunately she decided to emigrate to Australia, although not before she had found a gold wedding ring around the middle of a carrot she had just gathered from the kitchen garden. From the inscription on its inside, we saw that it belonged to Mrs Early, who had lived in the house for a number of years and who was very pleased to be re-united with it, having lost it while gardening some 15 years previously.

Another gardener who was with us for about two years was an elderly man by the name of Calvert. It wasn't until he asked for a day off to go up to London for an interview with one of the daily papers that I discovered that he was 'Mad Mike' Calvert, who had made quite a name for himself during WW II.

Help in the house, quite definitely a must with 42 rooms to clean, we inherited so to speak, in the form of three ladies from the village. Sadly one by one these all retired over a few years, after which we had a succession of helpers. Mella hated having to employ someone new as it took her quite a long time to get them trained up to her satisfaction, but thankfully in the last few years we were fortunate enough to have the services of Barbara and Ann, both of whom now help Mella in our present, far smaller house in Haywards Heath.

One thing I have forgotten to mention earlier was our beehives. Soon after I planted the orchard in the Autumn of 1976, I thought that having bees on the premises would be beneficial to both the bee-keeper and to our fruit crop. With this in mind I contacted a local bee-keeper, who was delighted at the prospect of having six of his hives located in our spinney, where the bees had easy access to the hay fields on either side as well as to our orchard. It was a very good arrangement. The bee-keeper came along every now and then to tend his bees and each October he would pay his 'rent' in the form of 12lbs of honey. We also had the added benefit of better crops of fruit.

My earlier adventure in Meldreth, helping to catch a swarm of bees in my neighbour's garden, stood me in good stead as I was able to catch at least three swarms over the years and give them to our bee-keeper. At around £50 per swarm, this was not to be sniffed at!

The other amusing episode I forgot to include earlier concerned the chimney in the drawing room. In the Autumn of 1976 we decided that an open fire would be nice to sit around so logs were brought in and for a few weeks all was well. But then the chimney started to smoke and so I decided that I had better sweep it with the set of brushes and rods that came with the house. Having got everything prepared, I shoved a 'sweep's' brush up the chimney, using no less than 13 rods to get it to the top, and I was somewhat surprised to get only a couple of buckets of soot for my efforts.

Once again we started fires and this time the fire went well, but for only a couple of weeks. I thought this rather odd, so I rang up the previous owner, who laughed and apologised for omitting to tell me that many years previously he too had been sweeping the chimney and had managed to leave a sweeps brush up it. This had resisted all efforts to get it down and so was still up there. As part of the rod and brush kit, there was a drain brush (about 5 inches in diameter) so up it went and after a considerable amount of agitation down came the cause of the problem. Apart from the boss of the old brush, there were about a dozen bristles that had been keeping it stuck, most of the others having been burnt over the intervening years. Needless to say the fire burnt extremely well thereafter. YCNSTWLEM!

*An Autobiography
by Captain
D.B. Hopkins*

CHAPTER SIXTEEN

Inter Primos
Chauffeur Service

AVING FOUND MYSELF suddenly unemployed due to my heart attack in 1980, I needed to find some other way to keep myself occupied and to make a few shekels. As I had a Rolls-Royce, it seemed to be a good idea to use it for weddings.

First it was necessary to get it insured for hire or reward – not a difficult thing to do, I thought. I was wrong. After waiting for two weeks for the broker in Royston with whom I had done business for several years, to arrange the appropriate cover, I rang him, and to my amazement I was told that cover was only available if I was a bona fide hire operator.

Realising that this was a typical 'catch 22' situation, I tried all the local insurance companies and brokers only to be told the same thing. I was about to abandon the whole idea when Austen and Chris, both young drivers who had had the usual difficulty getting cover at a reasonable premium, suggested I try the local agent for the Co-operative Insurance Company, who had insured them. I went to see him straight away and to my surprise, not to say relief, got immediate cover. I stayed with the Co-op for many years until their premium rates rocketed, and from then on I found much more economic cover through the Ecclesiastical Insurance Company. This was most appropriate as by this time IPCS was providing limousines for over 30 of the funeral directors in Sussex and Surrey.

Having acquired insurance cover, it was necessary to think of a suitable name for the business. It just happened that many years ago we had bought a shield with the 'Hopkins' crest on it. This is not, I hasten to say, just for my family, but for any Hopkins anywhere. As you can see the family motto is INTER PRIMOS, Latin for 'among the first'. Being in that position had a certain appeal, and bearing in mind one of my mother's favourite sayings, 'the best is always good enough' and the fact that Inter Primos seemed to have a suitably international flavour, Inter Primos Chauffeur Service or IPCS for short, came into being. That it was a good choice was largely serendipity, but several of our foreign clients over the years have said what an excellent name it is for the sort of service we have provided.

The next thing was to find some customers, and this was when I found out to my cost that most advertising is a total waste of money and effort. I tried yellow pages, talking yellow pages (both very expensive and more or less useless), local newspapers (much more useful) and many other types of advertising, most of which yielded virtually no business. What is needed is personal recommendation, but this is another catch 22 situation, since you obviously need previous customers to do the recommending!

However the one thing that I tried that produced a fair amount of customers was the direct approach. I pored over the engagement announcements in the *Telegraph* and wrote to the parents of the daughter who had just announced her engagement in the locality and offered my services. This was effective and certainly better than any advertising.

After doing several weddings, it became apparent that I would have to get a second car to be able to transport not only the bride but also the bridesmaids and parents. To this end I purchased the first of my Audi's. I had originally gone to a local dealer with the intention of getting a Volvo that they had advertised, but fortunately the salesman, whom I knew, talked me out of that idea as not promoting the image I needed, and got me to buy an Audi they also had for sale. This was indeed a brilliant move for not only did the Audi project the right 'image', but it also had the biggest boot space of all the cars I considered, and this became an absolute godsend as soon as I started transporting customers, particularly Americans, to and from airports.

Of course having a second car means having a second chauffeur, so Mella was fitted out with a suitable uniform and together we did many weddings most successfully, earning many plaudits from satisfied customers. On the front of our 'wedding cars' we put a lucky horseshoe constructed from wire coat-hangers and white & red silk carnations. After a short time we got rid of the red bit in the horseshoes, because to some people, apparently, the combination of red and white together signifies ' blood and bandages' and is really not suitable for a wedding. YCNSTWLEM or, to put it another way – you learn by experience!

Quite soon we had a request to transport five or six people in the same car and this precipitated the purchase of a Daimler Limousine. We saw one advertised by a firm of funeral directors in Liverpool, so Mella

*An Autobiography
by Captain
D.B. Hopkins*

and I went up by train to see it. As it seemed to fit the bill, we bought it and drove it home. Like most secondhand vehicles, I've bought over the years, it needed a lot of TLC (tender loving care) including decoking the engine. I can honestly say I have never seen an engine with so much carbon deposited in it, presumably because it had always been driven slowly. Anyway, after close attention to a myriad of faults, which I later discovered were endemic in Daimlers, we had a limo fit to drive and hire out.

Before long I realised that if – say – the Audi, broke down I could substitute the Rolls, but if the limo fell by the wayside I could provide no suitable alternative. So it was that we purchased our second limo, but this meant that apart from Saturdays when most weddings are held, we had vehicles sitting around not earning. It so happened that a friend in the village was a funeral director and he became a regular user of our limos, and not only that, he recommended us to other funeral directors in the locality. In the end I think we worked for a total of 32 funeral companies in East and West Sussex and Surrey.

Now that we had all these vehicles (eventually we had six, the Rolls, three Daimlers and two Audis), it was vital to have a supply of chauffeurs. Because of the very nature of the business, much the same as any transport enterprise including flying, you either have vehicles sitting in the garage or you need more than those available. And because I could not afford to employ anybody full time, I began to employ semi-retired people on a casual basis, as and when I needed them. Since they were of the older generation, this had other advantages, for instance, they could be insured at a lower premium than young drivers and having experience, they were much more able to be good, informative guides to the many tourists we drove.

Often we were called upon to provide a car at short notice, usually for a hotel/airport transfer or a funeral, and because we made it a strict

rule never to send a vehicle out that had not been valeted, it became necessary to provide garage accommodation for all of them. Although we had four garages, seen in the above picture behind our cars in wedding regalia, none of them were long enough to house a Daimler limousine at just under 19 feet in length. Behind garage 2 (counting L to R) the vents at the top of the 'long shed' are discernible. I realised that if I were to knock out the back of this garage and part of the end of the shed, I could join them to make a really spacious area not only to store the cars, but also a place I could use for maintenance without worrying about the vagaries of the weather. The result was a great success and provided garaging for up to eight cars.

The fact that I did all my own maintenance, except for replacement of tyres and exhausts, meant that routine work could be done when the vehicles were not required rather than at the convenience of a professional garage and, just as importantly, it saved a vast sum of money in maintenance costs, without which I doubt if the business would have made much of a profit.

Fairly soon after the launch of IPCS, we had the good fortune to be asked by the owner of Gravetye Manor Hotel to be their regular supplier of chauffeur-driven cars, not only for airport transfers but, more interestingly, for tours of the local area, an area that is blessed with a great variety of historic houses, castles and gardens as well as beautiful scenery. In fact you would be hard pressed to find a better area in which to open a business such as IPCS, as Wivelsfield Hall was more or less equidistant from all the decent hotels in the area, such as Gravetye Manor, South Lodge, Horsted Place and Alexander House, to name but a few. Added to this was our proximity to Gatwick and access to the M23. Through contacts made at all these, we now have many good friends who come back to England time and time again and who also recommended our services to many of their friends and colleagues overseas, particularly in North America. Thus we were able to build up a considerable clientèle, which, together with our funeral and wedding hire, resulted in an annual turnover approaching £100,000 by the early 1990s.

Over time it was interesting to observe how the type of work varied. In the beginning most of the work was weddings, over 120 in our busiest year, but these gradually tailed off, so that by the time I retired we were lucky to be doing 35 per annum. Fortunately our funeral work was always there although the amount varied tremendously from month to month, from a maximum of 30 to a minimum of 2 or 3. In our best year for this side of the business we provided no less than 260 funeral limousines and while the average member of the public might think this would be pretty gloomy work to be engaged in, it quite often had its lighter side.

For instance I once collected five elderly ladies and an even more elderly gentleman from Lindfield to take to the Surrey & Sussex

*An Autobiography
by Captain
D.B. Hopkins*

Crematorium in Crawley. I had helped the ladies into the back of the limousine, which seated six, and was holding the door for the old gentleman when he said, 'I've got a gammy leg, I'll sit in the front with you as it will be easier for me to get in and out!' So after he was settled in his seat in the front off we went. The old boy never said another word all the way to the crematorium, but the five ladies all talked non-stop the entire 25 minutes of the journey, nobody listening, all jabbering away like a treeful of jackdaws.

After the ceremony I helped them all back into the limo and was just driving out of the crematorium grounds when the old boy turned to me and asked, referring to the deceased, 'did you know how old he was?' I indicated that I didn't. He said, 'Ninety, and I'm eighty-eight!' I felt like saying, 'Hardly worth you're going home, then.' But I politely restricted myself to something along the lines of, 'Had a good run for your money, then!' After that not another word from the old boy while the five ladies carried on jabbering away, nineteen to the dozen, all the way back to Lindfield. At their house I helped the ladies out first and then turned my attention to the old man, upon whose face there crept a slight smile and with a twinkle in his eye he spoke the memorable words, 'No need for us to talk, was there!'

Speaking of the Surrey & Sussex Crematorium, it was there I once witnessed what I can only describe as being an attempt at a DIY cremation. A hearse arrived from somewhere in Surrey, from where it had travelled at high speed in an attempt to arrive at the booked time, having departed well behind schedule. It screeched to a halt outside the chapel and while the funeral director went inside to check on the arrangements, it burst into flames, causing considerable panic while a fire extinguisher was found. YCNSTWLEM!

At a local burial during the summer one year, I was a member of the bearing party and as I was threading the strap through the coffin handle prior to lowering into the grave my spectacles fell out of the top pocket of my jacket, straight into the grave! Since I couldn't really say to the assembled mourners, 'Hang on a minute while I retrieve my glasses', I had to leave them in the grave. Before I left the graveyard, I mentioned my loss to the sexton in the faint hope that I might get them back, and to my astonishment the glasses were back at the funeral director's office by the time I had returned the mourners to their house. Fortunately not only were they completely undamaged, but also I didn't need them for driving, only reading! The moral? Keep them in an inside pocket whilst lowering coffins!

It was a pretty rare occurrence to be given a tip by a grateful mourner, although it did happen from time to time, usually a fiver or so. However, as my grandfather's saying goes, the unexpected does happen. I had taken just two mourners, an old lady and her son, back from the churchyard where her late husband had been buried and when we got to her house, she thanked me for my services and shook me by the hand, in which was a note folded up to the size of a postage stamp. Putting it in my pocket and thanking her I went about my business, only later discovering that it was a £50 note!

Likewise it was rare to get a gratuity at a wedding, but one of the best came from the father of the bride who had wanted two white Rolls-Royces, and to whom I had hired two black limousines on the grounds that they were much more elegant and that their contrasting colour showed the bride's dress to greater advantage in the wedding photographs. He gave the two of us £20 each, worth in today's money something like £50 apiece!

On the subject of colour, the vast majority of brides wore either a white or ivory dress, depending on the fashion at the time. One day early on in my career as a chauffeur I had two weddings booked for a particular Saturday. At the first, in the morning, the bride appeared in a candyfloss pink creation, and very beautiful she looked. At the second, in the afternoon, the bride appeared, equally beautiful, in candyfloss pink, remarking to me as she got into the back of the Rolls with her father, 'I suppose you think it's unusual for a bride to be wearing pink.' To which I was able to answer in all honesty, 'No, the bride I took to church this morning was also wearing pink.' In the entire nineteen years of weddings these were the only two in which the brides wore pink, although I did once drive a bride most elegantly attired in a white dress trimmed with black ribbon. YCNSTWLEM!

In April 1986 I received a call from the Girl Guides Association of Sussex East asking if I could provide a car to take HRH Princess Margaret to a church service in Brighton in June. To say that I was surprised would be a considerable understatement, but once I recovered from the shock I assured them that I would be delighted to do so. After two briefings with Special Branch and, as I later learned, after my driving ability had been checked, the great day dawned. Here we are arriving at St Peter's, the parish church, in Brighton, having brought the Princess from Withyham.

The occasion was the 21st Anniversary of the Association in East

Sussex, it being 21 years since Sussex was divided in two. The above picture shows the Princess being greeted by the Lord Lieutenant for East Sussex and being followed out of the limousine by Lady Buckhurst, the President of the Association.

This was my first experience of driving a member of the Royal Family and I thoroughly enjoyed the fun of driving with an escort of four motorcyclists from the Metropolitan Police Special Escort Group. As you will see, I had this pleasure on another occasion, and they are the only times I have been able to drive through red traffic lights with impunity! Great fun indeed! And the whole event was made all the more pleasurable by the letter I received from the County Commissioner. (See Annexe 'F')

The other fascinating part of driving HRH was her bodyguard, a tall young man of the variety who would shoot you first and ask questions afterwards! He sat with me in the front of the limousine with the division, of course, closed, so we were able to talk freely. In the course of the journey back to Withyham, he told me that his ambition was to become the proprietor of a nice teashop in the country. An understandable, if somewhat unexpected, reaction to his stressful life as a Royal bodyguard. YCNSTWLEM!

Whilst I'm name dropping, I must mention a few of the other famous names I've had the pleasure to drive. As I've already mentioned in connection with the hurricane in 1987, I often drove Sir Peter and Lady Hall at the time when they lived in Sussex. It was interesting to note that when Maria Ewing (Lady Hall) was on the way to a singing engagement, she would be very reluctant to talk, presumably to preserve her voice for the performance, whilst on the return journey she would engage in any amount of conversation.

We also provided the limousines for Harold MacMillan's funeral at Horsted Keynes parish church. This was a very high-security occasion, with some seven past and present Prime Ministers present. Some six months later we again provided limousines for the funeral of MacMillan's granddaughter.

I took several well known personalities to Gravetye Manor, where they were to be after-dinner speaker and these included Clement Freud, Diana Moran, Sheridan Morley and Ned Sherrin. I also drove David Hasselhoff from London to Sussex, where he was doing some recording, and I well remember him discussing with his agent the proposal that he take a part offered in some forthcoming production that required him to appear in drag. At six feet five inches tall, he thought that the prospect of appearing in high heel shoes was not on!

Another person I drove on several occasions, and who happened to live locally, was the late Sir David Hunt, first winner of the Mastermind competition and one-time ambassador. He and his Greek wife were a charming couple and I much enjoyed their company and conversation. Unfortunately I had to provide two limousines for his funeral in the late nineties.

One thing I learned early on in my career as a wedding car chauffeur is that most brides and grooms think you are part of the car and cannot hear what they are saying. While this might be true in a limousine with a division, it certainly isn't in a saloon such as our Rolls-Royce.

Hence it was not unusual to hear some funny remarks at times. One such came from a bride of all of half an hour to her new husband, a man with a very noticeable 'five o'clock shadow', even though he had no doubt shaved that morning. She looked at him very closely and said in an extremely stern tone, 'Have you shaved this morning?' I often wonder if they are still together!

On another occasion I was standing outside St. John's, the parish church of Burgess Hill, waiting for the bride and groom to finish having their photographs taken when I noticed a young man peering intently into the back window of the Rolls-Royce. I sidled up from the front, where I was standing, to see what he was up to and, as I got up to him, he said, 'You've done away with the white seat covers, Guv!' 'I beg you pardon,' says I! 'When you did my wedding 18 months ago you had white seat covers,' he repeated. I was about to tell him that I had never had white seat covers, when his wife, who was standing next to him with a small child in a pram, expostulated, 'Don't be silly! That was my dress you were sitting on!'

During the early existence of IPCS I did a month's driving for the

*An Autobiography
by Captain
D.B. Hopkins*

MD of Whitbread's 'Take Home' division at Dorking during which I found that MD's are always late for their next appointment, necessitating doing an hour's travel in half that time. Great fun if you don't get caught by the fuzz exceeding the speed limit!

During this month I got in one Saturday just in time to take a phone call from a rough sounding individual asking, 'Can you do a wedding in the 'Roller' next Fursday, Guv?' As it happened my services were not required by the MD that day so I said I could, told him the price and asked if he would send me a cheque, to which he replied, 'I'll pay you cash when you get here, Guv!'

At the due time on the 'Fursday' I was approaching the house on a council estate in Lancing when a Ford came towards me containing a woman with an enormous hat and a host of children. As she passed me she screamed at me through the open window, 'Round the corner, Dearie!' I assumed from this that I was getting close to the house, which indeed proved to be the case. Once there, I got out of the Rolls to help the bride and her father into the car and by the time I had got them settled into their seats, the father had pulled out a huge roll of 'tenners' from which he extracted the relevant amount and handed it to me. Off we went towards Brighton and the registry office where the ceremony was to take place, but since we had a lot of time to spare, I suggested we went via the 'scenic route' to kill a bit of time. As we drove along the seafront, the father suddenly said, apropos to nothing, 'I nearly bought a 'Roller' the other day, Guv!' 'You didn't though?' I queried. 'Nah, got a Range Rover instead!'

Eventually we arrived at the registry office a minute or two before the ceremony was due to take place, only to find all the women standing in one group and all the men standing in another on the other side of the road among a mass of brand new Mercedes and other expensive cars. I stood by the Rolls trying to fend off what seemed like a million boys running around the car and trying to open doors, boot etc. I used expressions like, 'Please don't touch that sonny', which had absolutely no effect at all. Slowly I realised that I needed to talk their language, so I grabbed one by the front of his shirt, lifted him up to my eye level and said firmly, 'F**k off!' Immediately the whole million vanished like smoke in a hurricane!

About 20 minutes after start time the 'lady' with the big hat and host of children appeared in her car, and by the way she was driving I assumed she had filled in the time since I had seen her previously with a visit to the boozer. Finally everyone went into the RO, to reappear some short time later for the drive to the reception at a hotel on the outskirts of Worthing, where the photographer did his thing. After this was over I was taking the ribbon off the car, as I don't like driving with it on when its not necessary as it restricts one's vision, when the father came out and asked if I would like to 'Come in for a drink?' Thinking that I might never emerge alive I made some excuse, whereupon he produced the roll of tenners again, peeled one off and said, 'Have a drink on the way home, Guv!' This was my first experience of driving 'Travellers', but by no means the last. YCNSTWLEM!

Still on the subject of weddings, people have the strangest ideas of what makes a 'romantic' wedding. In January one year a young lady came to book a car for her wedding in the following November. The service, she said, was to be at 5.30 pm. I reminded her that it would be dark at that time and there would be little chance of outside photographs, but she told me that it had been a life-long ambition to walk to her wedding up a path lit by candles and this is precisely what she did!

To be perfectly snobbish, the 'quality' of a wedding is usually indicated by the number of lady guests wearing hats. For a bit of fun, Mella and I invented the 'Hat' scale for grading the type of wedding on a scale of 1 to 10. 1 for travellers up to 10 for royalty, and although I never had to provide cars for the latter, I was approached to provide two cars for the wedding of the daughter of the Duke of Norfolk at Arundel Castle. Regrettably we were already fully booked for the day in question.

At another wedding, which I knew was going to be about 4 on the hat scale, I was pleasantly surprised to see the groom, best man and ushers all attired in morning dress. The illusion was somewhat spoilt, however, when one of the ushers removed his top hat to reveal a 'mohican' hair style and an earring! Grandpa was right, life is full of little surprises.

Speaking of surprises, I was once providing one of the Daimlers for a wedding in Horsham. When I got into the town, I found the traffic at a standstill – neither the bride nor I had known that it was Horsham's Carnival day. Whilst I was pondering what to do to get to the bride's house on time a policeman on a motorbike appeared alongside. He asked me where I was trying to get to and as soon as I told him, he switched on his blue light and instructed me to follow him! When we got to the house, in excellent time, I thanked him for his assistance and also asked why he had been so kind as to help. He replied that I had done his wedding some 18 months previously and he had recognised the number plate. YCNSTWLEM!

Returning to funerals, I had considerable experience of 'gypsy' funerals, all of which were alike in one particular respect; flowers, or rather floral tributes to the deceased, on which they spend an inordinate amount of money. I have been present at several where a very conservative estimate of the cost of the flowers would be in excess of £20,000.

I learned early on that one needed to allow the whole day to attend one of these elaborate affairs. Once I was asked to provide a limousine for a double funeral near Swanley, Kent. The time I was given to be there was 11am, but with previous experience to fall back on, I arrived

*An Autobiography
by Captain
D.B. Hopkins*

at about 11.15 to find myself last in a line of 25 limousines garnered by the funeral director from all quarters of South East England. A message from the FD was passed back along the line that all the Daimler limousines were to go into the caravan site last. 'Good', I thought to myself, I'll be tail-end Charlie. How wrong can you be? When I got to the site I found that all the limousines had backed in making me number one instead of number 25!

This funeral was a double one for a young couple who had committed suicide, or rather he had shot her and then himself whilst under the influence of drugs. Thus I finished up with not one, but two sets of grieving parents in the back of my limo and somehow I sensed that there was going to be trouble of some sort. As with most gypsy funerals, we first toured all the places the deceased had been associated with, this done at a funereal pace and requiring a police escort for the 100 or so vehicles in the cortège, including no less than six flat-bed trucks covered with the floral tributes.

By the time we arrived at the church in St Mary Cray, we were about an hour and a half late, but the vicar was not phased by this since he was well acquainted with gypsy practices. After the service we proceeded slowly the short distance to the cemetery. Just after all the mourners had assembled around the double grave, there was a shout, 'Look out, he's got a gun!' I immediately took cover behind my limo, which was rather too close to the scene of the action for my comfort, and waited for events to unfurl. Before long one of the mothers, a very large woman of about 20 stone who had been in my limo, was carried by four burly men and virtually thrown into the nearest limo, thankfully not mine, and the burial was completed. I never did find out whether anyone really had a gun, but the reason for the large woman's rough removal from the graveside was that she had tried to hurl herself on top of the coffin of her son.

That was undoubtedly the most action-packed funeral I ever attended and I didn't get back home until around 5pm, having left at 9am. A full day's work indeed!

My own opinion of floral tributes is that they are a waste of money that could be put to a much better purpose, such a contribution to cancer research, etc. However I would not want to detract from the artistry of the florists who make up these creations. I have seen an enormous variety of structures made from flowers, including footballs, cricket bats, snooker tables, lorries, pearly gates, etc, all beautifully created.

At a funeral of a young lad of 18 who had committed suicide because he was about £1,000 in debt, there were flowers to at least twice that value, and I thought to myself how much better that money could have been spent getting the young man out of debt!

The activity I enjoyed most was touring, especially to gardens of note where I found I was well able to talk knowledgeably about many plants to the extent that many of my friends, as I like to call them, asked my advice on gardening problems.

Tours could be for anything from a day to two weeks, and one of the first I did was for five days starting at the Hilton Hotel, Park Lane with two American couples. I arrived at the hotel at the appointed time and made myself known to them, to be told that their luggage was on its way down. I sat in the lobby watching the world go by, so to speak, when an enormous amount of bags went by on a hotel trolley. Quite why I should have thought these belonged to my party I don't know – sixth sense perhaps – but sure enough they did. All told there were 42 pieces of luggage plus the four people to go into the Daimler limousine. When Mr & Mrs Dickey and friends arrived, I said that it would be impossible to get all their luggage and them into the limo, to be told that part of the load was only going as far as their factory in Wokingham, where it would be stored. A London taxi was hired to take this while the remaining 22 bags were carefully loaded into the limo. To this day I am not sure how I got them all in, but there seemed to be bags everywhere, in the boot, on the front seat, and all around my passengers, who seemed quite comfortable with the arrangements, although I felt quite embarrassed having them packed in like the proverbial sardines. The fact that some 16 years later I still get a Christmas card every year suggests that they found their sardine experience great fun!

On this and most other tours I was expected to arrange my own accommodation in local B & B's, but with one couple I drove for over a week they insisted I stay with them in such luxury hotels as Chewton Glen. This was the lifestyle I could quite easily have got used to on a regular basis, although I must say that being with clients throughout the day can be a little overwhelming, not to say tiring.

Of all the tours I did, and there were a great many, only on one occasion did I not enjoy acting as chauffeur/guide. That one occasion was with an American couple and their two teenage children. I think the parent's idea was to broaden their son's and daughter's education. It was an utter failure, particularly in the son's case, as all he did was sit in the back of the limo with his 'walkman' clamped firmly over his ears and stare into space. Also his diet consisted entirely of hamburgers and Coca-Cola.

Another couple, whom I still see from time to time, have become firm friends since we all have the same intense interest in all things horticultural, and through several tours with them I have visited many gardens all over England that I might not otherwise have had the opportunity to see. Not only did I enjoy these tours immensely, but I was getting paid for the pleasure.

Every year for about five years I had the pleasure of driving a couple

*An Autobiography
by Captain
D.B. Hopkins*

from Vancouver, who always came with the husband's mother – a youthful 90 year old! Over the years I toured with them all over England, Wales and Scotland, but because of mother's great age we usually just drove around, only occasionally going on 'shank's pony' to look at some house or garden. The other thing I remember about them was that we had to stop at a greengrocers quite regularly to purchase a supply of fresh lemons to go with their evening G & T's. I once expressed surprise that the hotel couldn't provide them with lemons, to be told that although this was the case, they liked to have their own supply so as to be able to scrape zest into their drinks. YCNSTWLEM!

Some time ago I met a lady and gentleman from Texas and drove them a lot over a period of several years. Sadly the gentleman died some five years ago, but the lady still comes over to England every year. She is convinced that England saved the world from dictatorship and disaster in 1939/45 and because of this she has an extremely high regard for England and everything English. I would have been driving her yet again this year, 2001, but for the fact that the day she arrived from Ireland I had just got home from hospital after my re-plumbing. She had invited Mella and me to go and have dinner with her at Gravetye Manor, but since this was out of the question, she sent us a token allowing us to have dinner at Gravetye at a later date and at her expense! I feel justified in saying that we must have been doing something right over the past 20 years!

Over the years we were quite often asked to provide limousines to help with State Visits. Usually this meant sitting in the Royal Mews 'in reserve' in case anything went awry with the standard arrangements. The only time this actually happened was with the arrival of the President of Egypt, whose aircraft for some reason landed at Heathrow instead of Gatwick. So this became the second occasion on which I had the pleasure of driving through red lights with an escort of police motorcyclists. Coming back from Heathrow, the M4 was completely blocked (no bus lane then!) and so we had the fun of driving along the hard shoulder past hundreds of frustrated 'ordinary' motorists. YCNSTWLEM!

CHAPTER SEVENTEEN

I Become A Rotarian

I T IS DIFFICULT TO KNOW quite where to relate how and when I became a Rotarian without it getting lost in my day-to-day life, so I feel quite justified in devoting a separate chapter to the subject. For the benefit of readers who have no idea what Rotary is about, I shall start by quoting the Object of Rotary, which is as follows:

To encourage and foster the ideal of service as a basis of worthy enterprise and, in particular, to encourage and foster:

1. The development of acquaintance as an opportunity for service.
2. High ethical standards in business and professions; the recognition of the worthiness of all useful occupations; and the dignifying by each Rotarian of his occupation as an opportunity to serve society.
3. The application of the ideal of service by every Rotarian to his personal, business, and community life.
4. The advancement of international understanding, goodwill, and peace through a world-fellowship of business and professional men united in the ideal of service.

At this point it is interesting to note the history of Rotary. It was conceived by the late Paul P. Harris, a Chicago lawyer. The idea came to him out of his own loneliness as a stranger in a great city. His original conception was simply that of a Club for businessmen who had some use for each other beyond that of merely making money out of each other.

He mentioned the idea to three friends: Silvester Schiele, Hiram Shorey and Gus Loehr and the first meeting among these members took place on 23rd February 1905. The name 'Rotary' was used since the meetings took place in rotation at each member's place of business.

An Autobiography by Captain D.B. Hopkins

Although one of the original ideas was that members should benefit from business given by one member to another, this was quite quickly dropped in favour of a much more altruistic approach. Nowadays any attempt to use Rotary for the purpose of getting business is positively frowned upon!

Since 1905 Rotary has, like 'Topsy', grown out of all recognition, so that today there are clubs in practically every country in the world and one of the privileges of being a Rotarian is that one can attend any meeting of any club at any time, so if one is away from home one can 'make up' one's attendance by visiting a club in the country one is visiting.

I mentioned 'making up' attendance, because one is obliged to attend a minimum of 60% of meetings throughout the year, and since each club meets weekly this is a commitment not to be taken lightly.

In about May 1990 I was asked by a friend if I would like to go along to a meeting of the Cuckfield & Lindfield Rotary Club with a view to becoming a member. I went along to several meetings, all of which I thoroughly enjoyed and eventually I applied to become a member. After a time – during which it is customary for the current members to be given the chance to veto an application, I was 'inducted' into the Club on 3rd July 1990.

Since that time I have served on the Vocational Service Committee and then become editor of the Club's monthly magazine, which in most clubs is called *The Bulletin*. However each club is autonomous and so when I took over as editor, I changed the name of our *Bulletin* to *The Gazette*, which it has remained ever since. The fact that each club is autonomous makes it very interesting when you visit another club, as the procedures and atmosphere at each vary quite a lot, although all clubs adhere to the same basic constitution.

I carried on as editor of *The Gazette* for three years before I was asked to become Secretary, a post I held for just one year before I was asked to become Junior Vice President. Becoming JVP means that you are destined to become the President Elect the following year and The President the year after that. This is a considerable honour as well as being a position of responsibility, for the health of the Club is in your hands for a year, and naturally one wants to hand over the Club to the next President in at least as good a shape as it was when one took it over!

As with most enterprises, success is only guaranteed by having an excellent team to assist you. In this I was very lucky and the team I chose worked extremely hard to help me achieve my aim of raising around £15,000 for the three charities I had designated as 'President's Charities' for the year. It is the privilege of the president to be able to choose which charities to support during his year of office. The three I chose were a local one, Hollyrood House, located in Lindfield, that was to provide a home for 24 autistic adults. Autistic children are, in the main, well catered for, but when they leave school at the age of 18, they can be pitched into society with little or no further support. Hollyrood House was set up to give young autistic adults support to try to integrate them into society and even enable them to hold down some sort of job.

My second charity, a national one, was the Motor Neurone Disease Association. I chose this for two main reasons. One was that the son of one of my fellow Rotarians is a sufferer from this terrible disease and the second stems from my admiration for Professor Stephen Hawking.

My third charity, an international one, was the Rotary Eye Hospital in Hooghly, near Calcutta. I was introduced to this very worthwhile scheme by an Indian ophthalmic surgeon, Mr Samar Das (a member of the Rotary Club of Guildford). He regularly visits Hooghly and operates at this hospital, which is entirely funded by the Rotary Club of Hooghly. By joining forces with several other Rotary clubs in UK, France and Hooghly, we were able to raise a sum of $33,500 for the purchase of operating microscopes and ancillary equipment for use in the hospital.

Besides fund raising for charities, Rotary, and in particular our club, also provides hands-on support for various organisations. Over the years we have erected a summerhouse in the garden of an old people's home, painted several rooms at the same home, and also painted a goodly part of another building. This last year one of our members has been very active in helping the Headway Hurstwood Park Trust for people with head injuries, supervising and instructing in their woodwork facility.

I mentioned earlier that the Club meets every week and that it is a duty of each member to attend a minimum of 60% of the meetings. Our programme for the month starts with a 'Vocational' evening at which we hear from one of our members about their job or hobby or whatever. At the second meeting we have a speaker, and over the eleven years I have been a member I have heard some really good speakers on most interesting topics. In particular I recall a most entertaining talk from the late Sir David Hunt (the first winner of 'Mastermind'), who told us about his experiences serving under Sir Winston Churchill and Clement Atlee.

Our third meeting is 'Business', during which we discuss items of interest regarding support for charities, fundraising and so on. The fourth week is, like the second, a speaker meeting. Occasionally we have a visit to a local place of interest and in those months in which there is a fifth Tuesday, we have a 'Ladies Night', at which we try to provide a speaker of interest to the fairer sex.

On the subject of ladies, members wives are invited to join a companion organisation to Rotary called 'Inner Wheel', and most of our wives are indeed members of this.

The fun and fellowship to be derived from being a Rotarian is immense and also the support of fellow members during times of crisis is a wonderful benefit as I can testify. As you will see in chapter 19, I had occasion to be hospitalised for a quadruple coronary by-pass. During this time neither Mella nor myself had to drive back and forth to Brighton, as transport was provided every day by various members of the Club. This was a great help as Mella dislikes driving in Brighton and I was able to relax in the knowledge that Mella's needs were being well looked after, which I am sure greatly speeded my recovery.

Having completed my year as President, I have reverted to my previous position as editor of the *Gazette*, something that I find most stimulating, especially when I can persuade fellow members of the Club to contribute items for publication.

On an international level, Rotary has been largely responsible for the eradication of polio worldwide, through a programme called 'Polio Plus'. Also Rotary is almost invariably involved in providing aid to people unfortunate enough to be stricken by natural disasters such as hurricanes, earthquakes, etc, etc.

Because there are Rotary Clubs in most corners of the world, it is gratifying to know that when we provide funds for, say, disaster relief in some country or another, we can rely on the local Rotary club to ensure that it all goes where it is intended to go and is not siphoned off by the local 'mafia', as is so often the case. It is for this reason that both Mella and I refuse to support charities that are not administered locally by Rotary.

Just to show that our Club is moving with the times, I must tell you that one of our members has set up a most wonderful website to inform all and sundry of our activities. The site has just won an award, one of only three in the UK, for its brilliance. Judge for yourself by logging on to www.rotarysussex.org

So you can see that if one is minded to be of service to ones fellow human beings, being a member of Rotary is a very good , and fun, way of going about it.

CHAPTER EIGHTEEN

Retirement, If That's
What it's Called!

By 1996 MELLA BEGAN TO FIND looking after Wivelsfield Hall a considerable burden and I was having great difficulty keeping the garden in order, so we decided to sell and move to something more manageable for our retirement years. However the best laid plans of mice and men don't always pan out as you would like them to, and it was October 1998 before a sale was arranged and we then had to find something to move into. Here good fortune was on our side for once and within a week we found our current house. Like Wivelsfield Hall in 1976, it had been on the market for a considerable time, which was surprising as it was one of a few available houses with a *large* double garage capable of housing both the Rolls and Audi. In fact it has the biggest double garage I've ever seen attached to a modern house. Once again I made what I considered a cheeky offer, some £5,000 less than the asking price, and to our amazement (and relief) this was accepted, leaving us wondering what the snag was!

The snags were, in the main, twofold. Firstly the décor was, to say the least, 'tired', and secondly all three doors and seventeen windows were in need of a lot of work to make them all function properly.

As this was to be our retirement home, our policy was to make the place as maintenance-free as possible. To this end we had all the doors, windows, bargeboards and soffits replaced with modern upvc ones that will require no maintenance and are guaranteed for 10 years. We also had the walls filled with rockwool to reduce heating costs, part of the front garden made into a parking area and the garage door was fitted with an electric opening device to make it easier for Mella to open.

The downstairs décor I re-did myself, together with the stairs and landing. Looking ahead to the time when one of us may find getting into a normal bath less than easy, we had the shower unit replaced with a 'walk-in' bath. (I kept the shower pan to convert into a 'sink-garden'). The upstairs décor I left until I had fitted out the garage and completely

*An Autobiography
by Captain
D.B. Hopkins*

redesigned the garden. Fortunately my second heart attack (see Chap. 19) occurred after I had done the garage and garden, but before I had time to redecorate upstairs. This should be done as my next retirement project!

Many of my retired friends have told me how busy they are and that they never seem to have enough hours in the day to do all that they want. How true! And it reminds me of the story of two friends, both retired, who met each other for the first time for a year or two. One asked the other how he was enjoying his retirement, to which he replied that he was extremely busy: 'I play golf, bowls and bridge. I do lots of gardening and crosswords and I walk the dog twice a day. I'm busy all the time! How about you?' To which enquiry his friend said he too was busy, doing research. 'Research?' says the first man. 'Well, its not so much research as investigation,' says his friend, 'I investigate where I've left my spectacles, I investigate where I put my slippers……..!' Nuff said!

However, to get back to my story. Once the garage was fitted out so that I could find the tools or equipment I needed without having to search through the dozens of containers in which everything had been stored during the move, I turned my attention to the garden.

The only 'plan' I had was to make the gardens into easy maintenance areas. I say 'easy' as opposed to 'low' maintenance, as I like gardening and 'low' implies that there will not be a lot to do once the initial redesign has been done. No, my intention was to have a nice interesting garden with seats to relax in, but something to keep my enthusiasm alive over the coming years without too much hard work. Rather than describe in detail the renovation of the gardens (front and rear) as it was carried out, I thought it might be more interesting to take the reader on a tour of the garden with explanations of the plants, plantings and work carried out.

Starting at the front of the house, which faces more or less North (345° if you want to be precise) we have a Hydrangea Petiolaris that had been neglected for many years, so that it had much dead wood to be cut out and practically no flowers because the poor thing had been starved.

After removal of the dead wood and two seasons growth with suitable food, it has now (2001) rewarded us with a magnificent display. The creamy-white corymbs come out in June and the little white male flower petals stay on right through the summer and autumn, although they gradually turn brown.

To the right is a lovely magenta Clematis that is cut down to ground level every winter and which grows to around 9 feet high by mid-summer, sending out side growths that climb through the Hydrangea Petiolaris so that by mid-August it too appears to have magenta flowers. Next we come to the front door that is flanked by two bushes of

Hydrangea Macrophylla. I am uncertain of the variety, but it could well be 'Deutschland'. These two bushes had also been neglected for a number of years, so much so that when we first went to see the house after a shower of rain, both Mella and myself got significantly wet squeezing through the ten-inch gap to get to the front door. It is a very vigorous grower and even after severe pruning each spring, it grows to a considerable height and spread.

On either side are gravel paths crossing the path to the front door, which was made of concrete paving slabs – very dull – until I replaced them with brindle pavers. I found the latter surprisingly easy to do with the aid of a hired plate vibrator, although I must have picked the hottest few days of the year to do it, with the result that Mella had to keep me well supplied with large quantities of cold drinks!

When 'Window Wise' were installing our new doors and windows, they asked if they could display their trade board in the front garden. I was most willing for them to do this, but when they tried to sink a stake in the ground, it would not go in more than about three inches. Bearing this in mind, it did not come as a complete surprise to find what I did when I came to prepare the ground for what is now the Rose garden. Everywhere I tried to dig I hit something extremely solid and what I eventually uncovered was an area about 14 x 6 feet of very thick concrete. After unsuccessfully hitting it with a sledge hammer I had to enlist the help of a local contractor to break it up with a pneumatic drill. I was left with an 18 inch deep hole to fill after the concrete and underlying hard-core had been removed. I will probably never know what its original purpose was, but I reckon it would have been strong enough to park a Boeing 707 on, although the neighbours might have objected to that idea!

Eventually I managed to have a suitable site to make into the rose garden, digging out in the process many red pavers that are now part of the surrounds for the beds containing miniature conifers. The rose garden is divided by narrow paths into four rectangular beds with a circular one in the middle. Each of the beds has one variety of David Austin roses, namely: Gertrude Jekyll, Pat Austin, L.D.Braithwaite, Teasing Georgia, and, in the centre circle, Francois Juranville. The good point about these roses is that they have a repeat-flowering capability, so that one gets blooms from June onwards until October and the coming of frosts.

On coming through the gate into the back garden, the first thing you see is the sink garden made from the old shower pan. The picture shows it as it is now in July 2001. A certain amount of replanting has taken place as some of the plants I put in originally turned out to be unsuitable. It now has something in flower most of the year. How the shower pan was converted may be of interest. First it was covered with a coating of Evostick, followed by a layer of sand/cement in the ratio of 3/1. Then I made up a mixture of sand, peat and cement (4/2/1) and plastered this on by hand rather than a trowel to get the 'antique' look. In the picture you can perhaps see that it is now looking reasonably 'natural'.

To the left of the sink garden is a decked area with a bench seat and a water feature. The latter was not well designed because the water remained in the top bowl, which promptly cracked with the first severe frost. My second effort resembles a stone cairn with water coming through a hole in a large rock on the top, the water being pumped from a sump below by a solar-powered pump. This is very effective and provides sufficient 'water noise' to have a cooling effect on a hot day, without being loud enough to annoy our neighbours.

As you walk up the right hand side of the decking, you can see a number of plants, including Kerria Japonica Pleniflora (Bachelor's Buttons), through which is growing Lonicera Japonica Henryii, Hebe Franciscana Variegata, Dierama Pendulum (Angel's Fishing Rod), Cytisus Burkwoodii (Broom with lovely dark red flowers), Enkianthus Campanulatus (Pagoda Bush), Bergenia Cordifolia (Elephant's Ears), Pulmonaria Saccharata (Lungwort) and Trachelospermum Jasminoides with its white Jasmine-type scented flowers from July to October.

The Pagoda bush is in front of an electricity pole and it is hoped it will disguise it when it grows to its full size of about nine feet. Behind the wall at the back of the decking are some hardy Fuchsia, and behind them is Mahonia 'Charity'. Beyond this is another wall, built entirely of bricks dug up during the renovations, above which is the top terrace. I dug up over 400 of the red bricks and they came in very handy for the beds in the gravel garden, although I must admit to a bit of 'blue air' production while I was digging them up!

On the top terrace there is a quite large red Camellia that I removed from in front of the window to the utility, room from which it was blocking not only the light, but also the path to the back door. I didn't really expect the Camellia to survive the move for two reasons. Firstly it was in full flower and all the best gardening advice is never to move anything in full flower. Secondly, when I dug round the root ball, I found I was quite unable to even rock the bush. This was due, I eventually discovered, to the roots having grown round both sides of a piece of builders rubble weighing some two hundredweights, making it

necessary to cut the roots very severely. Now some two years on it is growing very happily in its new home, proving that the pundit's advice is not always right!

The picture on the right shows the gravel garden, replacing what was a so-called lawn. In the small beds are dwarf conifers of various shapes and colours, some of which change colour between summer and winter. On the left is the pergola garden, which divides the decking 'room' from the patio etc. Wisteria Chinensis is growing up two of the five poles and now, in summer 2001, it is spreading along the top rail and so I hope to have a 'curtain' of sweet

smelling blue flowers next spring. On the left of the shot, between the sunshade and bird table, the solar panel that powers the water feature can be seen attached to the wall of the house.

Around each conifer is a selection of bulbs including: Eranthis Hyemalis (Winter Aconite), Galanthus Nivalis (Snowdrop), Crocus; Fritillaria Meleagris (Snake's Head Fritillary), Muscari (Grape Hyacinth) and some miniature daffodils. I must admit to having second thoughts as to the planting of bulbs around the conifers because the dying foliage tends to look a bit of a mess after the flowers have gone. On balance, though, I think the lovely flowers early in the year out-weigh the disadvantages!

On walking down the path and turning round, you see the view below of the summerhouse/garden shed, with the cold frame I built last year.

Behind the wall on the right is where the big beech tree stood, which we had to have removed for there to be any light in the garden. Fortunately it was not 'preserved' nor are we in a conservation area, but its removal left behind a large stump that was more or less impossible to remove. To cover this I planted a Buddleia Alternifolia, which has

spread as advertised about ten feet in all directions and is a sight for sore eyes when in full bloom in late spring.

Behind this beautiful bush is a Fothergilla Major (Bottle Brush), planted not for its flowers, though these are sweetly scented, but for its autumn foliage, which has orange/yellow/red tints. At the moment it is too small to see, except from the bedroom windows or by a

passing helicopter, having been planted only last spring. In front of this is a Weigela 'Briant Rubidor' which has yellowish foliage and dark red flowers, also too small to see as yet.

Half way down the path back towards the garden gate is a perennial sweet pea, Lathyrus Latifolius, that came with the house so to speak, although it didn't flower much until I gave it some TLC (tender loving care), for which I have been well rewarded.

In my opinion all gardens should have a greenhouse as well as some sort of water feature, and since there was not a lot of room and I had a supply of glass from the secondary glazing taken out when the windows were replaced, I decided to 'custom build' my own. I found out the hard way that you cannot cut old glass with any degree of success, so the structure is designed around the sizes of glass that I had. In the picture of the summerhouse/shed you can see one of these panels in use as the top for the cold frame. This is how it looked before I took off the aluminium surround. Of course 'Sods Law' meant that no two panels were the same size, so construction was rather like a chinese puzzle! However, it provides me with enough space to store my tender Fuchsias during the winter and to start various seeds into growth in the spring. It also collects rainwater – what more could you ask when the cost was virtually nothing?

If you are a gardener, you will know that a garden is never *finished* and mine is no exception. I already have plans for a few changes – in particular where I made the mistake of planting some Rhododendrons in the front, where it is far too dry for them to do any good at all. I said the garden was 'easy' maintenance, but that doesn't mean there is nothing to do!

How else am I going to keep busy, when I already know where my slippers and spectacles are?

CHAPTER NINETEEN

The Forsyth Saga

I N CHAPTER 14 I related how my flying career came to an untimely end due to a heart attack. That was in 1980/81 and fortunately for the next 20 years or thereabouts I had no further trouble, despite exerting myself in no small measure in maintaining my fleet of cars, moving house in 1998, and getting my new house and garden into order.

Early in 2000 I started to get very much out of breath walking back uphill with my dog, something I did twice every day. On the 23rd February this breathlessness was accompanied by a severe chest pain that did not go away when I stopped walking. The net result of this was that I found myself in the Princess Royal Hospital for six days recovering from heart attack number 2!

After presenting myself in A & E, I was set upon by a whole team, and some three hours later, after numerous tests (blood pressure; ECG; chest X-ray; blood test; etc) I was given an injection of a warfarin-type drug to thin the blood and then taken to the Coronary Care Unit (CCU), where I found myself in a bed next to a delightful old gentleman of 89 called Edgar Spillett. After we had introduced ourselves, I discovered that he used to be head gardener to Sir Stephen Tallents (Director General of the BBC during WW II and well known contributor to the *Sunday Times*, particularly on the subject of moles) who lived at St. John's Jerusalem in Sutton-at-Hone, near Dartford in Kent. This made my ears prick up, since my parents had a house in this very village and it was where I lived from 1949 to 1952 until I left home to join the RAF. It transpired that Edgar had been born in and lived in a cottage next to where I lived, making us neighbours some 50 years ago. Small world isn't it? Edgar was quite a philosopher and remarked to me one day that although getting old had many disadvantages, he found it quite delightful to be able to look back on so many happy memories.

All the four days we were ward mates, neither Edgar nor I could walk further than around our beds, since we were tethered to a monitor to record the behaviour of our hearts. If one accidentally, or on

An Autobiography
by Captain
D.B. Hopkins

purpose, disconnected the lead, a nurse would dash in and remonstrate with the offender. I was moved out of the main ward to a side ward so that a bed with a monitor was available for somebody else. This somebody turned out to be an Irishman, as t'ick as the proverbial Kerryman! First of all he decided that he wanted to go to the loo, so he just pulled off the three plugs and was wandering out of the ward by the time the nurse caught and re-tethered him.

The following day no less than three (only two allowed at one time) of his fellow 'Kerrymen' arrived – outside visiting hours – and proceeded to unfasten his tether and start to take him 'for a walk'! To the pub I imagine.

Another patient, an elderly lady, who was quite obviously 'past it', kept wandering around the entire ward, so much so, that one of the nurses was permanently employed to shepherd her back to her bed, demonstrating that nurses need to have the patience of saints!

There was seldom a dull moment in the CCU. As the 29th of February approached, the talk turned to the opportunity the ladies, both patients and nurses, would have to propose to any eligible bachelors. At this time one of my fellow inmates called Pamela announced that she had just celebrated her Golden Wedding and that now she was no longer married. This seemed odd as her husband had visited the evening before. All became clear when she informed us that when she gave wedding vows it was 'until death us do part or 50 years, whichever was the sooner'!! Her husband had played along with this and presented her with a beautiful eternity ring that she was proudly wearing instead of her wedding ring.

Now that I was able to wander about freely, I witnessed each evening a remarkable sight. My room looked out over an enclosed area planted with a variety of shrubs and trees. At dusk I could hear the clamour of many birds coming to roost. They turned out to be pied wagtails, hundreds of them, that gathered on the roof before flying down to the bushes, where they were safe from predators and sheltered from the worst of the weather. The noise they made jostling for the best positions to spend the night was almost deafening. I never saw them in the morning, so I imagine they all left at first light.

Each day I was given injections of 'warfarin', to the extent that my tum looked like a pin-cushion. When I got home I joined up all the dots, rather like a child's drawing book and found that it read 'EAT LESS FAT'. Point taken!

In May I went down to the Royal Sussex County Hospital in Brighton for an angiogram, or cardiac catheterisation as I believe it is now called. I must say that many advances in this technique had been made since my first one at Kings College Hospital in 1981. In June I was seen by Mr Andy Forsyth, senior cardiothoracic surgeon, who informed me that I needed at least a quadruple, maybe quintuple, by-pass operation and that the waiting list was about six to eight months.

During the waiting time I kept myself as fit as possible by walking up to two or three miles a day, albeit with a degree of breathlessness, and on the 21st February 2001 I went down to the RSC hospital for a pre-admission clinic. At this my chest x-ray revealed an inexplicable shadow on the bottom of my right lung, so on 5th March I was yet again at the RSC hospital, this time for a CT scan, which showed that the 'shadow' was nothing more than a cyst on my right kidney, apparently a quite common phenomenon at my age!

Great news came on 15th March when I was told that my operation would take place on 3rd April, but on 30th March I learned that due to the large number of emergencies that had been admitted, my admittance was delayed until 23rd April. Very disappointing, but when I did get into the RSC on the 23rd April and saw the condition of some of those who were waiting, I could quite see why my relatively non-urgent case could safely be postponed.

On my admittance on 23rd April, I was told that my operation would not take place until the 25th, then this was put back to the 26th and on Friday 27th I was sent home on leave for the weekend with instructions to return on 30th. During this week I was able to observe at first hand the reasons for all these delays. For instance the High Dependency Unit (HDU) has four beds and each patient is expected to spend around 24/48 hours there after their operation. One man who came into the bed opposite mine had been in the HDU for no less than eight days, from which you can see why these unforeseen delays occur. One could argue that the HDU should have double the number of beds, but then when things were going normally many of them would be empty and that, it is obvious, would be a complete waste of resources.

However I made good use of my waiting time by acting as paper boy for the ward together with a fellow patient, Peter, who was in much the same boat as me. One morning a lady from the next bay came in to order her paper and asked Peter to get the SUN instead of the MIRROR as the latter was too intellectual! That has to be the classic comment of the year, especially as she meant it!

On 30th April I returned to my bed in bay 3 of ward 6A and when Mr Forsyth came to tell me that my operation would not be on the Tuesday I took the opportunity to ask him if he would object to my title for this chapter. Fortunately he was quite amused by the idea. The following day Dr Bedda told me I would be first in theatre on Thursday 3rd May. Hooray! At last I'll be on the road to to recovery and to being my normal self! Mr Ramanan came along to get me to sign the consent form and asked if I had any questions about the procedure, to which I replied that I was somewhat mystified as to how the actual grafts were made 'blood tight'. He explained that it was done entirely by stitching with <u>very</u> fine sutures and that when complete was, as he put it, 'Water tight, blood tight and rat tight'!

Accordingly on the Wednesday night I had yet another shower using 'hibiscrub', a type of antiseptic liquid soap, and after a good night's sleep, I was awoken at 0530 to have another hibiscrub shower and a notice was displayed on my bed, 'NIL BY MOUTH'. Just before 0800 I was transferred to a trolley for the trip upstairs to the anaesthetic room and after my arrival there I remember nothing more until I came round in the HDU. I learned later that the operation lasted from 0800 until 1330 and that I had, in fact, had four grafts not five. To my relief I also found that the necessary new 'pipework' had been found by utilising two arteries from my left arm plus the two mammary arteries from inside my chest wall. As someone pointed out, the latter are somewhat surplus to requirements among us chaps, but of course my tits are now useless!

I was accompanied up to theatre by a young trainee nurse called Sue, who had been to see me the previous evening to ask my permission for her to watch the entire procedure as part of her training – of course I said yes – and her happy smiling face together with that of Tracey, my HDU nurse, was one of the first things I saw when I came round afterwards.

At about 0800 on the Friday Mr Ramanan appeared at my feet, grabbed hold of both of them and said, 'Feel these!' Then Mr Forsyth had a go and agreed that they were lovely and warm and that I could go back to ward 6A forthwith. It was only later, when I was more 'compos mentis', that I worked out that warm feet meant that the 'pump' was working well. So back to 6A I was taken having been out of it for barely 24 hours, proving that sometimes things do go according to plan, or even better! Come lunchtime I selected fish and chips from the menu and when Mella arrived later to find me sitting in a chair, having had a brief walk around the ward with the physio, I think she thought I was joking when I told her of my lunch! Well Friday's fish isn't it?

On Saturday I was taken off oxygen and by evening all my drips had also been taken away, leaving only the stitches to be removed from where the drains were at the bottom of my chest. These were in fact removed just before I went home on the Tuesday, only five days after the operation.

I've gone into the details of my by-pass at some length in the hope that it might lend encouragement to anyone reading this before they too have the same. I would say that two things under my control contributed greatly to my rapid recovery – firstly I was as fit as could be in the circumstances and secondly I had a very positive attitude. With these and a wonderful team of surgeons, doctors and nurses, you are more or less guaranteed to make a full and rapid recovery to normal.

Whilst I was waiting, from 3rd April onwards, one of my friends asked why I didn't have the operation privately, something which I could quite easily have afforded. There are several reasons why I would not have pursued this option. Firstly I have been paying into the NHS since it started and I have a rooted objection to paying for something twice, but much more importantly is the fact that by sticking with the NHS I could be sure that I would be treated in what I believe to be the most up-to-date facility in the country and by the best surgeons. Another reason for not going private, as far as I'm concerned, is the fact that privately one would be in a private ward with virtually no-one to talk to, whereas in a NHS ward there is always going to be a number of others who are in the same boat and in my limited experience I have found many interesting people to talk to. All this helps to make the time pass more quickly, keeps up one's morale and generally speeds one's recovery. The proof of the pudding is in the eating and I am writing this just 18 days since my operation. Already I am able to walk my dog twice a day and generally lead a pretty normal life. What more could I ask?

The morning of 3rd May was a beautiful one with clear blue skies, the sort of morning that makes you glad to be alive, and while I was waiting to be taken up to the anaesthetic room, I was humming the Eton Boating Song to myself and thinking that I might adapt it to become a tribute to everyone in the Royal Sussex County Hospital's Cardiothoracic unit who had made my stay successful and enjoyable:

BRIGHTON PLUMBING SONG

Jolly plumbing weather,
And a heart by-pass breeze,
Scalpels at the ready,
Surgeons just like these,
Plumb, plumb together,
Working in teams of threes.

Twenty years hence this weather
Will remind me of Andy Forsyth,
And I'll be quick to remember
Ramanan, Bedda and pals,
Who all plumbed together
At the best of hospitals!

*An Autobiography
by Captain
D.B. Hopkins*

That's more or less the end of the Forsyth Saga, and now my ambition is to outlive my paternal great-grandmother, who lived to be four months short of 100. I see no reason why I shouldn't achieve it, but you will have to hang around for the next 30 years to see if I do manage it!

There is one other thing I want to mention, however, and that is the reason why I should have had this problem with my plumbing. In the excellent booklet provided by the Brighton Health Care NHS Trust for the benefit of patients attending the cardiac centre, there is a list of the 'risk factors' in relation to heart disease. They are as follows, with my comments as to how they apply to me:

Smoking – I have never smoked;
Family history – None;
High blood pressure – Mine has always been around normal;
Not coping with stress – Not a problem with me;
Lack of exercise – I've always taken loads of exercise;
High cholesterol – maybe;
Overweight – No;
Too much alcohol – I've only ever drunk in moderation.

So from the above I cannot be said to be a prime candidate for heart disease and the reason (there must be one!) why I have suffered in this direction has puzzled me ever since my first episode in 1980/81. I have said to several doctors that I consider that there must be another factor, as yet unknown, that could have a bearing on the subject.

Now I think I may have stumbled across a possible causal factor. I read in the paper shortly before I had my operation of some research in the USA that suggested that any baby that was breast fed for more than four months was likely to have a propensity for furring of the arteries in later life. Unfortunately I cannot prove that I was breast fed for more than this length of time since both my parents are dead, but it seems highly probable given their circumstances in 1930. I know for certain that my mother had to sell her engagement ring to be able to buy baby food for me, so it seems to be highly likely that she breast fed me for a long time out of sheer economic necessity. At the moment this theory appeals to me as the most likely reason for my problem and until I hear of some better idea, I shall consider this to be the most plausible cause of my situation.

If this be the case, it will be a relief to my three sons and four grandsons who should not have cause for concern that they might inherit the condition from me.

27th June 2001. As a postscript to this chapter I must mention, with a great deal of satisfaction, that I had my final check-up with Mr Forsyth today and he told me I was 'disgustingly healthy' and there is absolutely no reason why I shouldn't achieve my ambition to live to be 100! He told me that I should forget I've ever had an operation and to live my life as if I'd never had a problem in the first place. He also indicated that keeping the mind active was another vital factor.

I showed him my theory for my ever having a problem in the hope that he would tell me if he thought it was arrant nonsense – but he agreed with me that it was a perfectly possible theory, although as yet to be proved. YCNSTWLEM!

19th July 2001 – As a further postscript I am happy to tell the reader that after completing eight sessions of exercises at the cardiac rehabilitation centre of the Princess Royal Hospital, I am now fitter than at any time in the last 20 or more years. In order to stay in this happy state I have bought a bicycle and am frequently to be seen haring along the local highways and byways, although I'm not usually 'haring' on my way home as I live on the top of a hill and the return journey is inevitably uphill. Now that I'm getting used to riding again after a lapse of some 40 years, I often 'feel' the same age as I was when I last rode a bike, that is until I'm overtaken by some young blood in his or her twenties!

*An Autobiography
by Captain
D.B. Hopkins*

CHAPTER TWENTY

Highlights and How
I Stroked A Cheetah

T o ROUND OFF MY STORY, I'd like to mention a few my life's highlights, some of which I have already covered and some that I haven't. And finally, to satisfy your curiosity, comes the explanation for the rather odd title.

When I was six I had a small set of gauge 'O' Hornby trains and my most earnest desire was to have a guard's van, so you can imagine my delight on Christmas morning, at about 4 am, when after badgering my parents, I was allowed to open a most interesting-feeling box poking out of the top of the stocking fixed to the end of my bed. In it was my heart's desire – a brown guard's van complete with opening doors. Waiting from 4 am until I could get up and play with it seemed a very long time indeed, as time does when one is very young!

In the year following while I was still six and Steven was getting on for two, Father came home from Greenhithe one evening carefully carrying a brown paper carrier bag, in which we were very excited to find a tabby kitten. This had been given to us by Mr Fogg, who was the groundsman at HMS *Worcester*, which explains why we christened her 'Misty'! As far as I can remember, she lived to a ripe old age, for she was still part of the family when we moved to Sutton-at-Hone in 1951.

While we were at Sidcup, we acquired 'Panda', a cross between a spaniel and lord-knows-what. She was mainly white but had a black patch over one eye, hence her name, and she was a constant companion when we were out collecting food for the rabbits and goats during the war. The goats became quite tame and one in particular used to jump on to the coal bunker outside the kitchen and stick her head through the window.

Gaining my School Certificate and Higher School Certificate in 1946 and 1948 respectively, the latter giving me exemption from Inter B.Sc., were two memorable occasions, as was the letter of reference from Dr McGregor Williams, my headmaster, that is reproduced on page 205. I

UNIVERSITY OF LONDON
GENERAL SCHOOL EXAMINATION

SCHOOL CERTIFICATE

This is to certify that......HENRY BRYAN HOPKINS
born 8 December 1930... a pupil at...Chislehurst and Sidcup County
......Grammar School for Boys
was awarded the School Certificate of the University of London in Midsummer, 1946,
having satisfied the Examiners in the Examination as a whole and having attained in the
following five subjects the standards shown :—

English	Credit
Geography	Pass
French, written and oral	Pass
Elementary Mathematics	Credit
Physics	Pass

(The highest standard of award in individual subjects is "Very Good.")

Signed on behalf of the University of London,

Secretary for School Examinations.

The Ministry of Education accept the Examination as reaching the approved standard.

Signed on behalf of the Ministry of Education,

G. G. Williams

Deputy Secretary.

UNIVERSITY OF LONDON

HIGHER SCHOOL CERTIFICATE

This is to certify that.......HENRY BRYAN HOPKINS
born 8 December 1930 ...a pupil at...Chislehurst and Sidcup County
......Grammar School for Boys
passed the Higher School Examination of the University of London at Midsummer
1948, and in Group I... satisfied the Examiners in the following Main Subjects at
the standards shown :—

Physics	Pass
Chemistry	Pass at Subsidiary Standard
Pure Mathematics	Pass
Applied Mathematics	Pass

(In Main Subjects there are four standards of success :— Distinction, Good, Pass, and
Pass at Subsidiary Standard.)

Signed on behalf of the University of London,

Secretary for School Examinations.

The Ministry of Education accepts the Examination as reaching the approved standard.

Signed on behalf of the Ministry of Education,

Under-Secretary.

don't include this as any form of 'trumpet blowing', but solely to show the perspicacity of Dr Williams.

I find this letter, which I have only re-read during the time I've been writing my story, particularly interesting. Bearing in mind the fact that Dr Williams rarely, if ever, taught a class (I certainly cannot remember him ever teaching me) his character assessment was pretty spot on. Is this one of the attributes of a good headmaster? I think it must be. Certainly the school was very well run in spite of the fact that most of the young masters had been 'called-up' and their replacements were, it seemed to me at the time, beyond retiring age. Notwithstanding this, discipline at the school was never a problem and form size was always above the current trendy figure of thirty, except in the sixth forms where the figure was roughly half in each of the 'Arts' and 'Science' faculties. I have often wondered why such dogmatic emphasis is put on the magic 'thirty' as if achieving it would solve all educational problems.

Moving on, the next highlight was failing my degree in chemistry. You may think me odd considering a failure as a highlight, but it gave me a perfect excuse to abandon chemistry as a career and join the Royal Air Force. Thus my next real highlight was being accepted for pilot training. This was followed by being allowed to go solo in a Tiger Moth at the end of my 'grading', which, in turn, was followed by passing my basic and advanced flying courses and the award of my 'Wings'. A highlight indeed!

I've jumped ahead slightly because during my advanced course there was a highlight to beat all other highlights. I met Pamela Harley, who, as described in chapter six, I eventually married and we shall soon be celebrating our 46th anniversary. This was followed, in 1957, with the birth of Trevor, in 1959 with the arrival of Christopher and in 1963 that of Austen.

During the rest of my RAF career there were many highlights, such as becoming top of the bombing ladder on 9 Squadron; being selected to go to CFS and become an instructor; getting on the short list for a place on the Empire Test Pilots School course, which happened during my time instructing at Swinderby; becoming a CFS Examiner on

KENT EDUCATION COMMITTEE.

Dr. C. R. McG. WILLIAMS, M.A.
HEADMASTER.

CHISLEHURST & SIDCUP
COUNTY Grammar SCHOOL FOR BOYS,
FOOTSCRAY.
SIDCUP. KENT.

6th October 1948

It gives me great pleasure to say a few words in behalf of Derek Bryan Hopkins who was a pupil of this school from October 1940 to July 1948. He came here in the Pre-School and showed, immediately, the quality of his work. His school record proves that he was capable of very good work. He took the Form Prize in 1943-44. He was successful in gaining his School Certificate of London University in 1946, when his best performance was in English and Mathematics. He succeeded in gaining his Higher School Certificate in July 1948, with exemption from Intermediate B.Sc. (London). He took a full share in school societies, was a most energetic secretary of the Science Club, a member of the Chess Club and the School Committee 1947-48.

He was elected Vice-Captain of "C" House.

He preferred tennis to cricket and was a member of the swimming team.

I understand he wishes to pursue an Engineering course. He is a boy of forthright character, capable of great perseverance and application. He is of good address and very pleasant manners. He possesses qualities which should carry him a long way. I wish my former pupil and friend every success.

C. R. McGregor Williams
M.A., D.Litt.

Canberras and, somewhat vicariously, being told after it was cancelled that I was to have been the first instructor on the TSR2.

Next comes my appointment as a commander on CL44 aircraft with Tradewinds and during those years there were many memorable highlights involving the three boys, including the time when I took them all for a short flight on a CL44. I have been asked over the years if I was disappointed that none of the three wanted to follow in my footsteps and become a pilot. I can honestly say I wasn't, as I've always taken the view that it is better for sons to follow their own chosen career rather than try to live up to a standard set by their father's career. I always said to them, 'I don't mind what you do, as long as you do it to the best of your ability.' And they have!

Probably the last highlight of my flying career was flying the Boeing 707 and, in particular, being the only person to land one at night at Lasham. If you wonder why this is such a highlight, go and see the runway at Lasham – it is near Alton, Hampshire. Then imagine it pitch dark and lit only with wartime type goose-neck flares and you'll probably see my point!

The next highlight was my heart attack in 1980/81 – well I survived it, didn't I? This was followed by making a success of IPCS, in spite of one or two pessimists who predicted that I wouldn't! I must add here that without Mella running 'mission control' there is no doubt that our success would not have been so great.

Also there springs to mind the fun of winning the Section Prize of the RREC during my tenure as Section Secretary.

In more recent times our finding our present home at such a ridiculous price must definitely be called a highlight, as must my second heart attack in February 2000 – Well I've lived to tell the tale haven't I?

And the very latest is the success of my quadruple heart by-pass in May 2001, for which I shall be eternally grateful to the superb skills of Mr Forsyth, Mr Ramanan and all their team at the Royal Sussex County Cardiac Centre. I am writing this just nine weeks after the event and I am now as fit as I was when I was forty, with every chance, as Mr Forsyth told me, of achieving my ambition to live to 100!

The above are just a few of the highlights of an eventful and happy life and another is stroking a cheetah!

Some time in the mid 1970s I was scheduled to fly a full CL44 down to Nairobi. Unusually the charterer and his wife were to travel with us. I was able to see that they enjoyed their flight by having them on the flight deck as much as possible and when we eventually got to Nairobi after having refuelled in Cairo, they kindly invited us to have dinner with them at their farm outside Nairobi. Try as I may, I cannot remember their names, but their farm was called Whispers Farm. When the three of us, myself, the first officer and the flight engineer, got there, we were invited into the garden behind what was essentially two bunga-lows joined by a covered verandah. Almost immediately we were invited to meet Tigger, who was let out from his quarters in the verandah. Surprisingly, perhaps, I felt no fear of him, just wonderment and I went straight to him and stroked him on the neck and back, just as if he were a domestic cat. He immediately started to purr, a noise I can only equate with the sound of a powerful motorbike engine ticking over! This went on for some minutes until our hosts let out their two Labrador dogs, who thought it a good idea to 'wind up' Tigger. He was having nothing to do with them and, with his nose in the air, stalked off to find a quiet spot for a nap. Thus ended my meeting and stroking a cheetah. It seems that my hosts had found him as a kitten, more or less abandoned as he had been born with only one eye and would undoubtedly not have last-ed very long in the wild.

Unfortunately I did not have a camera with me when I met 'Tigger', so the picture is of a cheetah very like him.

In case you feel inclined to go out to Kenya and adopt a cheetah for yourself, I should mention that the law in that country will not allow you to do so unless the animal has been born with some defect that would cause it not to survive in the wild.

Stroking Tigger was probably the greatest privilege of my life and if nothing more of note happens during the rest of my time, I shall be content to look back at my memories, which Edgar Spillett reckons is one of the benefits of getting old. And now you know the reason for the strange title of my book. I do hope you have enjoyed living some of my adventures with me!

*An Autobiography
by Captain
D.B. Hopkins*

ANNEXE A

Low Flying Instructional Guide

STRIKE SQUADRON EXERCISE No 23 Reconnaissance Squadron Exercise No 32

References

A – MoD Flying Orders 102, 311 to 315 incl
B – No 3 Group Air Staff Instructions, Section 3, Order 7
C – MoD Flying Orders No 119
D – MATO Low Flying Handbook
E – No 3 Group Air Staff Instructions, Section 3, Order 18

Introduction

1. Low flying is defined as flying sufficiently close to the ground to give a true impression of speed.
2. The present role of the Canberra Force requires a considerable amount of low flying and it is therefore imperative that all crew are thoroughly versed in the basic aspects of operating at low level.
3. Although modern aids and reliability of equipment make it unlikely there is nevertheless still the possibility of having to fly low because of bad weather. This aspect is covered briefly.

Regulations

4. The regulations pertaining to low flying may be studied in references A and B and are therefore not repeated here. Suffice it

*An Autobiography
by Captain
D.B. Hopkins*

to say that all low flying must be properly authorised and the appropriate low flying areas and routes booked at 'Operations'.

Public Relations

5. Although low flying practice is essential and special areas and routes are set aside for training, it is good manners and common sense to avoid disturbing the local population, both human and animal, as far as possible. Reference C should also be studied.

Pre-Flight Map Study

6. As high speed low flying demands absolute concentration from all crew members the area and route must be thoroughly studied before getting airborne. Such things as landmarks, towns, hazards, prohibited and danger areas should be memorized so that a brief look at the map is sufficient reminder whilst airborne. See reference D.

7. Although student navigators are instructed in map study during their ground school phase, it is the responsibility of the QFI to ensure that before the student crew fly on a low level exercise they know what to study on the map. It is worth bearing in mind that that most students will have little experience of low level map reading, especially at high speed.

Fuel

8. The fuel consumption of the Canberra at low level is 62 lb/min without tip tanks and 72 lb/min with tip tanks flying at 250 knots. This gives, in the T4, an endurance of little over 90 minutes if the aircraft is to be overhead base with 4000lb of fuel.

9. From the foregoing it is obvious that the student crew must become fuel conscious and that checks on the fuel state must be made at regular and frequent intervals.

Height

10. The height at which a particular sortie will be flown will depend on the weather, terrain, operational necessity and crew proficiency. At the OCU the minimum heights are laid down in

current orders and may be varied from time to time. However the dual exercise should be flown at 250 feet AGL if possible to obtain maximum benefit.

11. Because of its errors, the pressure altimeter cannot always be relied upon. Therefore in the absence a radio or radar altimeter the pilot must maintain the correct height <u>Above Ground Level</u> by use of his own judgement, which can be perfected only by experience. Before descending to low level, Regional QNH must be set on all altimeters.

Effect of Wind

12. Movement over the ground is more apparent when low flying than at more normal altitudes. When flying at low speed upwind or downwind the decrease or increase in ground speed may be noticeable, but at the normal operating speeds of the Canberra the effect will be negligible.

13. Turns made near the ground will also be affected by the wind and, in particular, turns into wind from downwind will have a larger effective radius than would normally be expected. This must be allowed for when turning to avoid an obstacle.

Turning Performance

14. It is only when low flying that the size of the turning circle becomes evident and, because of the need to avoid obstacles, of real importance. As a rule of thumb it can be said that in a rate 1 turn the radius of the turning circle in miles is approximately equal to one third of the TAS in miles per minute. For example, at 240 knots or 4 miles per minute, the radius is one and one third miles.

Minimum Radius Turns

15. Consider a hypothetical 'ideal' aircraft, that is one without 'g' or structural limitations, or compressibility effects and with a very high thrust weight ratio. To achieve a minimum radius turn a combination of the following is required:
    a. Maximum angle of bank
    b. Maximum angle of attack (i.e. at the verge of the buffet)
    c. Maximum IAS obtainable

*An Autobiography
by Captain
D.B. Hopkins*

d. Maximum thrust.

Because the Canberra is by no means 'ideal', the conditions for minimum radius have to be modified to:

a. Maximum angle of bank consistent with b, c and d below

b Maximum loading with maximum angle of attack (i.e. 4g at the verge of the buffet)

c. An IAS that will enable 4g to be held at the verge of the buffet

d. Sufficient thrust to maintain c in a level turn. This may be full throttle.

Theory states that the manoeuvre stalling speed (V_{sm}) is a function of basic stalling speed (V_s) and load factor (LF). The equation is $V_{sm} = V_s \times LF^{-2}$. For a Canberra at 32,500lb AUW V_s = 85 kts. Therefore for a turn at maximum loading, $V_{sm} = 85 \times 4^{-2} = 170$ kts. In practice however, it is found that a higher speed is required to hold 4g on the verge of the buffet and in the T4 it is in the range of 180 to 200 kts, depending on AUW. This is because the aircraft is held at the verge of the buffet and not stalled.

Turning to Avoid an Obstacle

16.   When turning to avoid an obstacle the main consideration is the distance travelled while the turn is being initiated rather than the radius of the turn that is eventually established. This distance depends on the speed because of the inertia problem and the length of time required to roll on bank. Because of the adverse yaw produced when aileron is used, and the aileron control system, judicious use of rudder will greatly facilitate entry into turns. When the need arises to turn quickly whilst flying at high speed, the following technique is recommended. Close the throttles and open the airbrakes, start applying bank using rudder to assist aileron and as the speed approaches the optimum (180 – 200 kts), close the airbrakes, increase RPM to maximum and loading to 4g, whilst maintaining maximum angle of bank. The restriction of not more than 2g with aileron applied must be observed.

Turbulence

17.   Low flying in conditions of moderate or severe turbulence should be avoided as the fatigue life of the aircraft will be drastically reduced and the crew will tire quickly. When operational

circumstances demand low flying under these circumstances, if at all possible, fly at the appropriate turbulence speed as given in Pilots' Notes.

Flying over the Sea

18.   Flying low over the sea presents two problems that are not encountered over land, namely: height judgement can be difficult especially over a glassy calm and salt spray from a rough sea may cover the canopy and impair visibility from the cockpit. For obvious reasons, it may be advisable to fly a little higher than normal when the above conditions exist. On relatively frequent occasions there may be no definite horizon and extra care must be taken, especially when turning.

Flying over Sand

19.   The two main problems associated with low flying in sandy regions are firstly, the possibility of rising sand which will drastically reduce visibility and secondly, lack of relief makes it possible to approach rising ground without appreciating it. In particularly featureless areas it is inadvisable to fly below 250 feet AGL not only because of these problems, but because it is possible to become hypnotised and get much closer to the ground than one realises.

Flying over Snow

20.   Flying low over snow is similar in many respects to flying low over sea or sand. Lack of relief and a changed terrain after fresh snow must be allowed for. Many landmarks may be obliterated or completely changed in appearance and in certain conditions the snow-covered ground and the sky may merge into a single white surface known as a 'white out'. If faced with these conditions and the exact whereabouts of the ground is in doubt, the aircraft must be climbed away on instruments. Reference E should also be studied.

*An Autobiography
by Captain
D.B. Hopkins*

Radio Aids

21. Radio reception is adversely affected by low altitude and the higher the frequency the more it is affected. Thus if radio reception or transmission is vital the aircraft may have to be climbed to get the necessary range from the radio equipment.

Lookout

22. It is stating the obvious to say that a sharp lookout is very important when low flying. Nevertheless it must still be said. In order that the minimum time is spent looking inside the cockpit while at low level, a careful check should be made before descending. Special attention must be paid to such things as fuel state, stowage of loose articles and ensuring that harness is tight.

Birds

23. The hazard of bird strikes is well known but no method of avoiding them has yet been found. However, avoiding areas where birds are known to congregate and the times when they leave from and return to nesting or roosting sites, i.e. dawn and dusk, will reduce the chances of a bird strike. Similarly flying in certain areas during the migratory seasons, which are notified by NOTAM, should be avoided whenever possible. If following other aircraft along a route, one should expect to encounter more bird activity, as the leading aircraft will have disturbed the bird population.

24. By the time a bird is seen to be in the flight path of the aircraft, it is usually too late to take effective avoiding action. Turning is out of the question in the time available and descending is obviously dangerous. This leaves climbing, which may be useful especially as birds usually break downwards when a collision is imminent.

Low Level Map Reading

25. A comprehensive précis on low level technique is issued to navigators during the ground school phase and they have some five lectures on the subject. However, as this is their first opportunity to put theory into practice it is important that the

QFI discusses with the whole crew the methods of map reading as a crew.

26. Because the navigator cannot see outside from the back of a T4 he should be encouraged to use the 'commentary' system, where he map reads and the pilot looks for the features. This system can be adapted for use in the B2/PR3 Where both pilot and navigator can see out, but where it is impractical for the pilot to hold a map and fly the aircraft. Nevertheless, the pilot should carry the appropriate maps with him.

27. The system used on the squadron will depend on the mark of the aircraft and whether the crew has one or two navigators. Therefore crews must be prepared to be adaptable when they leave the OCU.

Bad Weather Low Flying

28. If forced to fly low because of poor weather conditions speed should be reduced to 170 kts and the flaps kept up. This gives best endurance and good manoeuvrability.

Weather Deterioration

29. If the exercise has to be discontinued because of bad weather, climb to at least the minimum safe flight level and return to base. NB: If flying under controlled airspace when the sortie is abandoned, the appropriate rules must be observed and control obtained as soon as possible from the appropriate authority.

Procedure When Uncertain of Position

30. If at any time the navigator becomes uncertain of his position, climb to 3000 feet AMSL or to the nearest quadrantal above safety height. If an accurate position using all available aids can be determined within ten minutes, a descent may be made to continue low level; otherwise return to base.

*An Autobiography
by Captain
D.B. Hopkins*

Low Flying Air Exercise

Sequence	Observations

Sequence

Observations

1. Book area and route at Operations.

  a. Ensure the student understands the method of booking, the significance of his clearance number and the importance of estimating his entry time accurately.

2. Study the route with the whole crew.

  a. Point out the likely hazards including:
    1. High ground
    2. Pylons and TV masts
    3. Airfields
    4. Known areas of bird activity

  b. Point out the features that are most likely to be of use at low level, noting particularly which can be used for timing and which for track checks.

3. Fly to the appropriate low flying area and let down.

  a. If weather permits fly between 2000 and 3000ft on Regional QNH and map read to the low flying area.

  b. If weather is unsuitable for 3a fly to a convenient airfield and descend under their control, remembering that this will need arranging before the flight.

  c. Before descending below 2000ft:
    1. Check position and that Regional QNH has been set.
    2. Select fuel pumps as required and check fuel contents.
    3. Ensure harness is tight and that loose articles are stowed.
    4. Check compasses.
    5. Inform controlling authority of entry time into low flying area.

  d. Descend in a turn keeping a good lookout on both sides

The Extraordinary Story of a Very Ordinary Person

4.. Descend to 250 ft AGL (this can be done in stages, levelling off at 1000ft and 500ft initially if the instructor wishes).	a. Height is estimated by reference to ground features. b. Compare radii of turns at 30° and 45°. (NB 30° gives a radius of approximately 13 miles, which is the radius used by navigators for planning a low level sortie).
5. Starting at a convenient point fly round the low level route. Assist with map reading as required.	a. Accurate headings and speeds are most important. b. Absolute reliance must be put on the navigator's timing if a turning point is not found. c. If seemingly off track make no attempt to regain it until a second observation confirms the fact, then alter heading to regain track at the next check point, or, if a well defined feature known to be on track can be seen far enough ahead 'S' turn to fly over it. d. The navigator reminds the pilot of what to look for at the next turning point early during each leg. e. Fuel must be checked after each turning point but not during the turn when 'eyes must be outside the cockpit'. f. Before turning, set the new heading on the G4B compass. g. After turning carry out a compass check. h. Turns are made with 30° to 40° of bank, the aim being to keep on track by using the correct (13 miles) radius of turn.
6. Pick an easily discernable ground feature and fly over it at 250' and 150, 250 and 350kts in turn, each time starting a turn of 60° of bank as the aircraft passes over the ground feature.	a. At 150kts the aircraft is easily turned and has a small radius of turn. The time and effort needed to apply bank is small. b. At 250kts bank is more difficult and takes longer to apply, and the radius of turn is increased. However the aircraft can still be flown with one hand.

An Autobiography
by Captain
D.B. Hopkins

c.   At 350kts bank takes a considerable time and effort to apply and the radius of turn is very much increased. The aircraft now needs to be flown with both hands on the control column.

d.   The LABS modified aircraft is lighter on the elevator and aileron controls than the unmodified version.

7. Allow the student to reduce speed to 170kts.

a.   This is endurance speed. The aircraft's also very manoeuvrable so 170kts is the speed recommended for bad weather low flying.

8. Demonstrate and let the student practice a minimum radius turn.

a.   Maximum angle of bank is required (about 85°)

b.   Full power is required once bank is applied.

c.   The aircraft is flown just on the buffet with 4g registered on the accelerometer.

d.   Not more than 2g must be applied while large amounts of aileron are being applied.

e.   Speed increases to and stabilises at around 180 to 200 kts.

f.   A little rudder may be used to assist entry.

g.   If the aircraft is not held on the verge of the buffet it will accelerate above minimum radius speed and it is impossible to regain the minimum radius turn without first decelerating or overstressing the aircraft.

h.   Note the ability to 'turn on a sixpence'.

i.   If the turn is entered at a higher speed, it is possible to over-stress the aircraft and so great care must be taken.

9. Allow the student to practice entering a minimum radius turn at a high speed, say 300kts.

a.   Close the throttles and extend the airbrakes.

b.   Enter the turn as in sequence 8, taking care not to exceed 4g, closing the airbrakes and applying full power as the speed approaches the optimum for a minimum radius turn.

c.   Rudder will greatly reduce the time taken to initiate the turn.

*The Extraordinary
Story of a Very
Ordinary Person*

10. Set heading for base and while still at low level throttle back an engine simulating a bird strike, fire or mechanical failure.	a. The aircraft should be climbed using no more than 1½ g so that 1000ft is reached as quickly as possible consistent with the navigator being able to get back to his seat.
	b. Speed should not be allowed to decrease below the minimum recommended for hatch jettison, i.e. 150kts.
	c. If simulating a bird strike, carry out a low speed handling check at a safe height by lowering the undercarriage and flaps and reducing speed to threshold speed or the speed at which control becomes difficult, whichever is the higher. Note: the speed found above plus 5–10 kts, should be the minimum used on the approach after an actual bird strike.
11. Return to base.	a. Let the student rejoin by one of the standard methods according to the weather conditions and his training requirements.

DBH February 1966

*An Autobiography
by Captain
D.B. Hopkins*

Canberra Braking Techniques

Introduction

IN THE INTERESTS of both safety and economy it is important to be able to stop an aircraft in the most efficient manner. To be able to do this under all prevailing conditions, a pilot should understand the theory upon which the braking techniques outlined in Pilot's Notes are based. It is with this in mind that the following paragraphs have been included in the Instructor's Handbook.

Considerations

The Nature of the Problem. In order to stop a Canberra after landing, it is necessary to dissipate a very large quantity of energy (approximately 17,700,000 ft lb at the maximum AUW for landing and 12,630,000 ft lb at 30,000lb AUW) through one or more of the following media:

Rolling Drag;
Aerodynamic Drag;
Wheel Brake.

The effectiveness of these three media is governed by a number of factors, namely:

Tyre pressure and condition;
Type of runway surface and its condition, e.g. wet or dry;
Aircraft attitude and configuration, e.g. position of the flaps;
The distribution of the AUW between the nose and main wheels;
Condition of the wheel brakes;
Method of using the wheel brakes;
Ambient temperature – this affects the amount of energy to be dissipated, the total drag of the airframe and the cooling of the wheel brakes and tyres.

Wheel Slip. The difference between the speed of rotation of a braked wheel and an unbraked one, where the axles of both wheels are travelling over the same surface at the same rate, is known as 'wheel slip'. The amount of slip is a function of the total friction between the tyre and the surface upon which it is running, i.e. it will be greater the more slippery the surface. It has been found from trials that the maximum braking efficiency is obtained when the wheel slip is 4 to 6 ft/sec.

Wheel Spin Up. When the brakes are applied to a rotating wheel the wheel tends to spin down and if the frictional forces are low the spinning down may result in a locked wheel with consequent loss of braking. In order to minimise the chances of this happening it is essential to ensure that the wheels are given time to spin up <u>before</u> the brakes are applied. The time needed for this to happen is proportional to the 'slipperiness' of the runway.

Rolling Drag. Rolling drag depends on the amount of flexing of the tyres and the frictional effects between the tyre and the runway, and the wheel and its axle. The temperature rise in a tyre due to flexing is of the order of 20°C per mile of travel. (This applies to aircraft tyres only). The total value of rolling drag is approximately 2% of the vertical load on the axle, which means, for instance, that a Canberra at an AUW of 50,000lb would have a rolling drag of approximately 1000lb when just moving from rest. Because the main wheels are bigger than the nose wheels, the rolling drag for any given speed is greatest when the greater part of the effective weight of the aircraft (AUW minus lift) is distributed about the main wheels.

Aerodynamic Braking. When aerodynamic braking is employed, lift is produced, thus reducing the effective weight of the aircraft. This happens to such an extent that although the weight is distributed about only two wheels, as opposed to four when the nose wheels are on the runway, the weight on each main wheel is less than it would be with all four wheels on the runway.

The 'Stick Back' Braking Technique. From the foregoing it can be seen that rolling drag will be increased when the tyres are squashed as much as possible. This can be achieved by having the nose wheels on the runway and by bringing the control column backwards as soon as the aircraft decelerates under the influence of the wheel brakes. When the wheel brakes have been applied <u>and</u> the aircraft is decelerating the nose of the aircraft pitches down (figure 1). This has the effect of making the

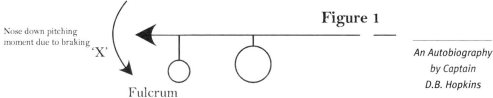

Figure 1

Nose down pitching moment due to braking

'X'

Fulcrum

*An Autobiography
by Captain
D.B. Hopkins*

point of contact of the nose wheel on the runway a fulcrum. The fact that it is a travelling fulcrum does not affect the argument.

If we now apply 'up' elevator, we get a down load on the tailplane and thus a nose up pitching moment (figure 2).

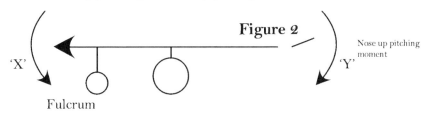

Figure 2

Nose up pitching moment

'X'   'Y'

Fulcrum

This has a 'nut-cracker' action on the main wheels, squashing them and increasing the rolling drag **provided that 'Y' does not exceed 'X'**. This is most important, and in practice care must be taken to ensure that the nose wheel oleo does not even start to extend, for this is a sign that 'Y' is greater than 'X'. Another effect of this technique is that the main wheels slip less and more nearly reach the optimum of 4 to 6 ft/sec, thus increasing braking efficiency. Furthermore, because the wheels now have less tendency to spin down and lock, more braking can be applied, increasing 'X', then more 'up' elevator can be applied, increasing 'Y', and so on until a point is reached where the wheels are rotating so slowly that the brakes must be gradually released in order to prevent the aircraft stopping with a jerk. It can be seen that the three pre-requisites for using this technique are:

The aircraft must be decelerating under the influence of the wheel brakes;
Continuous braking must be employed;
Elevator response must be optimum. This is ensured by correct use of the tailplane trimmer.

Wet Runway Braking. When the runway is wet, there is a reduced coefficient of friction between the tyres and the runway. This means that the wheels will take longer to spin up, be more prone to spin down and locking, and less likely to reach the optimum wheel slip. Thus the overall braking efficiency will be reduced.

Maximum Braking. The wheel brake system of an aircraft is designed to accept a given amount of energy in a given period of time. If either of these limits is exceeded, then the system will fail. What will happen at the moment of failure depends on the nature of the brake system. In the case of the Canberra, it is considered that the surface of the copper rotors will melt causing total loss of braking. As this happens, there is a rapid loss of heat input, the copper will solidify and may jam the brakes, locking the wheels and bursting the tyres. In all probability this will be accompanied by fire in and around the brakes.

The maximum indicated speed at which the brakes can be used to stop the aircraft using the maximum braking technique, is known as the Emergency Maximum Brakes On Speed (EMBS). It is important to remember that EMBS will be lower if the brakes are already hot (from a recent landing for instance) than it would be if the brakes were cold. If the brakes are used at speeds in excess of EMBS then they will fail before the aircraft has stopped. As an illustration the following example is given: AUW = 53,000lb; ISA; nil wind; nil slope; dry runway; EMBS = 100kts. If the brakes are applied at 135kts they will be completely destroyed by the time the aircraft has decelerated to 90kts. (The recommended procedure for this type of situation is contained in Exercise 4 to the Standardisation Notes under the heading 'Abandoning Take-off'.

Practical Application

Normal Braking. After the aircraft has touched down and the nose wheel has been lowered onto the runway, allow a second or so for the wheels to spin up. Then apply sufficient braking to slow the aircraft to walking pace by the time the end of the runway is reached. In a well executed landing run the amount of braking can be reduced progressively as the run continues. This method ensures maximum safety and minimum wear and tear of brakes and tyres.

Maximum Braking – Without Maxaret Units. After the wheels have been allowed to spin up apply as much brake as possible *without skidding* and bring the control column backwards, simultaneously increasing the application of brakes. The process should be continued throughout the landing run. The great difficulty with this technique is detecting the tendency of the wheels to spin down, because it must be remembered that maximum braking is no longer being obtained once the optimum wheel slip is exceeded. If the amount of deceleration appears to be decreasing, even though a fairly large amount of braking is being applied, release the brakes, move the control column forward, allow the wheels to spin up again and then restart the 'stick back' technique.

Maximum Braking – With Maxaret Units. In this case there is no difficulty with regard to the detection of spin down as the Maxaret units are designed to do just this. Therefore after the wheels have been allowed to spin up, apply maximum braking, simultaneously bringing the control column progressively backwards. This process may be continued until the aircraft has stopped.

Wet Runway Braking – With or Without Maxaret Units. As pointed out in paragraph 5 a longer time is needed for the wheels to spin up when the runway is slippery. As a guide, some 2 to 4 seconds should be

*An Autobiography
by Captain
D.B. Hopkins*

allowed during which time the aircraft will travel about 150 to 300 yards. Applying the brakes sooner than this is absolutely pointless, as it will result in wheel locking and subsequently a further period of time for the wheels to spin up. After the wheels have been allowed to spin up, apply light *intermittent* braking with the control column held forward. As soon as some deceleration is felt, start light *continuous* braking and use the 'stick back' technique. It is important to remember that the purpose of the intermittent braking is solely to determine whether the wheels have spun up sufficiently to allow the brakes to function without excessive spin down and wheel locking. If the wheels are felt to skid, or if a large puddle is about to be entered, release the brakes, move the control column forward, allow a further period for the wheels to spin up and start again with intermittent braking. Continue the process as above.

November 1967 DBH

ANNEXE C

Airfields/Airports Visited

THE FOLLOWING IS A LIST of all the airfields and airports the author operated from during his flying years, 1952 to 1981, with the location of each either by County or Country. The names are those extant at the time of the visit.

Abingdon – Oxfordshire
Abu Dhabi – Oman
Accra – Ghana
Adelaide – Australia
Aden – South Yemen
Akrotiri – Cyprus
Aldergrove – Northern Ireland
Algiers – Algeria
Alhorn – Germany
Alicante – Spain
Almeria – Spain
Amman – Jordan
Amsterdam – Holland
Andoya – Norway
Ankara – Turkey
Asmara – Eritrea (Ethiopia)
Bahrain – Bahrain
Baghdad – Iraq
Ballykelly – Northern Ireland
Bangkok – Thailand
Bangor – Maine, USA
Barcelona – Spain
Basel – Switzerland
Bassingbourn – Cambridgeshire
Bathurst – Gambia
Bedford – Bedfordshire
Beirut – Lebanon

Belgrade – Yugoslavia
Benghazi – Libya
Benson – Oxfordshire
Bentwaters – Suffolk
Biggin Hill – Kent
Binbrook – Lincolnshire
Birmingham – Warwickshire
Bodo – Norway
Bombay – India
Booker – Buckinghamshire
Boston – Massachusetts, USA
Bovingdon – Hertfordshire
Brisbane – Australia
Brize Norton – Oxfordshire
Bruggen – Germany
Bruntingthorpe – Leicestershire
Brussels – Belgium
Buenos Aires – Argentina
Burtonwood – Cheshire
Butterworth – Malaya
Cairo – Egypt
Calcutta (Dum Dum) – India
Casablanca – Morocco
Chicago – Michigan, USA
Changi – Singapore
Charlotte – North Carolina, USA
Church Fenton – North Yorkshire

An Autobiography by Captain D.B. Hopkins

Colerne – Wiltshire
Colombo – Ceylon
Coltishall – Norfolk
Coningsby – Lincolnshire
Copenhagen – Denmark
Cosford – Shropshire
Cotonou – Benin
Cottam – East Yorkshire
Cottesmore – Rutland
Cranwell – Lincolnshire
Croydon – Surrey
Dacca – Bangladesh
Dallas/Fort Worth – Texas, USA
Dar-es-Salaam – Tanzania
Damascus – Syria
Darwin – Australia
Delhi – India
Detroit – Michigan, USA
Dhahran – Saudi Arabia
Digby – Lincolnshire
Dishforth – North Yorkshire
Djibouti – Afars and Issas
Doha – Saudi Arabia
Dubai – United Arab Emirates
Dusseldorf – Germany
East Kirkby – Lincolnshire
El Adem – Libya
Entebbe – Uganda
Fairford – Gloucestershire
Feltwell – Norfolk
Fort Lamy – Chad
Frankfurt-am-Main – Germany
Frobisher – Baffin Island, Canada
Gamston – Nottinghamshire
Gander – Newfoundland, Canada
Gardermoen – Norway
Gatwick – West Sussex
Gaydon – Warwickshire
Genoa – Italy
Geilenkirchen – Germany
Gibraltar
Habbaniya – Iraq
Halifax – Nova Scotia, Canada
Hamble – Hampshire

Hamburg – Germany
Heathrow – Middlesex
Hal Far – Malta
Hawarden – Clwyd
Helsinki – Finland
Heraklion – Crete
Honington – Lincolnshire
Hucknall – Nottinghamshire
Hurn – Dorset
Idris – Libya
Istanbul – Turkey
Istres – France
Jeddah – Saudi Arabia
Johannesburg – South Africa
Kai Tak – Hong Kong
Kano – Nigeria
Karachi – Pakistan
Kemble – Gloucestershire
Khartoum – Sudan
Kigali – Rwanda
Kilimanjaro – Tanzania
Kinloss – Grampian
Kinshasa – Congo
Kuala Lumpur – Malaya
Kufra Oasis – Libya
Kuwait City – Kuwait
Laarbruch – Germany
Labuan – Pulau, Malaysia
Lagos – Nigeria
Langar – Nottinghamshire
Larnaca – Cyprus
Lasham – Hampshire
Las Palmas – Canary Islands
Lisbon – Portugal
Lindholme – South Yorkshire
Little Rissington – Gloucestershire
Liverpool – Merseyside
Long Beach – California, USA
Long Marston – Warwickshire
Luanda – Angola
Lubumbashi – Congo
Luqa – Malta
Lusaka – Zambia
Luton – Bedfordshire

Luxembourg
Luxor – Egypt
Lyneham – Wiltshire
Maastricht – Holland
Madras – India
Madrid – Spain
Manchester
Manila – Philippines
Manston – Kent
Marham – Norfolk
Mauripur – Pakistan
Melbourne, Essendon – Australia
Melbourne, Tullamarine – Australia
Mezoon – Oman
Milan, Linate – Italy
Milan, Malpensa – Italy
Mogadishu – Somalia
Mombasa – Kenya
Montreal (Mirabelle) – Canada
Munich – Germany
Nairobi – Kenya
Ndola – Zambia
Negombo – Ceylon
Nuremberg – Germany
New York, JFK – USA
Niamey – Niger
Nicosia – Cyprus
Northolt – Middlesex
Nutts Corner – Northern Ireland
Oakington – Cambridgeshire
Oklahoma City – Oklahoma, USA
Odiham – Hampshire
Ontario – California, USA
Oran – Algeria
Orland – Norway
Osaka – Japan
Ostend – Belgium
Panshangar – Hertfordshire
Paris, Charles de Gaulle – France
Paris, Orly – France
Pershore – Worcestershire
Perth – Australia
Pisa – Italy
Point-à-Pitre – Guadeloupe

Poona – India
Prestwick – Strathclyde
Radlett – Hertfordshire
Ras Al Khaimah – UAE
Recife – Brazil
Rio De Janeiro – Brazil
Riyadh – Saudi Arabia
Rome, Ciampino – Italy
Rome, Fiumicino – Italy
Ronaldsway – Isle of Man
Rotterdam – Holland
Rygge – Norway
Sal – Cape Verde Islands
Salalah – Oman
Salonika – Greece
Salmesbury – Wiltshire
Sana'a – Yemen
Sao Paulo – Brazil
Scampton – Lincolnshire
Sebha – Libya
Seville – Spain
Shannon – Ireland
Sharjah – UAE
Shawbury – Shropshire
Shiraz – Iran
Singapore International – Singapore
Southend – Essex
St Mawgan – Cornwall
Stansted – Essex
Stapleford Tawney – Essex
Stockholm – Sweden
Strubby – Lincolnshire
Sturgate – Lincolnshire
Swinderby – Lincolnshire
Tangmere – West Sussex
Taipeh – Taiwan
Teeside, Middle-St-George – Durham
Tehran – Iran
Tenerife – Canary Islands
Tengah – Singapore
Thorney Island – West Sussex
Tokyo – Japan
Topcliffe – North Yorkshire
Toronto – Canada

**To Stroke
A Cheetah**

*An Autobiography
by Captain
D.B. Hopkins*

**To Stroke
A Cheetah**

Tunis – Tunisia
Turin – Italy
Turnhouse – Lothian
Valencia – Spain
Vancouver – Canada
Vienna – Austria
Volkel – Germany
Waddington – Lincolnshire
Wattisham – Suffolk
Watton – Norfolk
Weston Zoyland – Somerset
West Raynham – Norfolk
White Waltham – Berkshire
Wigsley – Nottinghamshire
Wildenrath – Germany

Wisley – Surrey
Wittering – Cambridgeshire
Wombleton – North Yorkshire
Worksop – Nottinghamshire
Wunsdorf – Germany
Wyton – Cambridgeshire
Zaragosa – Spain
Zurich – Switzerland

*The Extraordinary
Story of a Very
Ordinary Person*

Birds Seen at Wivelsfield Hall

IN THE YEARS we were at Wivelsfield Hall (1976 to 1998) we recorded the following birds over, in or around the garden. They are in no particular order and those marked with * we have seen in our town garden since October 1998 to the time of writing:

Starling *
House Sparrow *
Swift *
House Martin *
Collared Dove *
Song Thrush
Mistle Thrush
Blackbird *
Robin *
Hedge Sparrow (Dunnock) *
Tree Sparrow
Wren *
Great Tit *
Blue Tit *
Coal Tit
Long Tailed Tit *
Greenfinch *
Chaffinch *
Bullfinch
Goldfinch *
Spotted Flycatcher
Hoopoe
Lapwing
Pheasant *
Golden Pheasant
Partridge
Wood Pigeon *

Stock Dove
Tawney Owl
Barn Owl
Little Owl
Rook *
Carrion Crow*
Magpie *
Jackdaw *
Fieldfare
Swallow *
Skylark
Kestrel
Cuckoo
Yellowhammer
Curlew
Green Woodpecker
Lesser-Spotted Woodpecker
Great Spotted Woodpecker *
Nightingale
Blackcap
Chiffchaff *
Willow Warbler *
Black Headed Gull
Tree Creeper
Nuthatch
Jay *
Gold Crest *

*An Autobiography
by Captain
D.B. Hopkins*

**To Stroke
A Cheetah**

Fire Crest
Heron *
Pied Wagtail *
Mute Swan
Mallard
Moorhen
Alpine Swift
Canary
Grey Wagtail
Brent Goose
Lesser Redpoll
Sparrowhawk *
Redwing
Siskin

Buzzard *
Red Legged Partridge
Woodlark
Kingfisher
Hobby
Pied Flycatcher
Green Sandpiper
Guinea Fowl
Parrot
Cormorant *
Woodcock
New house only:
Garden Warbler

asked the proprietor, an elderly man wearing a cloth cap and smoking a self-rolled fag, if I could have a piece of tinplate about 4' by 2'. After much sucking of teeth and telling me how tinplate was in very short supply, he agreed to my request. Judging by the enormous stack he had of the stuff, I felt it couldn't be all that difficult to come by, but I let that pass without comment. When I enquired as to the price, there was a lot more tooth sucking and dire warnings about the supply and the cost thereof! Finally, after several minutes winding me up he said, 'A shilling!!' YCNSTWLEM.

Fourth was my first Jaguar – a 2½ litre Mark V, originally silver, but I felt it would look better resprayed black, and indeed it did. A great car with a flat floor that meant I was able to take out the front passenger seat to allow room for Trevor in his carry-cot for our six-hour journeys from Collingham to Eastbourne and back. During one of these epic trips the SU fuel pump decided to work only intermittently. It was time new points were fitted, but as the pump was under the car, it was not 'get-attable' en route, so every now and then I had to reach under and give it a 'technical tap' with a blunt instrument, after which it kept going for a few more miles. Ah, the delights of motoring in secondhand cars!

Fifth came an elderly Hillman, bought for Mella to learn to drive in 1959. We didn't keep it very long as my attempts to teach Mella nearly resulted if not in World War III, then divorce! Her next three cars were a Morris Minor van called 'Matilda', that had a large hole in the floor which necessitated the use of a travelling rug and hot water bottle on long journeys in winter to avoid the onset of frostbite! Then came two Morris Minor estates, the first of which I restored and presented to her complete with red ribbon. The red ribbon deserves an explanation – when we were first married and relatively penniless, living on my officer's salary of £25 per month, we did a lot of window shopping. Whilst engaged in this pursuit in Grimsby one day we saw a lovely dark green Triumph TR2 in a showroom window, round the bonnet of which was a large red ribbon. Mella said that if she ever had a car she would love to have it delivered with red ribbon round it. So naturally…!

Ninth, then, was my second Jaguar, a Mark VIII in two-tone grey, and the first of several I had with the famous 4.2 litre twin overhead camshafts engine. What I learned about Jaguars from this car stood me in good stead in later years when I had three Daimler limousines to maintain, as the engine remained virtually unchanged for many years. We took this one over to Northern Ireland in 1962 and kept it until 1965 or thereabouts, when I changed it for a Mark X.

The Mark X Jaguar, appropriately the tenth car, was in dark green livery with red upholstery. A grand mode of transport, provided petrol was reasonably cheap, which it was in 1965. About 4 shillings and six-

ANNEXE E

My Cars

THROUGHOUT MY BOOK I have mentioned various cars th
have owned during my life, but here I am listing them in o
in which I owned them, together with some points that ma
of interest to car enthusiasts.

My first car was a 1932 Wolseley Hornet 'Daytona Special', b
with red upholstery when I bought it in 1950 and pale green with
leather after I resprayed it. I drove it for many miles as describe
chapters 1 and 2. One thing it lacked was half the sliding window ir
driver's door. Instead the gap was filled with a piece of cork linoleu:
keep the rain out when it was parked. Of course I had to take this
when driving in order to see and as the other thing it lacked w
heater (cars didn't have heaters in those days), it was extremely
driving it in winter! I was sorry to part with it in exchange foi
Royal Enfield motorbike, but I was unable to keep it roadworthy.

Second a 1955 Hillman 'Minx' coupe, cream with red uphols
This had a pretty poor performance, even by the standards of the
However, by the use of numerous 'bolt on' accessories, I manage
raise the top speed to around 68mph and improve the fuel consump
I also built and installed a primitive heater by ducting air past
exhaust pipe into the car.

Third another Hillman 'Minx', also in cream with red uphols
but this time a saloon with the express intention of keeping our {
born safe and warm! At one time it had the most irritating sq
emanating from somewhere under the dashboard. It took ages to
the source, which turned out to be just two pieces of metal rubbin;
the time there was much talk in motoring circles of the benefit of v
injection, presumably based on the fact that a car seemed to run 1
sweetly at night when the air was cold and damp. I decided to do :
experiments, for which I needed to make a 'water tank' of a parti
shape to fit into the boot. I thought that I could manufacture one c
tinplate that I could easily solder together. I eventually tracked do
factory in Grimsby that made kettles, funnels and so on from tinpl

pence per gallon if my memory serves me, the equivalent of 22.5p (i.e. under 5p per litre), less than a fifteenth of today's price! This one was the only version of the 4.2 litre engine to have triple SU carburettors (as far as I'm aware), and these were very difficult to tune accurately and quite frankly I feel they were an unnecessary refinement.

Eleventh came the Jaguar XJ6, circa 1966 vintage in willow green with dark green upholstery. Still the same 4.2 litre engine but now back to having twin SU carburettors and with much improved disc brakes. As with the previous two Jags, the main problem was that the bodywork rusted very quickly from the inside out and when I traded it in on my next purchase, the salesman remarked how well the mechanics had been looked after even though the bodywork was falling apart.

Mella's fifth car, a Morris Estate, which became very useful when we moved house in 1976 and her next car was yet another Morris, this time an 1100 saloon with the registration GUF and known to all three boys as the 'Guffmobile'.

It had long been an ambition to have a Rolls-Royce so there was much rejoicing when I bought my first in 1977. This was a 1967 Silver Shadow and it turned out to be something of a 'bad un'. I kept it for only six months, during which it was roadworthy for only six weeks, so I exchanged it for a 1969 one coloured Seychelles blue that I kept for about nine years and how it looked after I resprayed it can be seen in chapter 15.

Then came six Audis and five Daimler 7-seater limousines in connection with Inter Primos Chauffeur Service.

My third Rolls-Royce, a 1978 Silver Shadow II that I've had for fifteen years and my sixth Audi, an A6 2.4 Special Edition, I still have residing in the garage.

Letters Etc

OVER THE YEARS Inter Primos was being operated we received a large number of letters of appreciation and a selection are reproduced hereunder. Even now (in 2001), after my recent heart by-pass, I have received offers of financial help from one of our very long-standing Arab clients, and although I was thankfully in a position not to need his assistance, the offer touched me deeply. Similarly, from a Texan lady we received a token allowing Mella and myself to have dinner at her expense at Gravetye Manor. I think it fair to say that we must have been doing something right over the years!

> September 3th 1982
>
> Dear Mrs Hopkins,
> I should like to record my appreciation for your particular contribution towards the smooth running of the arrangements at my daughter's wedding on Saturday last.
> It really turned out to be a the happiest day in every way.
>
> with my sincere thanks,
> Gavin Rowe

GIRL GUIDES ASSOCIATION

COUNTY OF SUSSEX EAST
President: The Lady Buckhurst

County Commissioner:
MISS N. WEBBER

15th June 1986

Dear Captain Hopkins,

One of the best things about this job is that every so often someone makes a gesture of such thoughtfulness and generosity that suddenly everything seems worthwhile! We have rarely, if ever, however, had a gesture as warm and generous as yours, in offering your services to us on June 8th completely free of charge.

We are very very grateful to you. To have given up your Sunday to do the job at all was generous enough, to attend a lengthy and probably tedious briefing meeting was certainly over and above the call of duty - but to do all that and then to send us no bill leaves me speechless.

The question of a royal car had caused us considerable headaches and I was very relieved when the County Secretary told me that she thought she had found just the person and just the car. How right she was - we have some wonderful photographs of both you and the car looking properly dignified and royal and we are having some copies made and will send them to you.

Thank you again for all your help and generosity: we accept your offer, but on the condition that should we need your services again in the future, you will charge us the normal rate.

With all good wishes,

Yours sincerely,

Natalie Webber.

Natalie Webber
County Commissioner

Captain D.B. Hopkins,
Wivelsfield Hall,
Wivelsfield Green,
Haywards Heath
West Sussex

Denver Technological Center

George M. Wallace, P. E.
Executive Vice President
Chief Operations Officer

July 12, 1985

Captain D.B. Hopkins
Inter Primos Chauffeur Service
Wivelsfield Hall
Wivelsfield Green
Haywards Heath
West Sussex
RH177RG

Dear Derrick:

My only regret is that the trip was too short. You showed us a part of the world from your eyes that we would not have been privy to otherwise.

Thank you for your companionship. It was a pleasure for Betsy and I to spend those too short and too few days with you. My regards to your Rolls!

Sincerely,

George

George M. Wallace, P.E.
Executive Vice President
Chief Operations Officer

GMW:bh

7887 East Belleview Avenue, Suite 1100 · Englewood, Colorado 80111 USA
Telephone (303) 773-1700 · Telex WU 45-0261/RCA 216-176

Hamburg 17.10.96

Dear Mrs. and Mr. Hopkins,

sorry it took us so long to
send you the picture of our short
stay in your wonderful home.
We often think of our days
in England: Glyndebourne, Gravetye Manor
with its beautiful gardens and of course
our drive to Brighton.

With many good wishes we are

Yours
... heinz and
...

Dear Capt Hopkins,

I am writing
to thank you for the splendid
job you did for us at our
wedding at Scaynes Hill on Aug 30th.
The car looked very elegant
and although I was not
lucky enough to ride in it
myself all the ladies said it
was lovely and remarked how
kind and helpful you were to
them.
With thanks once again for
getting everyone there safe and
on time.

Yours sincerely

In all the 20 years during which we were providing cars for weddings, this below was without a shadow of a doubt the wettest one we ever did.

Although we evidently kept the bridal party dry, we got totally soaked, literally to the skin, so much so that when we finally returned home we both had to have a bath and a complete change of clothes!

Whilst driving the German lady standing between Mella and myself, page 243, I discovered that like Mella, she was an avid collector of paperweights. Consequently I invited her and her companion to visit us to see Mella's collection, one or two of which are visible in the cabinet behind.

We didn't often have 'clients' to visit Wivelsfield Hall, but on those occasions when we did, we always found them to be most interested in what one might call the 'British way of life'.

The letter on page 239 bears this out quite vividly!

Looking again at the letter from Catherine Reiman – the first time I've read it for five years – makes me realise that I was definitely doing something right! Well, wouldn't you like to get *paid* to drive three charming ladies around the Cotswolds, having to all intents and purposes, an all-expenses-paid holiday? Ah, happy days!!

Dear Captain Hopkins,

I am enclosing our cheque for £50 being the balance due to you.

My husband and I would like to thank you and Mrs. Hopkins for your efforts to try to keep the bridal party dry, in fact I think you were most successful. In spite of the rain the wedding day was a very happy one.

Yours sincerely,

Vera Torton

Capt. D.B. Hopkins,
Wivelsfield Hall,
Wivelsfield Green,
Haywards Heath,
West Sussex, RH17 7RG.

Enc:

Tuesday
May 26, 1987

Dear Mela & Derrick,

I want to thank you for having us over to your home for tea last Thursday afternoon. That was so kind of you! Your home and gardens are lovely! We so enjoyed the tour you gave us around the gardens.

We've been to England a few times before, but this was the first time

over

We'd ever been invited in an English home. I feel it helps to understand better a people and their country to have contact with the people and what better place than in their home—

It was a real treat for all of us and we thank you for this opportunity.

Sincerely,

Joan Rechter

ANGUS & ASSOCIATES

BARRISTERS AND SOLICITORS

#203, 47 COLBORNE ST.
TORONTO, CANADA M5E 1P8
TELEPHONE (416) 864-1028
TELECOPIER (416) 864-1549

IAN W.M. ANGUS, B.ENG, LLB, P.ENG
IN ASSOCIATION WITH
DAVID J.M. RENDEIRO

MONTREAL
3468 DRUMMOND ST
MONTREAL, CANADA H3G1Y4
TELEPHONE (514) 849-4134
TELEX 055-62340 TRAMLAW MTL
TELECOPIER (514) 849-4137

July 4, 1989

Inter Primos Chauffeur Service
Wivelsfield Hall
Wivelsfield Green
Haywards Heath
West Sussex
RH177RG

ATTENTION: Capt. D. B. Hopkins

Dear Captain Hopkins:

I wanted to thank you for driving us around when my wife and I
were in England in April, a feeling that I perhaps did not
adequately express when you left us off at the airport. I have
therefore enclosed something that I am sure will be useful the
next time you have to buy car wax or something similar!

After our tribulations concerning my time in West Africa, it was
so reassuring to be so graciously looked after. I look forward
to meeting you again, which, knowing our peripatetic nature, will
be in the not too distant future.

Best regards.

Yours very truly,

ANGUS & ASSOCIATES

Ian W. M. Angus, B. Eng., LL.B., P. Eng.
IWMA/mls
encl.

Dear Capt. Hopkins,

Herewith my cheque for £73.50 in settlement of the enclosed two invoices.

Everyone was impressed with your professionalism and good humour, as always. Thank you very much for helping to make Saturday such a special occasion for Elizabeth.

Sorry about the "decibals" when the Danes were taken home late on the Saturday evening. I hope your hearing has now recovered from the shock!

Yours sincerely,

Pete Hop

CATHERINE M. REIMAN

BRENTWOOD, R.R. 1 - BOX 10
YARMOUTH, MAINE 04096

Dear Derek:

We were already home before I realized I had not asked for your business card so here I am writing to you minus an address and trusting that this will eventually reach you.

Our twelve days in England in early June were delightful - fantastic weather, beautiful gardens, intriguing Cotswold villages AND the perfect guide and perfect driver.

Thank you so much for taking such good care of the three women from New England. Thank you for your patience and your good humor, for sharing your gardening knowledge and for giving us such a lovely picture of your very special country.

Sarah and her Vermont family are just beginning a trip to Colorado; Anne is completing her move into a new condominium and I'm keeping busy with my writing but whenever we talk, our principle subject is THE TRIP. Anne and I are already dreaming of another trip, perhaps to Cornwall, perhaps...perhaps.

Thank you again Derek. We hope to enjoy your company again one day.

Most sincerely,

Catherine M. Reiman

July 13, 1996